Lecture Notes in Computer Science 6963

Commenced Publication in 1973
Founding and Former Series Editors:
Gerhard Goos, Juris Hartmanis, and Jan van I

Anant Madabhushi   Jason Dowling
Henkjan Huisman   Dean Barratt (Eds.)

Prostate Cancer Imaging

Image Analysis
and Image-Guided Interventions

International Workshop
Held in Conjunction with MICCAI 2011
Toronto, Canada, September 22, 2011
Proceedings

 Springer

Volume Editors

Anant Madabhushi
Rutgers University
Piscataway, NJ 08854, USA
E-mail: anantm@rci.rutgers.edu

Jason Dowling
CSIRO Australian e-Health Research Centre
Herston, QLD 4029, Australia
E-mail: jason.dowling@csiro.au

Henkjan Huisman
Diagnostic Image Analysis Group
6525 HK Nijmegen, The Netherlands
E-mail: h.huisman@rad.umcn.nl

Dean Barratt
University College London
London WC1E 6BT, UK
E-mail: d.barratt@ucl.ac.uk

ISSN 0302-9743   e-ISSN 1611-3349
ISBN 978-3-642-23943-4   e-ISBN 978-3-642-23944-1
DOI 10.1007/978-3-642-23944-1
Springer Heidelberg Dordrecht London New York

Library of Congress Control Number: 2011935945

CR Subject Classification (1998): J.3, I.4, H.5.2, I.5, I.2.10, I.3.5

LNCS Sublibrary: SL 6 – Image Processing, Computer Vision, Pattern Recognition,
and Graphics

Typesetting: Camera-ready by author, data conversion by Scientific Publishing Services, Chennai, India

Printed on acid-free paper

Springer is part of Springer Science+Business Media (www.springer.com)

Preface

Prostatic adenocarcinoma (CAP) is the second most common malignancy and the most frequently diagnosed cancer among men, with an estimated 190,000 new cases in the USA in 2010 (Source: *American Cancer Society*). If CAP is detected early, men have a high five-year survival rate. Unfortunately, there is no standardized image-based screening protocol for early detection of CAP (unlike for breast cancers). In the USA high levels of prostate-specific antigen (PSA) warrant a trans-rectal ultrasound (TRUS) biopsy to enable histologic confirmation of presence or absence of CAP. TRUS biopsy incorporates significant random and systematic error. Random error occurs because the prostate is biopsied without knowledge of the cancer location; systematic error because certain areas (apex, transition zone, anterior fibrostroma) are undersampled.

There have been recent rapid developments in multi-parametric radiological imaging techniques (spectroscopy, dynamic contrast enhanced MR imaging, diffusion-weighting, PET, and ultrasound) that allow high-resolution functional and metabolic imaging of benign and malignant prostate tissue. Distinct computational and technological challenges for multi-modal data registration and classification still remain in leveraging these multi-parametric data for optimizing biopsy and directing therapy.

The Workshop on Prostate Cancer Imaging aims to bring together clinicians, computer scientists and commercial partners of novel prostate cancer imaging tests to (1) discuss the clinical challenges and problems, (2) present state-of-the-art research in quantitative image analysis and visualization methods for prostate cancer detection, diagnosis, and prognosis from multi-parametric imaging and digitized histopathology, and (3) discuss advances in image-guided interventions for prostate cancer biopsy and therapy. The workshop aims to acquaint radiologists, urologists, oncologists, and pathologists on the role that quantitative and automated image analysis can play in prostate cancer diagnosis, prognosis and treatment. It also allows imaging scientists in academic and commercial sectors to understand the most pressing clinical problems. The talks also provide a thorough introduction to novel imaging techniques and their diagnostic capabilities and create new connections and focus academic effort within the medical imaging community. The workshop built on the successful 2010 workshop on prostate imaging hosted in Beijing, China, under the auspices of the MICCAI 2010 conference.

The workshop hosted two invited talks. The first on the benefits of multi-parametric MR imaging and analysis of prostate cancer by Masoom Haider, MD, Department of Radiology, Princess Margaret Hospital, Toronto, Canada. The second invited talk was given by David Jaffray, PhD, Ontario Cancer Institute, who spoke about image-guided radiation therapy for prostate cancer.

A total of 19 papers were received in response to the call for papers for the workshop. This year, the call for papers allowed for submission of regular papers (8–12 pages) and short abstract papers (1–2 pages). While regular papers were eligible for oral or poster presentations, the short papers were only considered for poster presentations, the new short paper format being intended to motivate clinicians to submit their research work.

Each of the 19 papers underwent a rigorous, double-blinded peer-reviewed evaluation, with each paper being reviewed by a minimum of two reviewers. Based on the critiques and evaluations, 15 of the 19 papers were accepted for presentation at the workshop. The papers cover a range of diverse themes, including (a) prostate segmentation, (b) multi-modal prostate registration, (c) computer-aided diagnosis and classification of prostate cancer. The clinical areas covered included (1) radiology, (2) radiation oncology, and (3) image-guided interventions.

The organizers would like to acknowledge the assistance with both the workshop and reviewing websites offered by Rob Toth and Pallavi Tiwari, who are graduate students in the Laboratory for Computational Imaging and Bioinformatics, Rutgers University.

Special thanks also to the MICCAI 2011 Workshop Chairs (Randy Ellis and Purang Abolmaesumi) and to the authors for having submitted high-quality papers. The organizers are grateful to Springer for agreeing to publish the proceedings of the workshop in Springer's *Lecture Notes in Computer Science* (LNCS).

The organizers are also thankful to the CSIRO Australian e-Health Research Centre for sponsoring the workshop.

August 2011

Anant Madabhushi
Jason Dowling
Henkjan Huisman
Dean Barratt

Organization

Organizing Committee

Anant Madabhushi	Rutgers University, USA
Jason Dowling	CSIRO Australian e-Health Research Centre, Australia
Henkjan Huisman	Radboud University Nijmegen Medical Center, The Netherlands
Dean Barratt	University College London, UK

Program Committee

Olivier Salvado	CSIRO Australian e-Health Research Centre, Australia
Richard Levinson	CRI, USA
Lance Ladic	Siemens Corporate Research, USA
Ali Khamene	Siemens Corporate Research, USA
Mark Rosen	Hospital at the University of Pennsylvania, USA
Dinggang Shen	University of North Carolina, Chapel Hill, USA
Gabor Fichtinger	Queens University, Kingston, Ontario, Canada
Ernest Feleppa	Riverside Research Institute, USA
Hashim Uddin Ahmed	University College London, UK

Table of Contents

A Learning Based Hierarchical Framework for Automatic Prostate Localization in CT Images

Shu Liao and Dinggang Shen

Department of Radiology,
Biomedical Research Imaging Center,
University of North Carolina at Chapel Hill
liaoshu.cse@gmail.com, dgshen@med.unc.edu

Abstract. Accurate localization of prostate in CT images plays an important role in image guided radiation therapy. However, it has two main challenges. The first challenge is due to the low contrast in CT images. The other challenge is due to the uncertainty of the existence of bowel gas. In this paper, a learning based hierarchical framework is proposed to address these two challenges. The main contributions of the proposed framework lie in the following aspects: (1) Anatomical features are extracted from input images, and the most salient features at distinctive image regions are selected to localize the prostate. Regions with salient features but irrelevant to prostate localization are also filtered out. (2) An image similarity measure function is explicitly defined and learnt to enforce the consistency between the distance of the learnt features and the underlying prostate alignment. (3) An online learning mechanism is used to adaptively integrate both the inter-patient and patient-specific information to localize the prostate. Based on the learnt image similarity measure function, the planning image of the underlying patient is aligned to the new treatment image for segmentation. The proposed method is evaluated on 163 3D prostate CT images of 10 patients, and promising experimental results are obtained.

1 Introduction

External beam radiation therapy is a major treatment method for prostate cancer and it consists of the planning stage and treatment stage. During the planning stage, the planning image is obtained from the patient. The prostate is then manually delineated in the planning image and a specific treatment plan is designed. In the daily treatment stage, a new treatment image is obtained from the patient and the prostate is localized such that the treatment plan designed in the planning image can be adjusted accordingly and applied to the patient. Therefore, the key to the success of external beam radiation therapy lies in the accurate localization of prostates.

However, accurate localization of prostates in CT images is a challenging task due to the two main issues. The first issue is due to the low image contrast, which is illustrated by Figures 1 (a) and (b). Figure 1 (a) is a slice obtained

A. Madabhushi et al. (Eds.): Prostate Cancer Imaging 2011, LNCS 6963, pp. 1–9, 2011.

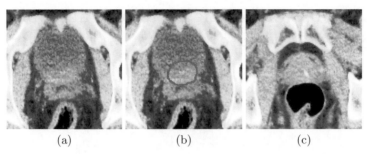

Fig. 1. (a) An image slice obtained from a 3D prostate CT image. (b) The prostate boundary highlighted by the red manually-delineated contour superimposed on the image in (a). (c) An image slice with bowel gas obtained from a different 3D prostate CT image of the same patient as in (a).

from a 3D prostate CT image, and the prostate boundary delineated by the clinical expert is shown by the red contour in Figure 1 (b). It can be observed that the contrast between the prostate and its surrounding tissues is low and no obvious boundary can be identified. The other issue is due to the uncertainty of the existence of bowel gas. Figure 1 (c) is a slice obtained from a 3D prostate CT image of the same patient but from a different treatment day. It can be observed that the existence of bowel gas in Figure 1 (c) changes the image appearance significantly. In order to address these two issues, many novel approaches have been proposed. For instance, profile based features and region based features are used in [1,2] to localize the prostate, and Davis *et al.* [3] proposed a deformable image registration based prostate segmentation method by combining a deflation algorithm to deal with the bowel gas area.

In this paper, we propose a learning based framework for automatic prostate localization in CT images. The proposed method extracts anatomical features from input images, and adaptively learns the best features at distinctive image regions to localize the prostate. Regions with salient features but irrelevant to localize the prostate such as regions filled with bowel gas are automatically filtered out. An online update mechanism is adopted to adaptively combine both the inter-patient and patient-specific information during the learning process. The alignment is performed in a hierarchical manner by first estimating the translational transformation and then estimating the deformable transformation from the planning image to the treatment image. The proposed method is evaluated on 163 3D prostate CT images of 10 patients; The experimental results show that high segmentation accuracy can be achieved by the proposed method and outperforms the state-of-the-art prostate segmentation algorithms.

2   Methodology

2.1   Preprocessing

In the preprocessing step, we remove the whole-body rigid motion of each patient in the planning and treatment images. More specifically, during this step the planning and treatment images are thresholded such that only the bone structure (i.e., the pelvis, which remains fixed) is visible. Then the bone structure in each treatment image is rigidly aligned to the bone structure in the planning image. After the bone alignment process, the remaining prostate shape differences between the planning and treatment images are mainly caused by the prostate motion.

2.2   Optimal Transformation Estimation for Training Set

After the bone alignment process, we need to obtain the optimal transformation from each training image to the planning image of the underlying patient to learn the similarity measure function in later stages. The training set contains both the inter-patient images as well as the available patient-specific treatment images. We denote each training image as I_i $(i = 1, ..., N)$. Moreover, for each training image, its corresponding segmentation groundtruth S_i $(i = 1, ..., N)$ is also available. We also denote the planning image of the current patient as I^{plan} and its segmentation groundtruth as S^{plan}. The optimal transformation to align each training image to the planning image of the current patient can be obtained by registering the binary images S_i to S^{plan}, and denote the corresponding estimated optimal transformation parameter as θ_i $(i = 1, ..., N)$. In the proposed hierarchical framework, we first estimate the optimal translational transform parameters and then estimate the optimal deformable transform parameters.

2.3   Combination of Inter-patient and Patient-Specific Information

The contributions of the inter-patient information and patient-specific information in the training stage should be dynamically changed. Initially, when only the planning image of the current patient is available, more weights should be assigned to the inter-patient information. As more treatment images of the current patient are segmented and collected in the training set, the patient-specific information should play an increasing role as intuitively it can capture the patient-specific prostate shape variations more accurately.

In this paper, the weight of the patient-specific information ω^{intra} is determined by a modified sigmoid function based on the current number q of available patient-specific treatment images in the training set. It is defined in Equation 1:

$$\omega^{intra}(q) = \begin{cases} 0, & \text{if } q = 0, \\ \frac{1}{1+\exp(-(q-5))}, & \text{if } q > 0, \end{cases} \tag{1}$$

The weight for the inter-patient information ω^{inter} can be calculated as $1 - \omega^{intra}$. The determined weights ω^{intra} and ω^{inter} will be used in later steps.

2.4   Feature Extraction and Training Sample Enrichment

In this paper, we use anatomical features as signature for each voxel to characterize the image appearance. More specifically, 14 multi-resolution Haar wavelet feature [4], 9 histogram of gradient (HOG) feature [5] and 30 local binary pattern (LBP) feature [6] are extracted from a small $W \times W$ window centered at each voxel. In this paper, we set $W = 21$. Therefore, each voxel is represented by a 53 $(14 + 9 + 30)$ dimensional feature signature.

In order to ensure the robustness of the learning process, sufficient number of training images should be used. However, on the other hand, to make our method practical in clinical application, the number of training images used should also be minimized. Therefore, in this paper, a simulation strategy in [7] is adopted to enrich the number of training images. Specifically, new training samples can be simulated based on Equation 2:

$$\hat{I}_i^j = T(I_i, \boldsymbol{\theta}_i + \boldsymbol{\epsilon}_i^j), \quad (i = 1, ..., N), (j = 1, ..., C_i) \tag{2}$$

where $\hat{I}_i^j$ denotes the jth simulated image generated from the ith training image I_i. $\boldsymbol{\theta}_i$ is the optimal transformation parameter for I_i estimated in Section 2.2, and $\boldsymbol{\epsilon}_i^j$ is the jth sample drawn from the zero mean uniform random variable $\boldsymbol{\epsilon}_i$. $T(I_i, \boldsymbol{\theta}_i + \boldsymbol{\epsilon}_i^j)$ denotes applying the corresponding transformation with parameter $\boldsymbol{\theta}_i + \boldsymbol{\epsilon}_i^j$ to image I_i. N is the number of training images available. C_i denotes the number of simulated images generated from I_i. If I_i is an inter-patient training image, then $C_i = \lceil B \cdot \omega^{inter} \rceil$, and otherwise $C_i = \lceil B \cdot \omega^{intra} \rceil$, where B is a constant and set to 40 in this paper. Equation 2 performs small perturbations on each aligned training images. The feature map calculated from each aligned training image can be permuted accordingly since all three types of features are robust against small perturbations.

It should be noted that in the deformable transformation estimation step, $\boldsymbol{\theta}_i$ has huge degrees of freedom. To lower the computational cost, we need to reduce the number of degrees of freedom in $\boldsymbol{\theta}_i$ for this step. In this paper, the weighted PCA is applied to the training set based on ω^{inter} and ω^{intra}. Denote the resulting top t eigenvalues as λ_h $(h = 1, ..., t)$, with their corresponding eigenvectors e_h, the original transformation parameter vector $\boldsymbol{\theta}_i$ can be approximated as:

$$\boldsymbol{\theta}_i \approx \bar{\boldsymbol{\theta}} + \sum_{h=1}^{t} c_h^i \sqrt{\lambda_h} e_h, \tag{3}$$

where $\bar{\boldsymbol{\theta}}$ denotes the mean parameter vector of $\boldsymbol{\theta}_i$ $(i = 1, ..., N)$, and c_h^i is the coefficient of $\boldsymbol{\theta}_i$ projected on the hth eigenvector e_h. In this paper, it is found that $t = 5$ is generally sufficient to accurately approximate $\boldsymbol{\theta}_i$, which can contribute over 80% of the cumulative energy of the original deformable transformation.

2.5   Feature Selection

The next step of our method to select the most informative features at distinctive image regions to localize the prostate. The most straight forward solution is to select the features which have the highest correlation coefficients with the Dice ratio measure based on the training set. However, the Dice ratio is an implicit function with respect to the transformation parameters and has many

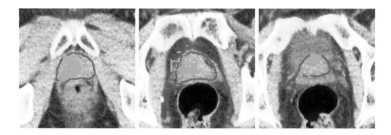

Fig. 2. Examples showing some selected distinctive regions. The selected regions are highlighted in green. The prostate boundary determined by the clinical expert is delineated in red.

local maxima. In order to overcome this problem, an explicit similarity measure function which has simpler form than the implicit Dice ratio measure function yet be able to reflect the overlap degrees of the current segmented prostates is defined by Equation 4:

$$F(\boldsymbol{\theta}_i, \boldsymbol{\epsilon}_i^j) = D(S^{plan}, T(S_i, \boldsymbol{\theta}_i)) \cdot \exp\left(-\frac{1}{2}((\boldsymbol{\epsilon}_i^j)^T \Sigma^{-1} \boldsymbol{\epsilon}_i^j)\right), \qquad (4)$$

where the first term $D(S^{plan}, T(S_i, \boldsymbol{\theta}_i))$ denotes the Dice ratio between the prostate in the planning image and the prostate in the aligned training image of I_i. The second term is an exponential function and Σ is a diagonal matrix whose diagonal elements are variances of the transformation parameters learnt from the training images. Thus the defined similarity function is a weighted Gaussian function. For simplicity, we denote the defined similarity function as the Gaussian score function in this paper.

The feature selection process is performed based on the defined Gaussian score function in Equation 4. Note that the feature map calculated for each training image in Section 2.4 encodes two pieces of information: feature value f_i of feature type i ($i = 1, ..., 53$) and voxel location $\boldsymbol{x}_j$ ($j = 1, ..., M$), where M is the number of voxels in the image. Thus the signature of each voxel is a pair $(f_i, \boldsymbol{x}_j)$. For a given feature type i and a given voxel location $\boldsymbol{x}_j$, a distance vector can be obtained for $(f_i, \boldsymbol{x}_j)$ based on all the simulated images: $\boldsymbol{V}(f_i, \boldsymbol{x}_j) = [d_1^1(f_i, \boldsymbol{x}_j), ..., d_1^{C_1}(f_i, \boldsymbol{x}_j), ..., d_t^s(f_i, \boldsymbol{x}_j), ..., d_N^{C_N}(f_i, \boldsymbol{x}_j)]$, where $d_t^s(f_i, \boldsymbol{x}_j) = f_i(\hat{I}_t^s(\boldsymbol{x}_j)) - f_i(I^{plan}(\boldsymbol{x}_j))$ and C_k ($k = 1, ..., N$) is the number of simulated images generated from the kth training image defined in Equation 2. The corresponding Gaussian score vector can be constructed by Equation 5:

$$\boldsymbol{G} = [F(\boldsymbol{\theta}_1, \boldsymbol{\epsilon}_1^1), ..., F(\boldsymbol{\theta}_1, \boldsymbol{\epsilon}_1^{C_1}), ..., F(\boldsymbol{\theta}_t, \boldsymbol{\epsilon}_t^s), ..., F(\boldsymbol{\theta}_N, \boldsymbol{\epsilon}_N^{C_N})]. \qquad (5)$$

Therefore, the most salient features at the most distinctive image regions can be determined by selecting the pairs $(f_i, \boldsymbol{x}_j)$ with the largest correlation coefficients with $\boldsymbol{G}$. Figure 2 shows examples of the selected distinctive regions, and it can be observed that regions with salient features but irrelevant to the localization of prostate such as regions filled with bowel gas are automatically filtered out.

2.6   Image Similarity Function Learning

Suppose there are m pairs of $(f, \boldsymbol{x})$ selected in Section 2.5, denote them as $(\tilde{f}_n, \tilde{\boldsymbol{x}}_n)$, where $n = 1, ..., m$. For each simulated training image $\hat{I}_i^j$, its corresponding feature distance vector is: $\boldsymbol{U}_i^j = [d_i^j(\tilde{f}_1, \tilde{\boldsymbol{x}}_1), ..., d_i^j(\tilde{f}_m, \tilde{\boldsymbol{x}}_m)]$, and its corresponding Gaussian score $F(\boldsymbol{\theta}_i, \boldsymbol{\epsilon}_i^j)$ is also available. The next step is to learn a image similarity measure function Φ which establishes a mapping from $\boldsymbol{U}_i^j$ to $F(\boldsymbol{\theta}_i, \boldsymbol{\epsilon}_i^j)$ based on all the simulated training images. In the treatment stage, when a new treatment image comes in, Φ takes the distance vector calculated from the new treatment image and estimates the corresponding Gaussian score to guide the alignment procedure from the treatment image to the planning image. In this paper, Φ is obtained by support vector regression (SVR) with the Gaussian radial basis function (RBF) kernel based on $\boldsymbol{U}_i^j$ and $F(\boldsymbol{\theta}_i, \boldsymbol{\epsilon}_i^j)$ from all the simulated training images. Grid search is performed to determine the optimal kernel parameters in SVR.

2.7   Predict Optimal Transformation for New Treatment Images

After learning the image similarity measure function Φ in Section 2.6, we can use Φ to estimate the optimal transformation to align the new incoming treatment image I^{new} to the planning image of the current patient. Similar to Section 2.6, we can calculate the feature distance vector from the transformed treatment image $T(I^{new}, \boldsymbol{\theta})$ with the current transformation parameter $\boldsymbol{\theta}$ based on the selected features, denoted it as $\boldsymbol{U}_{\boldsymbol{\theta}}^{new}$. Then the corresponding Gaussian score can be calculated as $\Phi(\boldsymbol{U}_{\boldsymbol{\theta}}^{new})$; the higher the score, the better the alignment is expected. Therefore, the parameter $\boldsymbol{\theta}$ which can maximize $\Phi(\boldsymbol{U}_{\boldsymbol{\theta}}^{new})$ is determined as the optimal parameter, denoted as $\boldsymbol{\theta}_{opt}^{new}$. The grid search optimization method is adopted in this paper to estimate $\boldsymbol{\theta}_{opt}^{new}$. After getting $\boldsymbol{\theta}_{opt}^{new}$, we can localize the prostate in the new treatment image by transforming the segmented prostate in the planning image via the inverse transformation based on $\boldsymbol{\theta}_{opt}^{new}$.

3   Experimental Results

In this section, we evaluate the proposed method on a 3D CT prostate dataset consisting of 10 patients. Each patient has more than 10 CT scans. There are 163 images in total. Each image has in-plane resolution of 512×512, with voxel size $0.98 \times 0.98 \ mm^2$ and the inter-slice voxel size $3 \ mm$. The manual segmentation results provided by clinical experts are also available for each image.

The segmentation accuracy is evaluated based on two quantitative measures: The centroid distance and the Dice ratio between the estimated prostate and the manual segmented prostate. The Dice ratio between two segmented volumes S_1 and S_2 is defined as $DSC(S_1, S_2) = \frac{2|S_1 \cap S_2|}{|S_1| + |S_2|}$.

The box and whisker plots of the centroid distances with and without using the online update mechanism are given in Figure 3. Without using the online

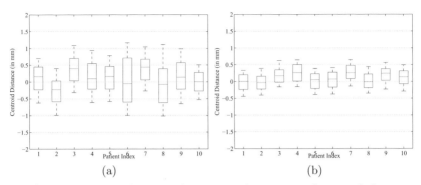

Fig. 3. Centroid distance between the estimated prostate volume and the manually segmented prostate volume (a) without using the online update mechanism, and (b) with the online update mechanism. The horizontal lines in each box represent the 25th percentile, median, and 75th percentile respectively. The whiskers extend to the most extreme data points.

updated mechanism means only the inter-patient information is adopted to segment each treatment image of the underlying patient, which is the most challenging case. It can be observed in Figure 3 (a) that even in the most challenging case, the proposed method can still achieve high prostate localization accuracy (i.e., for all the patients, the 25th and 75th percentiles of the centroid distances are within 1 *mm* error). Moreover, by using the online update mechanism, the centroid distance can be further minimized as illustrated in Figure 3 (b).

The average values and standard deviations of the Dice ratios for each patient are listed in Table 1. It can be observed that the proposed method achieves high segmentation accuracies (i.e., above 85% of the Dice ratio for each patient) *even in the case that only the planning image of the current patient is available to segment each treatment image*, and the segmentation accuracy can be further improved with the online update mechanism. It is also compared with two state-of-the-art prostate segmentation algorithms proposed by Davis *et al.* [3] and Feng *et al.* [8] and the average Dice ratios of different approaches are listed in Table 2. It can be observed that the Dice ratio of the proposed method is significantly higher than Davis's method [3], and the standard deviation of the Dice ratios of the proposed method is lower than Feng's approach [8].

To visualize the segmentation accuracy of the proposed method, Figure 4 shows a typical segmentation result of the proposed method. In Figure 4, the black contours and the white contours are the prostate boundaries determined by the clinical expert and the proposed method respectively. It can be observed that the prostate boundaries estimated by the proposed method are very close to those delineated by the clinical expert even in the cases of the presence of bowel gas, which implies the robustness of the proposed method.

Table 1. Mean and standard deviations of the Dice ratios of each patient. PA i denotes the ith patient. BA denotes before alignment. WU and WOU denote the proposed method with and without using the online update mechanism respectively. The highest value of the Dice ratio is bolded.

	PA 1	PA 2	PA 3	PA 4	PA 5
BA	0.64±0.06	0.46±0.13	0.71±0.08	0.69±0.07	0.40±0.05
WOU	0.88±0.01	0.87±0.01	0.88±0.02	0.85±0.07	0.88±0.02
WU	**0.89 ± 0.02**	**0.89 ± 0.01**	**0.90 ± 0.01**	**0.87 ± 0.08**	**0.90 ± 0.02**
	PA 6	PA 7	PA 8	PA 9	PA 10
BA	0.78±0.10	0.79±0.02	0.80±0.07	0.47±0.10	0.73±0.08
WOU	0.85±0.01	0.86±0.02	0.87±0.03	0.86±0.02	0.88±0.01
WU	**0.88 ± 0.01**	**0.88 ± 0.02**	**0.90 ± 0.01**	**0.89 ± 0.02**	**0.89 ± 0.01**

Table 2. Comparisons of the proposed method with two state-of-the-art deformable model based prostate segmentation algorithms in CT images based on the Dice ratios. WU denotes the proposed framework using the online update mechanism.

Methods	Mean	Median	Std. Dev.
Davis [3]	0.82	0.84	0.06
Feng [8]	0.89	0.90	0.05
WU	0.89	0.90	0.02

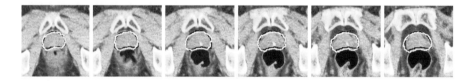

Fig. 4. typical performance of the proposed method on six slices of the 14th treatment image of the 8th patient. The Dice ratio of this treatment image is 90.42%. The black contours show the results of manual segmentation, and the white contours show the results obtained by the proposed method.

4   Conclusion

In this paper, we propose a new learning based framework for accurate localization of prostate in CT images. In the proposed framework, each input image is represented by anatomical feature maps, and a feature selection process is performed to determine the most salient features at distinctive image regions to localize the prostate. The underlying feature selection process also automatically filters the regions with salient features but irrelevant to the localization of prostates such as regions filled with bowel gas. An explicit image similarity measure is defined and learnt to avoid the local maxima problem. An online update mechanism is also adopted to adaptively combine the inter-patient information and patient-specific information in the learning stage. It is demonstrated that the proposed method can achieve high prostate segmentation accuracies in CT images and outperforms state-of-the-art prostate segmentation algorithms. Most importantly, the proposed method *is highly flexible in clinical application as high segmentation accuracies can be achieved even in the case that only the planning image of the underlying patient is available.*

References

1. Cosio, F.: Automatic initialization of an active shape model of the prostate. Medical Image Analysis 12, 469–483 (2008)
2. Stough, J., Broadhurst, R., Pizer, S., Chaney, E.: Regional appearance in deformable model segmentation. In: IPMI, pp. 532–543 (2007)
3. Davis, B.C., Foskey, M., Rosenman, J., Goyal, L., Chang, S., Joshi, S.: Automatic segmentation of intra-treatment CT images for adaptive radiation therapy of the prostate. In: Duncan, J.S., Gerig, G. (eds.) MICCAI 2005. LNCS, vol. 3749, pp. 442–450. Springer, Heidelberg (2005)
4. Mallat, S.: A theory for multiresolution signal decomposition: The wavelet representation. PAMI 11, 674–693 (1989)
5. Dalal, N., Triggs, B.: Histograms of oriented gradients for human detection. In: CVPR, pp. 886–893 (2005)
6. Ojala, T., Pietikainen, M., Maenpaa, T.: Multiresolution gray-scale and rotation invariant texture classification with local binary patterns. PAMI 24, 971–987 (2002)
7. Zhou, L., Liao, S., Shen, D.: Learning-based prostate localization for image guided radiation therapy. In: ISBI, pp. 2103–2106 (2011)
8. Feng, Q., Foskey, M., Chen, W., Shen, D.: Segmenting ct prostate images using population and patient-specific statistics for radiotherapy. Medical Physics 37, 4121–4132 (2010)

Fast Automatic Multi-atlas Segmentation of the Prostate from 3D MR Images

Jason A. Dowling[1,*], Jurgen Fripp[1], Shekhar Chandra[1], Josien P.W. Pluim[2],
Jonathan Lambert[3,4], Joel Parker[3], James Denham[3,4], Peter B. Greer[3,4],
and Olivier Salvado[1]

[1] Australian e-Health Research Centre, CSIRO ICT Centre, Australia
[2] University Medical Center Utrecht, The Netherlands
[3] Calvary Mater Newcastle Hospital, Australia
[4] University of Newcastle, Australia
Jason.Dowling@csiro.au

Abstract. A fast fully automatic method of segmenting the prostate from 3D MR scans is presented, incorporating dynamic multi-atlas label fusion. The diffeomorphic demons method is used for non-rigid registration and a comparison of alternate metrics for atlas selection is presented. A comparison of results from an average shape atlas and the multi-atlas approach is provided. Using the same clinical dataset and manual contours from 50 clinical scans as Klein et al. (2008) a median Dice similarity coefficient of 0.86 was achieved with an average surface error of 2.00mm using the multi-atlas segmentation method.

1 Introduction

During image guided radiotherapy of the prostate there is a need to accurately define the boundaries of the organs of interest to maximize dose to the target volume and minimize dose received by the bladder and rectum (to reduce post-treatment complications). This manual contouring can be a time consuming process and subject to intra- and inter-expert variability. Advances in prostate radiotherapy have led to improvements in the amount of dose delivered to target organs, while reducing the amount to organs at risk. Recent developments in MRI simulation and MRI accelerators [1, 2] bring the potential for MRI based adaptive treatment. MRI has a number of advantages over computed tomography (CT) for treatment planning which is currently required for treatment planning. These include improved soft tissue contrast, better definition of tumour margins [3] and prostate borders delineated on MRI scans by radiation oncologists have been shown to have lower inter-observer variability and are smaller than on CT [4, 5].

Atlas based segmentation methods are becoming increasingly popular for organ segmentation. The key idea is to use image registration to map a pre-labeled image (or

---

* Corresponding author.

A. Madabhushi et al. (Eds.): Prostate Cancer Imaging 2011, LNCS 6963, pp. 10–21, 2011.
© Springer-Verlag Berlin Heidelberg 2011

"atlas") onto a new patient image. Once a good correspondence between structurally equivalent regions in the two images is achieved the labels defined on the atlas can be propagated to the image. Rohlfing et al. [6] have identified four main methods to generate the atlas which is registered to a target volume: using a single labeled image (IND), generating an average shape image (AVG), selecting the most similar image from a database of scans (SIM); or finally to register all individual scans from a database and using multi-classier fusion to combine the pair-wise registration results (MUL).

Recent atlas based papers with good prostate segmentation results have been published by Martin et al. [7] and Klein et al. [8]. Martin et al. generated a probabilistic average shape atlas (AVE) from 36 patients and then used this to segment new cases by first using non-rigid registration to map the atlas to each patient, and secondly by using this result to initialize a spatially constrained deformable model. They have reported a median Dice similarity coefficient (DSC) of 0.86, with an average surface error of 2.41mm. Klein et al. used a multi-atlas fusion (similar to Rohlfing's MUL) method for prostate (including seminal vesicle) segmentation based on a BSpline free form deformation [9] and using localized mutual information to select the most similar images from an atlas set after pairwise registration. They reported a median DSC of 0.85, however each registration required approximately 15 minutes.

Our previous work (eg. [10-12]) has focused on the development of methods for the creation of MR-based pseudo-CT scans for external beam radiation therapy planning. However, the computational requirement for atlas based segmentation makes their usage clinically impractical. In this paper we aim to develop a fast and accurate method for prostate segmentation based around 3D diffeomorphic demons. For this we compare the accuracy of several atlas generation and three atlas selection methods to perform prostate segmentation and evaluate the computational cost.

2 Method

2.1 Data

The scans and contours reported in this paper are the same as those used in Klein et al [8]. The data consisted of 50 clinical scans acquired from patients (mean age 69) scheduled for external beam radiation therapy. Scans were acquired from a Phillips 3T scanner using a flex-M surface coil using a balanced steady-state free precession (bSSFP) sequence with fat suppression. The scans contain 512x512x90 voxels (size 0.49x0.49x1.0 mm).

Three different experts contoured the prostate (including seminal vesicles) in each scan, consisting of an experienced (ten years) radiation oncologist, a resident radiation oncologist, and a medical physicist specialized in prostate radiation therapy. As in Klein et al. we also generated a gold standard (L^G) segmentation by using majority voting to combine the three segmentations. As the use of STAPLE [13] to combine these manual contours has previously been investigated (having no significant difference with voting [8]), we did not include this method.

2.2 Preprocessing

As with Klein et al. [8], we also evaluated the registration similarity metric on a 271 x 333 x 86 voxel region of interest, Ω, which was sufficient to encompass the prostate, bladder and rectum in each scan. We also pre-processed this region of interest with:

1. N4 Bias field correction [14] (B-spline fitting = [160,3,0,0,5], convergence = [100x100x100,0,0.001], shrink factor = 3).
2. Histogram equalisation (ITK: levels = 1024, match points = 7, threshold at mean intensity).
3. Smoothing using gradient anisotropic diffusion (ITK: 10 iterations, time step = 0.03; conductance = 1.0).

2.3 Average Shape Atlas (AVE)

In order to objectively compare the multi-atlas approach, a single average atlas was built and evaluated. We have previously used this approach for prostate segmentation from MRI (for example, MICCAI 2009 prostate segmentation challenge[1])

This involved selecting an arbitrary case as the initial atlas defining the atlas space alignment. A probabilistic atlas (PA) for the prostate was generated by propagating the manual segmentations for each training case using the obtained affine transform and deformation field computed from the MR into the atlas space as per Rohlfing [6].

The first iteration involved the registration of every other case to the selected atlas case using rigid followed by affine registration. Subsequent iterations involved all subjects being registered to the average image using rigid and affine (ITK, based on 3 level pyramid up to ½ resolution, regular step gradient descent, Mattes Mutual Information, stochastic sampling) and non-rigid registration (diffeomorphic demons algorithm [15], 3 level pyramid, 10 iterations per level, max step length=2, smoothed deformation fields on, sd=3). At the end of each iteration a new average atlas was generated and used in the subsequent iteration. In the present study, five iterations were performed.

To evaluate the atlas, rigid, affine and non-rigid registration were used to map the average atlas onto each subject's MR scan and the affine transform and deformation fields were then used to map the prostate segmentation onto each scan. The prostate PA was then thresholded (50%) to provide an automatic segmentation for each individual subject.

2.4 Multi-atlas Decision Fusion

Multi-atlas decision fusion involves deformable registration of scans from a database to a new patient; selecting the closest matching scans; and finally combining their

---

[1] http://wiki.na-mic.org/Wiki/index.php/File:Dowling_2009_MICCAIProstate_v2.pdf

deformed organ labels to provide an automatic segmentation. The number of scans used to generate the automatic segmentation is variable.   We have modified the method from Klein et al. [8] to include a preprocessing stage, two levels of masking, a faster non-rigid registration method, and the use of alternate similarity measures. This approach involves two main steps: registration and label fusion.

First pairwise registration (rigid, affine, non-rigid as previous section) was performed between all cases. In this step all scans are considered atlases, A_i, and registered against an individual patient, P. Each resulting deformed atlas image is defined by $A_i \cdot T_i$. This step therefore generates 49 atlas scans for each patient in the dataset (and 2450 results in total). The same registration methods as the average shape atlas (section 2.1 above) were used.

In the second step, the most similar matching atlases for each patient scans from the first step are identified and fused to generate a patient specific atlas.

To calculate the similarity between each atlas image after registration and a target patient image, we evaluated three different metrics (Φ): normalized mutual information (NMI), normalized cross correlation (NCC), and the mean reciprocal square difference (MRSD) (ITK implementations). These metrics were calculated over a masked region, Ψ, of each registered atlas scan, consisting of a central 136x167x43 voxel area. This region was selected to speed up computation and to focus the evaluation on the central prostate area of the image (see also Fig. 1).

To select which scans and associated contours will be selected and fused for a new patient scan, we calculate the ratio r_i as:

$$r_i = \frac{\Phi\,(P, A_i \cdot T_i; \Psi)}{max_j\,\Phi\,(P, A_i \cdot T_i; \Psi)} \qquad (1)$$

(where $\Phi \in \{\text{NMI}, \text{MRSD}, \text{NCC}\}$)

As in [8], an atlas was selected if it satisfies $r_i \geq \varphi$ where $0 \leq \varphi \leq 1$. If φ is set to 0 all scans (ie. n=49) are included in the selection (MUL), and $\varphi =1$ means that only the most similar scan (SIM) is used for the automatic labeling.   In this paper we used majority voting to combine the selected atlases.

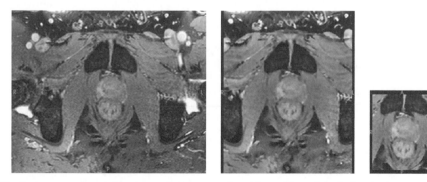

Fig. 1. An example axial is shown from one study subject. The original slice is shown on the left. The masked 271 x 333 x 86 voxel volume, Ω, is used for registration, is shown in the centre. The smaller 136x167x43 voxel volume, Ψ, used for metric calculation and atlas selection (equation 1) is shown on the right.

2.5 Validation

All results were obtained using a leave one out approach.   The automatic prostate segmentations were compared to the manual gold standard (L^G) segmentation using the Dice similarity coefficient defined as [16]:

$$DSC = \frac{2|X \cap Y|}{|X|+|Y|} \tag{2}$$

We also report the mean absolute surface distance between the automatic and manual segmentations by calculating the averaged forward and backward mean absolute Euclidean distance between surfaces (using MilxView, available at http://aehrc.com/biomedical_imaging/milx.html).

3 Results

Figures 2 and 3 show overlaid manual contours and segmentation results for two of the study cases. Qualitatively it can be seen that the automatic 3D method (multi-atlas, φ=0.98) has resulted in good segmentation accuracy in the apex and base areas of the gland.

Figure 4 shows a typical central axial slice from an original MR scan with the manual prostate contour overlaid. The result of multi-atlas fusion (section 2.4), and the associated automatic contour for this MR scan is shown in the centre image.   The image on the right hand side shows the result from the average atlas method (section 2.3) for this patient and the associated contour.   The purpose of this figure is to demonstrate the difference between the two segmentation methods.

Dice Similarity Coefficient (DSC) scores between automatic and manual prostate segmentations for the fifty clinical scans are summarised in Figures 5 and 6. The mean DSC across all 2450 (50 x 49) pairwise results was 0.66±0.16. All multi-atlas results received their highest median DSC score when φ=0.98. The highest result was found using NMI with the multi-atlas method, which used mean 16.39±7.1 atlas cases for each target and resulted in a median DSC of 0.86 (mean 0.83±0.09). The use of MRSD (median DSC: 0.83, mean: 0.81±0.11) and NCC (median DSC: 0.85, mean: 0.83±0.09) in multi atlas selection both outperformed the average shape atlas results (median DSC: 0.81, mean: 0.74±0.18).

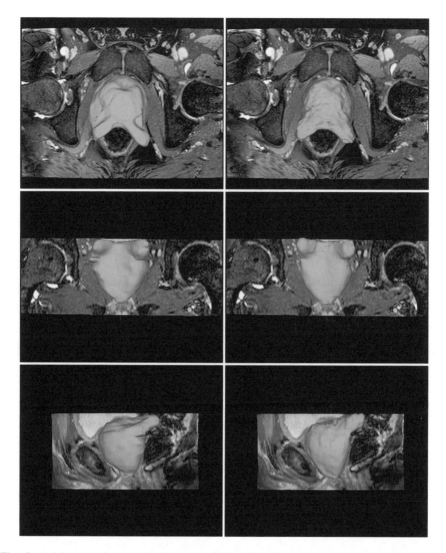

Fig. 2. Axial, coronal and sagittal views of the original expert contours (left column) and automatic best multi atlas (φ=0.98) (right column) prostate (with seminal vesicles) segmentation results overlaid over the original MR scan for one subject (case #5, DSC=0.915).

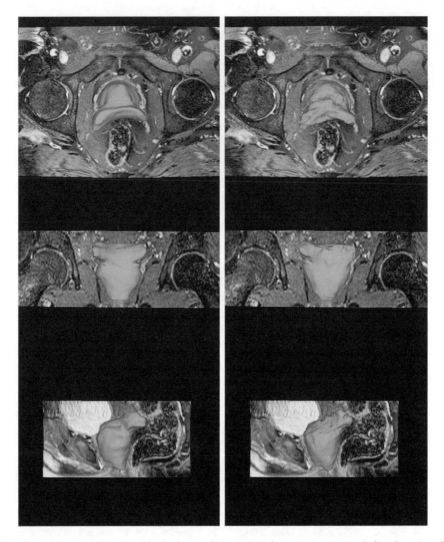

Fig. 3. Axial, coronal and sagittal views of the original expert contours (left column) and automatic best multi atlas (φ=0.98) (right column) prostate (with seminal vesicles) segmentation results overlaid over the original MR scan for one subject (case #11, DSC=0.92).

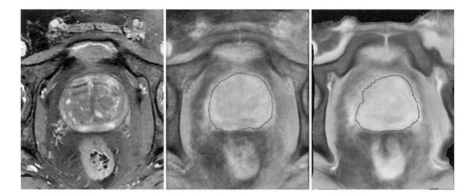

Fig. 4. Axial slice of (from left): an original patient MR scan with prostate contour overlay, (centre) the multi-atlas result ($\varphi=0.98$, DSC=0.88); and (right) the average atlas based segmentation result for this patient scan (DSC=0.81). Note that the multi-atlas approach (centre) only uses the fused contours, and the intensity image is shown for comparison purposes. The aim of this figure is to illustrate typical differences between atlas based segmentation methods.

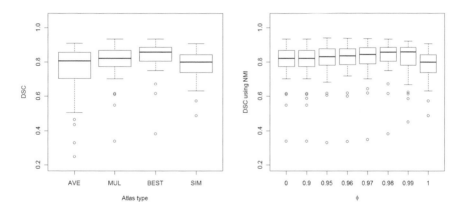

Fig. 5. (left) Comparison of DSC results for the average shape atlas (AVE), MUL ($\varphi=0$, NMI), best result ($\varphi=0.98$, NMI) and SIM ($\varphi=1$, NMI). (right) The DSC results for different threshold values of φ applied with NMI used for mutli-atlas selection. Note that it is possible to identify outlier results (DSC less than 0.7) by applying a selection threshold during the atlas selection process.

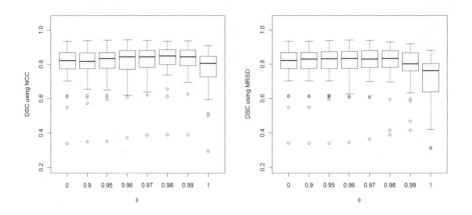

Fig. 6. (right) The DSC results for different threshold values of φ applied with (left) normalized cross correlation (NCC) and (right) mean root squared difference (MRSD).

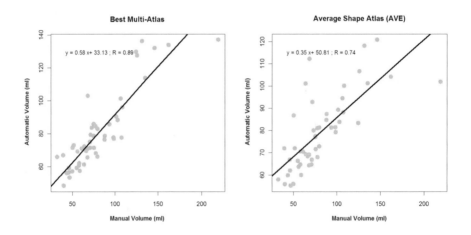

Fig. 7. Plots of automatic and manual prostate volume for (left) the best atlas (φ=0.98), and (right) the average shape atlas (AVE). Regression coefficients and Pearson correlation (R) are overlaid.

A mean surface error of 2.00±1.3mm was found for the multi-atlas method using φ=0.98 and NMI. This compares to 2.58±1.75mm for MUL; 2.59±1.37mm for SIM; and 3.53±3.39 from the average shape atlas (AVE). The correlation between the manual and automatic volume for the best multi-atlas result was found to be 0.89 compared to 0.74 for the average shape atlas (Fig. 7).

4   Discussion and Conclusion

During radiation therapy improved knowledge of the prostate border should result in less normal tissues receiving unnecessary and harmful high doses of radiation with subsequently fewer and less severe side-effects of treatment. Results from the multi-atlas approach using NMI for atlas selection and a selection threshold value of $\varphi=0.98$ were superior to all other methods. The average shape atlas performed worse than any multi-atlas selection method at that threshold.   The best median DSC result (0.86) was very close to the median interobserver DSC of 0.87, and slightly higher than the result reported in [8]. The median DSC is the same as that reported by Martin et al. using an average shape atlas and deformable model approach. Our average surface error of 2.00mm using the multi-atlas approach is an improvement on the 2.41mm reported in that paper [7].

The goal of atlas based segmentation is to segment any scan, however the training database can be too small to cover the range of morphology observed in the population. Therefore a further improvement to the selection process is to detect scans which are unlikely to find an adequate match in the database, and will not be segmented correctly. These can be detected by applying a threshold on the maximum atlas selection similarity metric. For example, one outlier case from the multi-atlas method had an average pairwise DSC=0.38, but also had the worst maximum NMI over the selection region, Ψ. This method can be used to identify patient scans which are unlikely to be accurately segmented (for example, the DSC scores below 0.7 in Figures 2 and 3). This will be explored in future work.

We are interested in quantifying how efficiently an automatic pipeline for prostate segmentation from MRI can be achieved using multi-atlas based methods. Using a local cluster it should be possible to perform the entire pipeline (including scan acquisition) in around 10 minutes using the steps in Table 1. Our preprocessing stage (which may not be included in other comparable papers) currently takes 3 minutes however it should be noted that no attempt at optimization has been made at this stage.

Table 1. Approximate time required for multi-atlas automatic prostate segmentation (timings based on dual CPU (each 2.4GHz i7) PC running Linux with 12Gb RAM).

Step		Time	*Notes*
1	Image acquisition	~2 mins	*Phillips 3T MR scanner. See [8] for details.*
2	Preprocessing	~3 mins	*The preprocessing methods have not been optimized and this time could be significantly reduced, particularly with the use of GPU technology.*
3	Pairwise registration	~1.5 mins * num atlases	*This is per atlas registration. These should be run in parallel on a local cluster or via the cloud.*
4	Atlas fusion	~2 mins	*Depends on the similarity metric used, and also the number of matching of atlas cases.*
5	Data transfer	~1 min	

Acknowledgments. This work was partially funded by the Cancer Council NSW, Project Grants RG 07-06 and RG-11-05.

References

1. Karlsson, M., Karlsson, M.G., Nyholm, T., Amies, C., Zackrisson, B.: Dedicated magnetic resonance imaging in the radiotherapy clinic. Int. J. Radiat. Oncol. Biol. Phys. 74, 644–651 (2009)
2. Raaymakers, B.W., Lagendijk, J.J.W., Overweg, J., Kok, J.G.M., Raaijmakers, A.J.E., Kerkhof, E.M., van der Put, R.W., Meijsing, I., Crijns, S.P.M., Benedosso, F., van Vulpen, M., de Graaff, C.H.W., Allen, J., Brown, K.J.: Integrating a 1.5 T MRI scanner with a 6 MV accelerator: proof of concept. Phys. Med. Biol. 54, N229–N237, (2009)
3. Prabhakar, R., Julka, P.K., Ganesh, T., Munshi, A., Joshi, R.C., Rath, G.K.: Feasibility of using MRI alone for 3D Radiation Treatment Planning in Brain Tumors. Japanese Journal of Clinical Oncology 37, 405–411 (2007)
4. Roach, M., Faillace-Akazawa, P., Malfatti, C., Holland, J., Hricak, H.: Prostate volumes defined by magnetic resonance imaging and computerized tomographic scans for three-dimensional conformal radiotherapy. Int. J. Radiat. Oncol. Biol. Phys. 35, 1011–1018 (1996)
5. Rasch, C., Barillot, I., Remeijer, P., Touw, A., Herk, M., van Lebesque, J.V.: Definition of the prostate in CT and MRI: a multi-observer study. International Journal of Radiation Oncology Biology Physics 43, 57–66 (1999)
6. Rohlfing, T., Brandt, R., Menzel, R., Maurer, C.R.: Evaluation of atlas selection strategies for atlas-based image segmentation with application to confocal microscopy images of bee brains. Neuroimage 21, 1428–1442 (2004)
7. Martin, S., Troccaz, J., Daanenc, V.: Automated segmentation of the prostate in 3D MR images using a probabilistic atlas and a spatially constrained deformable model. Med. Phys. 37, 1579–1590 (2010)
8. Klein, S., Heide, U.A., van der Lips, I.M., Vulpen, M., van Staring, M., Pluim, J.P.W.: Automatic segmentation of the prostate in 3D MR images by atlas matching using localized mutual information. Medical Physics 35, 1407–1417 (2008)
9. Rueckert, D., Sonoda, L.I., Hayes, C., Hill, D.L., Leach, M.O., Hawkes, D.J.: Nonrigid registration using free-form deformations: application to breast MR images. IEEE Transactions on Medical Imaging 18, 712–721 (1999)
10. Dowling, J., Lambert, J., Parker, J., Greer, P.B., Fripp, J., Denham, J., Ourselin, S., Salvado, O.: Automatic MRI atlas-based external beam radiation therapy treatment planning for prostate cancer. In: Madabhushi, A., et al. (eds.) MICCAI 2010. LNCS, vol. 6369, pp. 25–33. Springer, Heidelberg (2010)
11. Greer, P.B., Dowling, J.A., Lambert, J.A., Fripp, J., Parker, J., Denham, J.W., Wratten, C., Capp, A., Salvado, O.: A magnetic resonance imaging-based workflow for planning radiation therapy for prostate cancer. The Medical Journal of Australia 194, S24–S27 (2011)
12. Lambert, J., Greer, P.B., Menk, F., Patterson, J., Parker, J., Capp, A., Wratten, C., Dowling, J., Salvado, O., Hughes, C., Fisher, K., Ostwald, P., Denham, J.W.: MRI-guided prostate radiation therapy planning: Investigation of dosimetric accuracy of MRI-based dose planning. Radiotherapy and Oncology 98, 330–334 (2011)

13. Warfield, S.K., Zou, K.H., Wells, W.M.: Simultaneous truth and performance level estimation (STAPLE): an algorithm for the validation of image segmentation. IEEE Transactions on Medical Imaging 23, 903–921 (2004)

14. Tustison, N.J., Avants, B.B., Cook, P.A., Zheng, Y., Egan, A., Yushkevich, P.A., Gee, J.C.: N4ITK: Improved N3 Bias Correction. IEEE Transactions on Medical Imaging 29, 1310–1320 (2010)

15. Vercauteren, T., Pennec, X., Perchant, A., Ayache, N.: Non-parametric Diffeomorphic Image Registration with the Demons Algorithm. In: Ayache, N., Ourselin, S., Maeder, A. (eds.) MICCAI 2007, Part II. LNCS, vol. 4792, pp. 319–326. Springer, Heidelberg (2007)

16. Dice, L.R.: Measures of the Amount of Ecologic Association Between Species. Ecology 26, 297–302 (1945)

A Morphological Atlas of Prostate's Zonal Anatomy for Construction of Realistic Digital and Physical Phantoms

N. Makni[1,*], A. Iancu[1,2,3], P. Puech[1,2,3], S. Mordon[1,2], and N. Betrouni[1,2]

[1] Inserm, U703,152, rue du Docteur Yersin, 59120 Loos, France
[2] Université Lille-Nord de France, Loos, France
[3] Radiology Departement, Hopital Claude Huriez, CHRU Lille, France

Abstract. Validation of computer-aided detection and intervention procedures for prostate cancer is still a challenging issue. Despite the increasing accuracy of prostate image analysis tools, in vivo and in silico validations are necessary before they can be deployed in clinical routine. In this study, we developed a statistical atlas of prostate morphology for construction of realistic digital and physical phantoms. We have been interested in modeling the gland's zonal anatomy as defined by the peripheral zone and the central gland. Magnetic Resonance Imaging studies from 30 patients were used. Mean shape and most relevant deformations for prostate structures were computed using principal component analysis. The resulting statistical atlas has been used in image simulation and the design of a physical phantom of the prostate.

Keywords: Prostate, peripheral zone, transition zone, atlas, models, phantom, simulation.

1 Introduction

Prostate cancer (PCa) diagnosis has experienced an important development through the combination of prostatic specific antigen (PSA), digital rectal examination (DRE) and image-guided biopsy by transrectal ultrasound (TRUS) or magnetic resonance imaging (MRI). By the other hand, in addition to conventional treatment techniques (prostatectomy, radiotherapy and brachytherapy) a concept of focal therapies is emerging where the aim is to treat only the tumor. These focal therapies constitute an intermediate option between watchful waiting and radical therapy for small volume and low-grade prostate cancer. In all these procedures, imaging takes an increasingly growing position and image analysis has become crucial. Based on this observation and from the ubiquitous need for 3D data set with well-known ground truth to validate image processing tools/algorithms/methods, our motivation was to create a digital morphologic phantom of the prostate and its substructures. A similar solution had already been proposed for human brain [1]. Brainweb's phantom combines a statistical model and MR imaging simulator and is publically available (www.bic.mni.mcgill.ca/brainweb). A statistical atlas of prostate cancer distribution

---

* Corresponding author.

A. Madabhushi et al. (Eds.): Prostate Cancer Imaging 2011, LNCS 6963, pp. 22–34, 2011.

had been proposed by Shen et al.[2] for optimizing biopsies. It is also free and can be retrieved from the authors' website (www.rad.upenn.edu/sbia/projects/prostate.html). This atlas is limited to a statistical description of tumors' localization within the prostate, and does not model the gland's morphology or zonal anatomy. In fact, from a morphologic point of view, the prostate is an exocrine gland, shaped like a pyramid with an upward base. The zonal anatomy of the prostate has been described for the first time in the 60's, but the use of terms in anatomical practice was introducedin the 80's [3].It is composed of four zones: peripheral zone (PZ), central zone, transition zone (TZ) and fibro-muscular structure (figure 1). PZ and TZ are key structures, as 70% of prostate tumors are located within PZ. Inversely, benign hypertrophy (BPH) most often occurs in the transition zone, which becomes larger with age. From a radiologic point of view, for men aged over 50 years, only two areas of the prostate are considered: the central gland (hypertrophied transition zone and peri-urethral glands) and peripheral zone. In this study, transition zone (TZ) refers to the central gland. As shown by Figure 1, TZ is surrounded by the PZ, which thickness and size depend on patient's age and prostate pathological symptoms, like benign hypertrophy (BPH). The PZ is surrounded by vessels and is very likely tohost irregular tissues like tumors. In the next sections, we describe the statistical atlas construction and we detail how we use it to create realistic digital and physical phantoms of the prostate including the peripheral zone and the transition zone. Digital phantom can be used to simulate prostate MRI and to evaluate automatic segmentation methods. It also provides a statistical model of the gland's anatomy, which can be used in segmentation/registration techniques as an *a priori*. Physical phantom can be used in training and optimization of focal treatment therapies of prostate cancer.

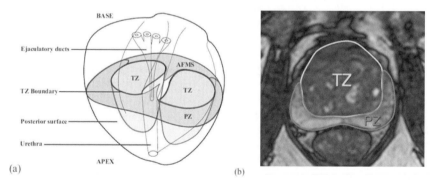

Fig. 1. (a) Anatomic description and (b) T2-weighted MRI of a 60cm^3 prostate showing its zonal anatomy with a transverse section at the verumontanum level (TZ:Transition zone, PZ: peripheral zone, AFMS: anterior fibro-muscular stroma).

2 Atlas Construction

2.1 Data

MR images database was collected based on patients' age and prostate volume considerations. The median age of patients is 74 years. 66% of cases are diagnosed after the age of 70 and 0.3%before the age of 50 [4]. The normal volume of a young man prostate is of 20cm^3 to 30cm^3. It was found that 50% of men have prostate benign hypertrophy before 60; this percentage increases to 90% for 85 years old men [5]. It was also shown that the sole factor influencing the prostate size was the age [6]. Our images database contains images from 30 patients, suspected with PCa. Each patient was screened using multi-parametric MRI that includes an axial 3D T2-weighted Balanced Turbo Field Echo (BTFE) sequence (voxel size 0.48x0.48x1.3 mm3), an axial T2-weighted sequence (Voxel size 0.31x0.31x4.0 mm^3) and a coronal T2-weighted sequence (Voxel size 0.31x0.31x4 mm^3). A TRUS guided biopsy was also realized. Table 1 summarizes characteristics of these patients.

2.2 Preprocessing

Subsol et al.[7] presented a global scheme for the construction of morphologic anatomical atlases and highlighted this operation needs to address two major issues: defining shape description parameters and handling large amounts of 3D data. The aim of the preprocessing is tomanage these issues and to make the data more suitable for analysis and modeling.

2.2.a Segmentation: this first step is performed to extract the structures (gland, PZ and TZ). Numerous automatic methods forprostate segmentationon MRI have been introduced [8-11]. However, these methods are very likely to fail at the apex and the base of the gland. Therefore, we preferred a manual delineation. An experienced radiologist involved in the diagnosis of prostate cancer used dedicatedhomemade software to segment the gland, the PZ and the TZ on the multi-parametric MR images. The software is able to register the sequences and provides a user-friendly interface allowingthe radiologist to display fusion of different series in three orientations: axial, coronal and sagittal (figure 2). This functionality allows checking prostate's boundaries at the level of its apex and base, which have better contrast with surrounding structures on coronal T2-w series.

At the end of this segmentation process, 30 glands, 30 PZ and 30 TZ were obtained. Marching cube surface reconstructionwas then performed to render 3D triangular mesh of these structures. These mesh were then down-sampled using Blender (a free open source 3D content creation software) and smoothed using [19].

2.2.b Normalization and correspondence solving: As the training set contains inter-patients data and the modeling process is based on the variation of the positions of surface mesh points (vertices) over the set, it is important to align these points in the same way according to a set of axes. Among the 30 patients, a patient with a prostate of 45cm^3 (mean value) of volume is chosen as reference and the 29 remaining prostates are aligned on this reference. A first alignment (rotation, translation and scaling) is achieved using the Iterative Closest Point (ICP) algorithm [12]. A second alignment is required tohaveeven moreaccurateand optimal solving of the correspondences. We used a non-rigid registration based on the algorithm of Chui and Rangarajan [13]. This method computes the optimal non-rigid mapping between 2 datasets using a local parametric transformation based on Thin Plate Splines (TPS) introduced by Bookstein [14]. Starting from these segmented, aligned and normalized data, a model can be computed for each structure (the gland, the peripheral zone and the transition zone).

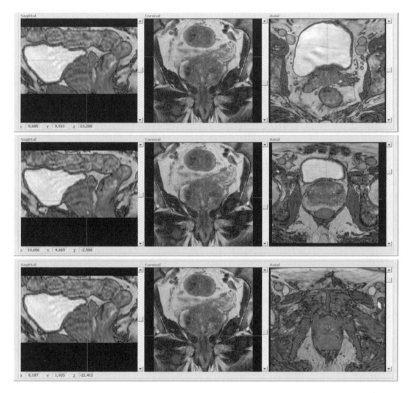

Fig. 2. A user-friendly interface used to delineate the structures (the gland, the PZ and the TZ). This interface allows the radiologist to load and to display a multi-planar MR study. Each row shows a display of T2-weightedcoronal acquisition, an axial 3D BTFE acquisition and a sagittal reconstruction from axial 3D BTFE. This navigation allows a better delimitation of prostate's base (first row) and apex (third row).

2.3 Statistical Shape Modeling

The model is deduced from the training set using Principal Component Analysis (PCA), which enables to extract the mean shape $\overline{X}$ and the most important deformation fields [15]:

$$\overline{X} = \frac{1}{N} \sum_{i=1}^{N} X_i \tag{1}$$

And

$$S = \frac{1}{N-1} \sum_{i=1}^{N} dX_i \overline{dX_i} \tag{2}$$

Wherein

$$dX_i = \overline{X} - X_i \tag{3}$$

Main variations around mean shape correspond to Eigen values of the covariance matrix S. Each eigenvector is responsible for a variance equal to its Eigen value. Its contribution to total shape variation can be expressed as:

$$\alpha_k = \frac{\lambda_k}{\sum \lambda_i} \tag{4}$$

Wherein λ_k and α_k are Eigen values and eigenvectors' contribution to shape variance, respectively.Thus, by considering the matrix $\phi = (\phi_1,..,\phi_m)$ composed by the m eigenvectors corresponding to the m most important eigenvalues, a structure shape could be expressed as:

$$X = \overline{X} + b.\phi \tag{5}$$

Wherein $b = (b_1,...,b_m)$ is an R^m vector of vectors' weights. By applying limits to the variation of these weights it can be ensured that a generated shape is similar to those contained in the initial training set. Usually variation fields are defined in the following interval:

$$|b_i| \leq 3\sqrt{\lambda_i} \tag{6}$$

3 Results

For the gland model, 16 deformation modes were retained. They allowed capturing 95% of the deformations. Table 2 shows the contribution each eigenvalue. For the transition zone, 17 deformation modes were selected to obtain a global deformations description of 95% (table 3). Note that, for convex structures (gland and transition zone), the first eigenvalue allows to describe a large field of the deformations (about 58%). It was not the case for the peripheral zone which form is not convex (table 4).The 6 first most important eigenvalues allowed capturing only 52% of the deformations. Figure 3 shows some of these deformations for the 3 structures.

Table 1. Characteristics of the selected patients

Patient	Age (years)	Volumetry (cm^3)		Biopsy	PSA (ng/ml)
		TRUS	MRI		
1	55	40	45	Normal	3,93
2	53	54	52	Gleason 7	15,58
3	68	56	58	Gleason 9	3,92
4	72	85	86	Normal	9,7
5	49	35	30	Gleason 6	5,54
6	60	42	41	Gleason 6	5,5
7	65	100	88	Normal	4.7
8	74	90	90	Normal	8.5
9	73	172	170	Normal	4,89
10	60	56	52	Normal	7,25
11	66	30	38	Gleason 6	10
12	73	70	72	Normal	9,28
13	77	44	49	Gleason 7	9,9
14	55	32	34	Gleason 7	9,7
15	56	55	37	Normal	6,15
16	68	83	111	Normal	4,89
17	56	65	75	Normal	6,6
18	74	60	61	Gleason 7	6,55
19	70	130	105	Normal	10,9
20	70	36	35	Gleason 7	2,9
21	71	56	70	Gleason 7	16,76
22	60	65	55	Gleason 6	12,1
23	59	45	46	Gleason 9	9,2
24	58	30	25	Gleason 7	10
25	69	45	40	Normal	9,81
26	56	77	81	Normal	7,09
27	73	45	46	Gleason 6	5,58
28	56	50	43	Normal	6,66
29	66	32	37	Gleason 6	54,63
30	68	35	37	Gleason 7	8,91

Table 2. Individual and cumulative contributions of the 16 eigenvalues retained to describe the shape variation of the gland

Eigenvalue	Individual contribution	Cumulative contribution
1	58.33%	58.33%
2	6.51%	64.84%
3	5.72%	70.56%
4	4.26%	74.81%
5	3.11%	77.82%
6	2.57%	80.50%
7	2.22%	82.72%
8	1.96%	84.68%
9	1.90%	86.58%
10	1.60%	88.18%
11	1.45%	89.62%
12	1.39%	91.02%
13	1.28%	92.30%
14	1.21%	93.51%
15	1.09%	94.60%
16	1.04%	95.65%

Table 3. Individual and cumulative contributions of the 17 eigenvalues retained to describe the shape variation of the transition zone

Eigenvalue	Individual contribution	Cumulative contribution
1	58.58%	58.58%
2	5.91%	64.49%
3	3.88%	68.37%
4	3.34%	71.72%
5	2.77%	74.49%
6	2.50%	76.99%
7	2.32%	79.31%
8	2.24%	81.54%
9	1.96%	83.50%
10	1.89%	85.38%
11	1.78%	87.16%
12	1.63%	88.80%
13	1.50%	90.29%
14	1.43%	91.72%
15	1.36%	93.08%
16	1.25%	94.33%
17	1.22%	95.54%

Table 4. Individual and cumulative contributions of the 19 eigenvalues retained to describe the shape variation of the peripheral zone

Eigenvalue	Individual contribution	Cumulative contribution
1	16.21%	16.21%
2	9.05%	25.17%
3	8.17%	33.34%
4	7.28%	40.63%
5	5.77%	46.40%
6	5.60%	52.00%
7	4.99%	56.99%
8	4.62%	61.61%
9	4.38%	65.98%
10	4.02%	70.00%
11	3.91%	73.91%
12	3.43%	77.35%
13	3.05%	80.39%
14	2.98%	83.37%
15	2.82%	86.19%
16	2.69%	88.88%
17	2.43%	91.31%
18	2.27%	93.58%
19	2.22%	95.80%

4 Applications of the Atlas

4.1 Digital Phantom

One of the main applications of these Atlas is the simulation of images with perfectly known Ground Truth for the validation of segmentation/registration/detection algorithms. For this purpose, the shape models are used to create empty structures (gland, ZP and ZT) then tissue intensities are mapped in the following way: TZ was filled with its mean MR value (issued from a specified MR sequence for instance T2-weighted, a Diffusion Weighted or Dynamic contrast). The PZ level is thendeducedusing a pre-determined contrast value, which is computed as:

$$C = \frac{|I_{TZ} - I_{PZ}|}{|I_{TZ} + I_{PZ}|} \tag{7}$$

Where ITZ and IPZ are mean MR signals of TZ and PZ. Gaussian noise, with a chosen standard deviation, is then added. Standard median filter was finally applied toreduce salt-pepper effect and smooth the images (figure 4). This process provides morphologically realistic images of the prostate and its substructures based on a known ground truth.

4.2 Physical Phantom

Current challenges in prostate cancer treatment concern the development of focal therapies to target only the tumor.These new therapeutics like Interstitial Laser Therapy, High Intensities Focused Ultrasound (HIFU) or cryotherapy require preclinical evaluation and simulation to accurately plan the intervention. These simulations can be performed on physical phantoms. However, existing commercial phantoms are designed to guide biopsies or global treatment as brachytherapies and do not allow precise description of the anatomy. We used the digital phantom to construct a physical phantom. It was composed of 2 parts: (i) a fixed part that contains

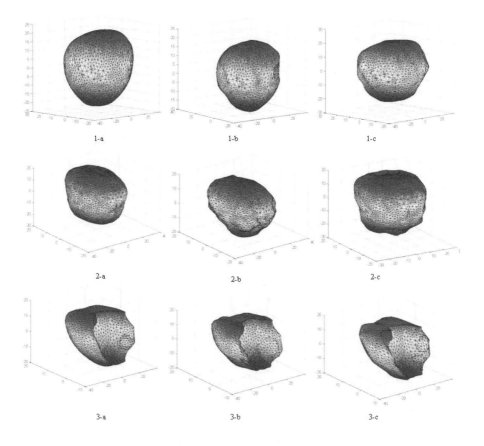

Fig. 3. Mean shapes and deformations of the structures. Plots1-a, 1-b and 1-c describe the gland mean shape and 2 deformation modes, respectively. Plots 2-a, 2-b and 2-c describe the model and 2 deformations for the transition zone. Plots 3-a, 3-b and 3-c describe the model and 2 deformation modes for the peripheral zone.

perineum and rectum, and (ii) a removable part with a prostate. The prostate form was created using a 3D printer system starting from the numerical generated model. Thus, different configurations with different prostate sizes were possible (figure 5). The phantom was evaluated using TRUS, MRI and real-time thermometry. Diffusing fibers were inserted into the model to simulate a focal treatment conducted by interstitial laser thermotherapy. Prostate cancer boundaries and laser fiber placement were assessed by TRUS sonography.

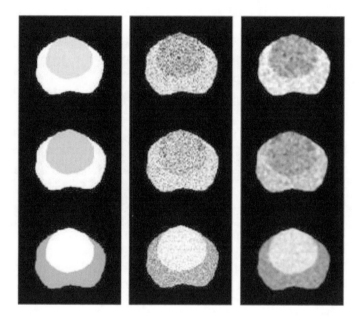

Fig. 4. Atlas-based image simulation. From Left to right: PZ and TZ labeled with their respective mean level, data with Gaussian noise, data after a smoothing median filter. First, second and third lines represent T2-weighted, DWI and T1-CEMRI respectively.

These experiments proved that this kind of phantoms allows a real simulation of laser therapy procedure: target definition and fibers placement optimization using MR imaging, treatment delivery and finally treatment monitoring using TRUS imaging.

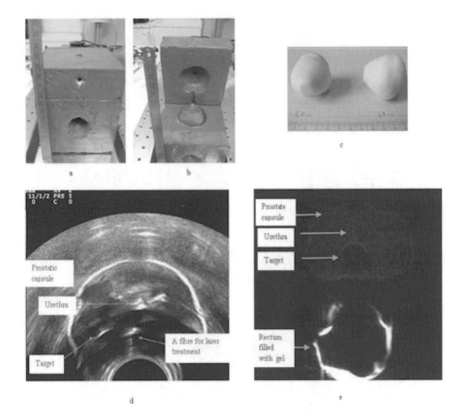

Fig. 5. Physical phantom for focal treatment planning of prostate cancer. (a) and (b) the phantom with the 2 parts and the prostate emplacement. (c) 2 different sizes prostate (40 and 45 cm3) that could be installed in the prostate place inside the phantom. (d) An ultrasound image of the phantom and visualization of the prostate capsule the urethra and a potential target. (e) MR T2 weighted acquisition of the phantom with the visualization of the structures.

5   Discussion and Conclusion

The rationale of constructing and using digital phantoms is that ground truth becomes available to optimize, control or validate different procedures. Many computerized and robotized procedures have been developed for prostate cancer management and it becomes crucial to have common tools for validation and comparison of these procedures. In this study we designed a morphological atlas of prostate's zonal anatomy. The atlas was constructed using data from a selected and representative group of patients. We focused on the prostate gland and two main structures: the Peripheral Zone and the rest of the gland, which is referred to as Transition Zone in this study. Principal component analysis allowed extracting a description of main deformations of each structure (table 2, 3 and 4).

We used the atlas for 2 applications. First, image simulation (figure 4).The purpose was to render simulated images of the prostate with a well-known ground truth to validate segmentation algorithms. The atlas can also be combined with the probabilistic tumors atlas proposed by Shen et al.[2] and include tumors' information in the simulation process. Simulation of prostate gland, its substructures and tumors distribution provides realistic simulated images to validate prostate cancer detection and staging algorithms.More relevant MR image simulators [17] will be used to produce closer-to-reality simulatedprostate MRI [16].

The second application involves planning of focal treatment. The purpose was the design of a physical realistic phantom to optimize a therapeutic approach consisting in introducing laser fiber inside the prostate (the tumor) to perform a focal ablation. Usually this kind of treatment is recommended for low-grade prostate cancer for glands from 30 to 60 cm^3. Thus, staring from the digital atlas, it was possible to create, Using 3D printing technology, different prostates were created based on atlas shape information and could be inserted in a mold that forms a pelvis (figure 5). This physical phantom was multimodality compatible and allowed focal targeting.Similar approach for the construction of an anatomically correct physical phantom was described in [18] to test imaging and ablation techniques of prostate cancer. This phantom allowed a good visualization of the prostate but it was designed to use only a fixed prostate size (80 cm^3) and did not permit the modeling of the 2 structures PZ and TZ.

References

1. Collins, D.L., Zijdenbos, A.P., kollokian, V., Sled, J.G., Kabani, N.J., Holmes, C.J., Evans, A.C.: Design and construction of a realistic digital brain phantom. IEEE Trans. Med. Img. 17(3), 463–468 (1998)
2. Shen, D., Lao, Z., Zeng, J., Zhang, W., Sesterhenn, I.A., Sun, L., Moul, J.W., Herskovits, E.H., Fichtinger, G., Davatzikos, C.: Optimized prostate biopsy via statistical atlas of cancer spatial distribution. Medical Image Analysis 8, 139–150 (2004)
3. McNeal, J.E.: The zonal anatomy of the prostate. Prostate 2, 35–49 (1981)
4. Villers, A., Grosclaude, P.: Epidemiology of prostate cancer. Médecine Nucléaire 32(1), 2–4 (2007)
5. Bushman, W.: Etiology, epidemiology, and natural history of benign prostatic hyperplasia. Urologic Clinics of North America 36(4), 403–415 (2009)
6. Bosch, J.L., Tilling, K., Bohnen, A.M., Bangma, C.H., Donovan, J.L.: Establishing normal reference ranges for prostate volume change with age in the population-based Krimpen-study: prediction of future prostate volume in individual men. Prostate 67, 1816–1824 (2007)
7. Subsol, G., Thirion, J.P., Ayache, N.: A scheme for automatically building three-dimensional morphometric anatomical atlases: application to a skull atlas. Medical Image Analysis 2(1), 37–60 (1998)
8. Pasquier, D., Lacornerie, T., Vermandel, M., Rousseau, J., Lartigau, E., Betrouni, N.: Automatic segmentation of pelvic structures from magnetic resoncance images for prostate cancer radiotherapy. International Journal of Oncology Biology Physics 68(2), 592–600 (2007)

9. Klein, S., Van der Heide, U.A., Lips, I.M., Van Vulpen, M., Staring, M., Pluim, J.P.: Automatic segmentation of the prostate in 3D MR images by atlas matching using localized mutual information. Med. Phys. 35(4), 1407–1417 (2008)
10. Makni, N., Puech, P., Lopes, R., Dewalle, A.S., Colot, O., Betrouni, N.: Combining a deformable model and a probabilistic framework for an automatic 3D segmentation of prostate on MRI. International Journal of Computer Assisted Radiology and Surgery 4(2), 181–188 (2009)
11. Toth, R., Tiwari, P., Rosen, M., Reed, G., Kurhanewicz, J., Kalyanpur, A., Pungavkar, S., Madabhushi, A.: A Magnetic Resonance Spectroscopy Driven Initialization Scheme for Active Shape Model Based Prostate Segmentation. Medical Image Analysis 15(2), 214–225 (2010)
12. Besl, P.J., Mckay, N.D.: A Method for Registration of 3-D Shapes. IEEE Transactions on Pattern Analysis and Matching Intelligence 14(2), 239–256 (1992)
13. Chui, H., Rangarajan, A.: A new algorithm for non rigid point matching. Computer Vision and Image Understanding 89(2-3), 114–141 (2003)
14. Bookstein, F.: Principal warps: Thin-plate splines and the decomposition of deformations. IEEE Transactions on Pattern Analysis and Matching Intelligence 11(6), 567–585 (1989)
15. Cootes, T.F., Hill, A., Taylor, C.J., Haslam, J.: The use of Active Shape Models For Locating Structures in Medical Images. Image Vision and Computing 12(6), 355–366 (1994)
16. Atalar, E., Ménard, C.: MR-guided interventions for prostate cancer. Magnetic Resonance Imaging Clinics of North America 13, 491–504 (2005); prostate carcinoma: Areview. Medical Image Analysis 10, 178–199 (2006)
17. Benoit-Cattin, H., Collewet, G., Belaroussi, B., Saint-Jalmes, H., Odet, C.: The SIMRI project: a versatile and interactive MRI simulator. J. Magn. Reson. 173(1), 97–115 (2005)
18. Lindner, U., Lawrentschuk, N., Weersink, R.A., Raz, O., Hlasny, E., Sussman, M.S., Davidson, S.R., Gertner, M.R., Trachtenberg, J.: Construction and evaluation of an anatomically correct multi-image modality compatible phantom for prostate cancer focal ablation. J. Urol. 184(1), 352–357 (2010)
19. Desbrun, M., Meyer, M., Schröder, P., Barr, A.H.: Implicit fairing of irregular meshes using diffusion and curvature flow. In: Proceedings of the 26th Annual Conference on Computer Graphics and Interactive Techniques, pp. 317–324 (1999)

Multiple Mean Models of Statistical Shape and Probability Priors for Automatic Prostate Segmentation

Soumya Ghose[1,2], Arnau Oliver[1], Robert Martí[1], Xavier Lladó[1],
Jordi Freixenet[1], Jhimli Mitra[1,2], Joan C. Vilanova[3], Josep Comet[4],
and Fabrice Meriaudeau[2]

[1] Computer Vision and Robotics Group, University of Girona, Campus Montilivi,
Edifici P-IV, Av. Lluís Santaló , s/n, 17071 Girona, Spain
[2] Laboratoire Le2I - UMR CNRS 5158, Université de Bourgogne, 12 Rue de la
Fonderie, 71200 Le Creusot, France
[3] Girona Magnetic Resonance Imaging Center, Girona, Spain
[4] University Hospital Dr. Josep Trueta, Girona, Spain

Abstract. Low contrast of the prostate gland, heterogeneous intensity distribution inside the prostate region, imaging artifacts like shadow regions, speckle and significant variations in prostate shape, size and inter dataset contrast in Trans Rectal Ultrasound (TRUS) images challenge computer aided automatic or semi-automatic segmentation of the prostate. In this paper, we propose a probabilistic framework for automatic initialization and propagation of multiple mean parametric models derived from principal component analysis of shape and posterior probability information of the prostate region to segment the prostate. Unlike traditional statistical models of shape and intensity priors we use posterior probability of the prostate region to build our texture model of the prostate and use the information in initialization and propagation of the mean model. Furthermore, multiple mean models are used compared to a single mean model to improve segmentation accuracies. The proposed method achieves mean Dice Similarity Coefficient (DSC) value of 0.97 ± 0.01, and mean Mean Absolute Distance (MAD) value of 0.49 ± 0.20 mm when validated with 23 datasets with considerable shape, size, and intensity variations, in a leave-one-patient-out validation framework. The model achieves statistically significant t-test p-value<0.0001 in mean DSC and mean MAD values compared to traditional statistical models of shape and texture. Introduction of the probabilistic information of the prostate region and multiple mean models into the traditional statistical shape and texture model framework, significantly improve the segmentation accuracies.

Keywords: Prostate Segmentation, Bayesian Framework, Multiple Statistical Shape and Posterior Probability Models.

A. Madabhushi et al. (Eds.): Prostate Cancer Imaging 2011, LNCS 6963, pp. 35–46, 2011.
© Springer-Verlag Berlin Heidelberg 2011

1   Introduction

An estimated 913,000 people worldwide were diagnosed with prostate cancer [1] in 2008. TRUS guided biopsy is commonly used to diagnose prostate cancer due to inexpensive real-time nature of the system and simplicity [15]. Accurate prostate segmentation in TRUS may aid in radiation therapy planning, motion monitoring, biopsy needle placement and multimodal image fusion between TRUS and magnetic resonance imaging (MRI) to improve malignant tissue extraction during biopsy [15]. However, accurate computer aided prostate segmentation from TRUS images encounters considerable challenges due to low contrast of TRUS images, heterogeneous intensity distribution inside the prostate gland, speckle, shadow artifacts, and presence of micro-calcifications inside the prostate. There is no global characterization for the prostate and the non-prostate regions in terms of pixel intensities and region appearance [15]. Moreover, inter patient prostate shape, size and deformation may vary significantly.

Often deformable models and statistical shape models are used in prostate segmentation. For example Badiel et al. [2] used a deformable model of warping ellipse and Ladak et al. [11] used discrete dynamic contour to achieve semi-automatic prostate segmentation. However, TRUS guided procedures should necessarily be automatic. Shen et al. [14] and Zhan et al. [16] presented an automatic method that incorporated a priori shape and texture information from Gabor filters to produce accurate prostate segmentation. However, the method is computationally expensive and probably unsuitable for TRUS guided prostate intervention [15]. In recent years Cosio et al. [6] reported an automatic method for prostate segmentation with active shape models [4]. However, the optimization framework of genetic algorithm used is computationally intensive and unsuitable for TRUS guided intervention.

To address the challenges involved with prostate segmentation in TRUS images we propose a multi-resolution framework using multiple mean parametric models derived from Principal Component Analysis (PCA) of prostate shape and posterior probabilistic values of the prostate region in TRUS images. The performance of our method is compared with the traditional AAM [5] and also with our previous work [9]. Compared to the use of intensity and one mean model as in [5] and to the use of texture from Haar wavelet features in [9], posterior probabilistic information of the prostate region obtained in a Bayesian framework is used to train, initialize and propagate our multiple statistical models of shape and texture. Statistically significant improvement is achieved with the use of multiple mean models in the Bayesian framework when validated with 23 datasets, that have significant shape, size, and contrast variations of the prostate, in leave-one-patient-out validation framework. Experimental results show that our method is unaffected by low contrast, heterogeneity of intensity distribution inside the prostate, speckle, shadow artifacts, micro-calcifications, and significant shape, size and intensity variations of the prostate gland between the datasets. Shen et al. [14] and Zhan et al. [16] proposed to use Gabor filters to model prostate texture and reduce heterogeneity of the prostate region in TRUS images. However, they often concluded that texture information inside the prostate region is unreliable. Hence, we adopt a probabilistic modeling of the prostate region based on both positional information and intensity distribution inside the prostate to reduce heterogeneity. The key contributions of this work are:

– The use of posterior probability information of the prostate region to build the statistical model of texture.
– Using such information in training, automatic initialization and propagation of the mean models.
– The selection of a mean model depending on the error of fitting of the posterior probability information of the prostate region for accurate segmentation.

2   Proposed Segmentation Framework

The proposed method is developed on three major components: 1) Bayesian framework to determine posterior probability of a pixel being prostate, 2) adapting multiple statistical models of shape and texture priors to incorporate the posterior probabilities of the prostate region for training, initialization and propagation of the parametric model and 3) selection of one of the mean models depending on the error of fitting of the posterior probabilities to segment the prostate. We present the Bayesian framework for determining posterior probability of the prostate region first followed by our statistical shape and probability model of the prostate region. The optimization framework is addressed thereafter, and finally the grouping of the datasets for building multiple mean models and selection of one among the mean models for segmentation is discussed.

2.1   Bayesian Formulation

In traditional AAM [5], the point distribution model (PDM) [4] of the contour is aligned to a common reference frame by generalized Procrustes analysis [10]. Intensities are warped into correspondence using a piece wise affine warp and sampled from a shape-free reference. Intensity distribution inside the prostate region may vary significantly from one dataset to another depending on the parameters of acquisition and nature of the prostate tissue of a patient. Hence, the use of intensity distribution of the prostate region to build the texture model, as in traditional AAM introduces larger variabilities producing an inaccurate texture model which adversely affects segmentation results. To reduce inter dataset intensity variabilities and intensity variabilities inside the prostate region, we propose to determine the posterior probability of the image pixels being prostate in a Bayesian framework and use PCA of the posterior probabilities of the prostate region to build our texture model. We use K-means clustering to roughly cluster the pixels into two classes (prostate and non-prostate) from the intensities. The class means and standard deviations obtained from this rough clustering are then used as the initial estimates in an expectation maximization (EM) [8] framework to determine the probability of a pixel being prostate from intensities. The E-step assigns the probabilities to the pixels depending on the

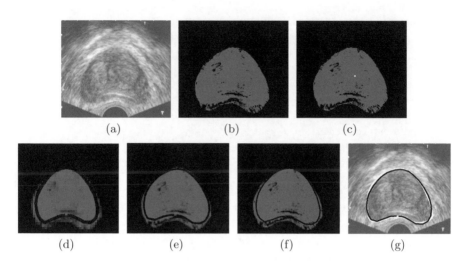

Fig. 1. Bayesian framework (a) TRUS image of a prostate (b) a posteriori of a pixel being prostate, (c) centroid (white dot) computed from posterior probability values for AAM initialization. On initialization, the AAM segments prostate in a multi-resolution framework 1(d), 1(e) and 1(f) to give final segmentation 1(g).

current mean and standard deviation values of the classes, while in M-step the means and standard deviation values are re-estimated. Maximum a posteriori estimates of the class means and standard deviations are used to soft cluster the pixels.

The likelihood of a pixel location in an image being prostate is obtained by normalizing the ground truth values of all the pixels for all the training images as

$$P\left(x_{ps}|C_{prs}\right) = \frac{1}{N}\sum_{i=1}^{N} GT_i \tag{1}$$

where $P\left(x_{ps}|C_{prs}\right)$ gives the probability of a pixel position being prostate with x_{ps} being the pixel location and C_{prs} denoting prostate. GT_i represents ground truth of the training images with N the total number of ground truth images. In our model the class prior probability is estimated from the frequency of the pixels (x) belonging to a class as

$$P\left(C_{Prostate}\right) = \frac{\sum_{i=1}^{pnm} x_i}{\sum_{j=1}^{m} x_j} \tag{2}$$

where $P\left(C_{Prostate}\right)$ gives the class prior probability of being prostate, x_i represents the pixels belonging to prostate region (total given by pnm) and x_j represents the pixels in all training images (given by m). The probabilities of intensity (being prostate) obtained in EM framework, location (being prostate) and class prior probability (prostate class) are used in a Bayesian framework to determine posterior probability of a pixel being prostate (Fig. 1(b)). According to Bayes rule,

$$P(C_i|X) = \frac{P(X|C_i)\,P(C_i)}{P(X)} \tag{3}$$

the posterior probability distribution $P(C_i|X)$ of a class is given by the prior $P(C_i)$ (i.e. $P(C_{Prostate})$) and the likelihood $P(X|C_i)$. $P(X)$ being equal for all classes can be removed from the formulation. Considering class conditional independence (as the probability of a pixel intensity being prostate is independent of the pixel location in the image and vice versa), the likelihood could be formalized as,

$$P(X|C_i) = P(x_{ps}|C_{prs})\,.P(x_{in}|C_{prs}) \tag{4}$$

In equation (4) the likelihood $P(X|C_i)$ is obtained from the product of the probability of a pixel intensity being prostate ($P(x_{in}|C_{prs})$) obtained from EM framework (x_{in} being pixel intensity) and the probability of a pixel location being prostate ($P(x_{ps}|C_{prs})$) obtained from (1). Our approach of using pixel location for determining prior position information of the prostate is based on the works of Cosio et al. [6] and Shen et al. [14]. Both used prior prostate location information in TRUS images for automatic initialization of their model. Cosio et al. [6] used a 3D feature vector of pixel location and intensity value to classify and localize prostate in TRUS images for initialization of their model. Similarly, Shen et al. [14] proposed to use the relative position of the prostate with respect to the TRUS probe (located at the center of the base line of the TRUS image) for initialization. These methods prove that prostate location in TRUS images is not random and provides meaningful information. Hence, we exploit the location information of the prostate in TRUS images in our Bayesian framework to determine the posterior probability of the prostate region.

2.2   Statistical Shape and Texture Model

The process of building the parametric statistical model of shape and texture variations involves the task of building a shape model, a texture model, and consecutively a combined model of texture and shape and prior learning of the optimization space from the combined model perturbation. To build the shape model, a PDM [5] is built by equal angle sampling of the prostate contours to determine the landmarks automatically. The PDM of the contours are aligned to a common reference frame by generalized Procrustes analysis [10]. PCA of the aligned PDMs identifies the principal modes of shape variations. Posteriori probabilistic information (of pixels being prostate) of the segmented region are warped into correspondence using a piece wise affine warp and sampled from shape free reference similar to the AAM [5]. PCA of the posterior probabilities from (4) is used to identify their principal modes of variation. The model may be formalized in the following manner. Let s and t represent the shape and posterior probability models, then

$$s = \bar{s} + \varPhi_s \theta_s, \quad t = \bar{t} + \varPhi_t \theta_t \tag{5}$$

where $\bar{s}$ and $\bar{t}$ denote the mean shape and posterior probability information respectively, then Φ_s and Φ_t contain the first p eigenvectors (obtained from 98% of total variations) of the estimated joint dispersion matrix of shape and posterior probability information and θ represent the corresponding eigenvalues. The model of shape and posterior probability variations are combined in a linear framework as,

$$b = \begin{bmatrix} W\theta_s \\ \theta_t \end{bmatrix} = \begin{bmatrix} W\Phi_s^T(s - \bar{s}) \\ \Phi_t^T(t - \bar{t}) \end{bmatrix} \tag{6}$$

where W denotes a weight factor (determined as in AAM [5]) coupling the shape and the probability space. A third PCA of the combined model ensures the reduction in redundancy of the combined model, and is given as,

$$b = Vc \tag{7}$$

where V is the matrix of eigenvectors and c the appearance parameters.

2.3   Optimization and Segmentation of a New Instance

In our model, we incorporate AAM optimization proposed by Cootes et al. [5]. The objective function of our model is similar to AAM. However, instead of minimizing the sum of squared difference of intensity between the mean model and target image, we minimize the sum of squared difference of the posterior probability of the mean model and the target image. The prior knowledge of the optimization space is acquired by perturbing the combined model with known model parameters and perturbing the pose (translation, scale and rotation) parameters. A linear relationship between the perturbation of the combined model (δc) and the residual posterior probability values (δt) (obtained from the sum of squared difference between the posterior probability of the mean model and the target image), and between the perturbation of the pose parameters (δp) and the residual posterior probability values are acquired in a multivariate regression framework as,

$$\delta c = R_c \delta t, \quad \delta p = R_p \delta t \tag{8}$$

R_c and R_p refer to the correlation coefficients. Given a test image, posterior probability values of the pixels being prostate is determined in the Bayesian framework 2.1. The sum of squared difference of the posterior probability values with the mean model is used to determine the residual value δt. The combined model (δc) and the pose parameters (δp) are then updated using (8) to generate a new shape, and combined model and hence, new posterior probabilities. The process continues in an iterative manner until the difference with the target image remains unchanged.

2.4   Multiple Mean Models

Statistical shape and texture model assumes the shape and the texture spaces to be Gaussian. However, inter patient prostate shape and their intensities may vary significantly. In such circumstances, a single Gaussian mean model is inefficient to

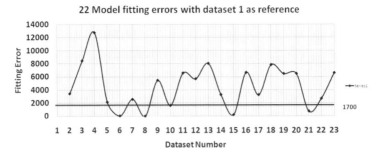

Fig. 2. Mean models fitting errors for with dataset 1 as reference

capture the variations of shape and texture spaces. To address this problem, we propose to use multiple Gaussian mean models. The sum of squared differences of the posterior probabilities between the mean models and a given test image is recorded as the fitting error after the final segmentation with each of the mean model. The segmentation results of the mean model with the least fitting error is considered as the optimized segmentation.

The scheme of building the mean models is as follows; initially the 1st dataset is chosen as the reference to register datasets 3 to 23 to produce a mean model of shape and texture. This mean model is used to test dataset 2. The sum of squared difference of the posterior probabilities between the mean model and dataset 2 is recorded as fitting error after the final segmentation. Likewise, with the fixed reference (dataset 1), we build the second mean model registering datasets 2 and 4-23 to test on dataset 3 and record the fitting error. The process is repeated for all datasets from 4-23. This provides 22 model fitting errors for the test datasets with dataset 1 as reference (Fig. 2). Consequently, the reference dataset is changed from 2 through 23 and the entire process is repeated for all the datasets (23 in total). The entire procedure yields 23 graphs of model fitting errors (one for each dataset).

We have analyzed these 23 model fitting error graphs and have observed that with less fitting error (< 2000 units, where units signifies the sum of squared differences of the probability values of the prostate region between the mean model and the target image) we have higher accuracy in segmentation (in terms of Dice similarity coefficient, mean absolute distance etc.). This is not surprising considering the fact that the objective function of our optimization framework tries to minimize the fitting error between the mean model and target image with respect to the pose parameters. Hence, an increase in fitting error indicates a reduction in segmentation accuracies. An empirical error value is determined from these graphs, above which, the segmentation accuracy is reduced (in our case the threshold value is 1700 units). The reference dataset that has a fitting error less than the empirical value for maximum number of test datasets is identified (dataset 1 in our case). The datasets below this fitting error are grouped together (datasets 1, 6, 8, 10, 15 and 21(Fig. 2)) and are removed from further grouping. The process is repeated until all the datasets are grouped.

Table 1. Prostate segmentation quantitative comparison (HD, MAD and MaxD in mm, Spec., Sens., and Acc., are for Specificity, Sensitivity and Accuracy respectively.) Statistically significant values are italicized

Method	DSC	HD	MAD	MaxD	Spec.	Sens.	Acc.
AAM [5]	0.92±0.04	3.80±1.98	1.26±0.76	3.81±2.00	0.91±0.04	0.98±0.01	0.97±0.05
Ghose et al. [9]	0.94±0.03	2.59±1.21	0.91±0.44	2.64±1.19	0.91±0.04	0.98±0.01	0.97±0.05
B-AAM	0.95±0.06	2.53±1.94	0.87±1.23	2.35±2.10	0.92±0.04	0.97±0.04	0.97±0.03
Our Method	*0.97±0.01*	*1.78±0.73*	*0.49±0.20*	1.72±0.74	0.95±0.01	0.99±0.00	0.98±0.00

These groups of datasets provide individual mean models (5 mean models in our case). However, increasing the number of mean models (decreasing the fitting error threshold) improves segmentation accuracy with additional computational time. Hence, the choice of optimum number of mean models depends on the segmentation accuracy and computational time requirement of the process.

3   Experimental Results

We have validated the accuracy and robustness of our method with 46 axial mid gland TRUS images of the prostate with a resolution of 348×237 pixels from 23 prostate datasets in a leave-one-patient-out evaluation strategy. During validation, a test dataset is removed and 5 mean model are built with remaining 22 datasets. All the 5 mean models are applied to segment the test dataset. The mean model with the least fitting error is selected for accurate segmentation. The ground truth for the experiments are prepared in a schema similar to MIC-CAI prostate challenge 2009 [13], where manual segmentations performed by an expert radiologist are validated by an experienced urologist. Both doctors have over 15 years of experience in dealing with prostate anatomy, prostate segmentation, and ultrasound guided biopsies. We have used most of the popular prostate segmentation evaluation metrics like DSC, 95% Hausdorff Distance (HD) [13], MAD [15], Maximum Distance (MaxD) [12], specificity [7], sensitivity, and accuracy [2] to evaluate our method. Furthermore, the results are compared with the traditional AAM proposed by Cootes et al. [5], to our previous work [9] and to B-AAM (that uses posterior probability of the prostate region and a single mean model for segmentation). It is observed from Table 1 that, a probabilistic representation of the prostate texture in TRUS images and using multiple mean models significantly improves segmentation accuracy when compared to traditional AAM and to [9]. We used posterior probability information for automatic initialization and training of our statistical shape and texture model. As opposed to manual initialization of traditional AAM and in [9], our model is initialized automatically. We achieved a statistically significant improvement in t-test p-value<0.0001 for DSC, HD and MAD compared to traditional AAM [5] and to [9]. A high DSC value and low values of contour error metrics of HD and

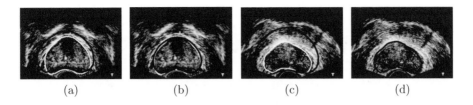

(a)   (b)   (c)   (d)

Fig. 3. (a), (c) Segmentation without multiple mean model (B-AAM), (b), (d) Segmentation with multiple mean model.

MAD are all equally important in determining the segmentation accuracy of an algorithm. In this context, we obtained better segmentation accuracies compared to [5] and [9]. As observed in Table 1 B-AAM produces better result compared to AAM justifying the use of posterior probability of the prostate region instead of intensity. However, our model which uses both posterior probability and multiple mean models produces superior results compared to B-AAM, suggesting that use of both posterior probability and multiple mean models are essential to improve segmentation accuracies. Quantitative improvement in segmentation accuracy with multiple mean model is evident from the last two rows in Table 1. Qualitative improvement in segmentation accuracy compared to B-AAM is illustrated in Fig. 3 for two datasets. In Fig. 3, we observe that segmentation accuracy of our model (in Fig. 3(b) and Fig. 3(d)) is better compared to B-AAM (in Fig. 3(a) and Fig. 3(c)). Improved qualitative results with our method compared to traditional AAM [5] are illustrated in Fig. 4. Our method is implemented in Matlab 7 on an Intel Core 2 Duo T5250, 1.5 GHz processor and 2 GB RAM. The mean segmentation time of the method is 5.97±0.55 seconds with an unoptimized Matlab code. Even with an unoptimized Matlab code in Table 2 we observe that our mean segmentation time is comparable to [3], better than [14] and [6] and inferior only to [15]. However, [15] used an optimized C++ code to achieve their results. We believe that speed up of computational time is possible with a parallelized optimized code in GPU environment. A quantitative comparison of different prostate segmentation methodologies is difficult in the

Table 2. Qualitative comparison of prostate segmentation

Reference	Area Accuracy	Contour Accuracy	Datasets	Time
Betrouni [3]	Overlap 93±0.9%	Distance 3.77±1.3 pixels	10 images	5 seconds
Shen [14]	Error 3.98±0.97%	Distance 3.2±0.87 pixels	8 images	64 seconds
Ladak [11]	Accuracy 90.1±3.2%	MAD 4.4±1.8 pixels	117 images	-
Cosio [6]	-	MAD 1.65±0.67 mm	22 images	11 minutes
Yan [15]	-	MAD 2.10±1.02 mm	19 datasets/301 images	0.3 seconds
Our Method	DSC 0.97±0.01	MAD 1.82±0.76 pixels/0.49±0.20 mm	23 datasets/46 images	5.9 seconds

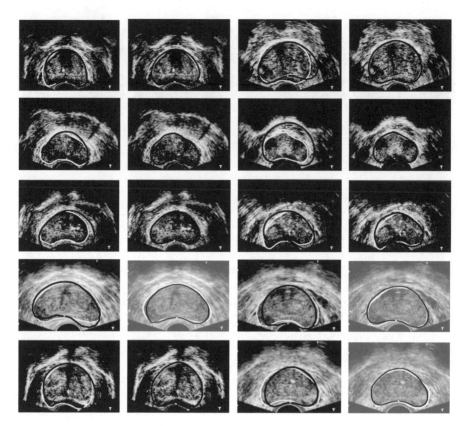

Fig. 4. Performance of our algorithm against shape, size and contrast variations. The white contour gives the ground truth and the black contour gives the obtained result. Columns 1, and 3 show segmentations with traditional AAM and 2, and 4 show corresponding segmentations with our model for 10 datasets.

absence of a public dataset and standardized evaluation metrics. Nevertheless, to have an overall qualitative estimate of the functioning of our method we have compared with some of the 2D segmentation works in the literature in Table 2. In Table 2 we may consider area overlap and area accuracy equivalent to that of DSC values and average distance equivalent to that of average MAD. Analyzing the results we observe that our mean DSC value is comparable to area overlap accuracy values of Betrouni et al. [3] and Ladak et al. [11] and very close to the area overlap error of Shen et al. [14]. However, it is to be noted that we have used more images compared to Shen et al. Our MAD value is comparable to [3], [14], [11], [6] and [15]. From these observations we may conclude that qualitatively our method performs well in overlap and contour accuracy measures.

4   Conclusion and Future Works

A novel approach of multiple statistical models of shape and posterior probability information of prostate region with the goal of segmenting the prostate in 2D TRUS images has been proposed. Our approach is accurate, and robust to significant shape, size and contrast variations in TRUS images compared to traditional AAM. While the proposed method is validated with prostate mid gland images, effectiveness of the method against base and apical slices is yet to be validated.

Acknowledgements. This research has been funded by VALTEC 08-1-0039 of Generalitat de Catalunya, Spain and Conseil Régional de Bourgogne, France.

References

1. Prostate Cancer Statistics - Key Facts (2011),
   http://info.cancerresearchuk.org/cancerstats/types/prostate (accessed on June 6, 2011)
2. Badiei, S., Salcudean, S.E., Varah, J., Morris, W.J.: Prostate segmentation in 2D ultrasound images using image warping and ellipse fitting. In: Larsen, R., Nielsen, M., Sporring, J. (eds.) MICCAI 2006. LNCS, vol. 4191, pp. 17–24. Springer, Heidelberg (2006)
3. Betrouni, N., Vermandel, M., Pasquier, D., Maouche, S., Rousseau, J.: Segmentation of Abdominal Ultrasound Images of the Prostate Using A priori Information and an Adapted Noise Filter. Computerized Medical Imaging and Graphics 29, 43–51 (2005)
4. Cootes, T.F., Hill, A., Taylor, C.J., Haslam, J.: The Use of Active Shape Model for Locating Structures in Medical Images. Image and Vision Computing 12, 355–366 (1994)
5. Cootes, T.F., Edwards, G.J., Taylor, C.J.: Active appearance models. In: Burkhardt, H., Neumann, B. (eds.) ECCV 1998. LNCS, vol. 1407, pp. 484–498. Springer, Heidelberg (1998)
6. Cosío, F.A.: Automatic Initialization of an Active Shape Model of the Prostate. Medical Image Analysis 12, 469–483 (2008)
7. Diaz, K., Castaneda, B.: Semi-automated Segmentation of the Prostate Gland Boundary in Ultrasound Images Using a Machine Learning Approach. In: Reinhardt, J.M., Pluim, J.P.W. (eds.) Procedings of SPIE Medical Imaging: Image Processing, pp. 1–8. SPIE, USA (2008)
8. Duda, R.O., Hart, P.E., Stork, D.G.: Pattern Classification, 2nd edn. Wiley Interscience, USA (2000)
9. Ghose, S., Oliver, A., Martí, R., Lladó, X., Freixenet, J., Vilanova, J.C., Meriaudeau, F.: Texture guided active appearance model propagation for prostate segmentation. In: Madabhushi, A., Dowling, J., Yan, P., Fenster, A., Abolmaesumi, P., Hata, N. (eds.) MICCAI 2010. LNCS, vol. 6367, pp. 111–120. Springer, Heidelberg (2010)
10. Gower, J.C.: Generalized Procrustes Analysis. Psychometrika 40, 33–51 (1975)

11. Ladak, H.M., Mao, F., Wang, Y., Downey, D.B., Steinman, D.A., Fenster, A.: Prostate Segmentation from 2D Ultrasound Images. In: Proceedings of the 22nd Annual International Conference of the IEEE Engineering in Medicine and Biology Society, pp. 3188–3191. IEEE Computer Society Press, Chicago (2000)
12. Liu, H., Cheng, G., Rubens, D., Strang, J.G., Liao, L., Brasacchio, R., Messing, E., Yu, Y.: Automatic Segmentation of Prostate Boundaries in Transrectal Ultrasound (TRUS) Imaging. In: Sonka, M., Fitzpatrick, J.M. (eds.) Proceedings of the SPIE Medical Imaging: Image Processings, pp. 412–423. SPIE, USA (2002)
13. MICCAI: prostate segmentation challenge MICCAI (2009), http://wiki.na-mic.org/Wiki/index.php (accessed on April 1, 2011)
14. Shen, D., Zhan, Y., Davatzikos, C.: Segmentation of Prostate Boundaries from Ultrasound Images Using Statistical Shape Model. IEEE Transactions on Medical Imaging 22, 539–551 (2003)
15. Yan, P., Xu, S., Turkbey, B., Kruecker, J.: Discrete Deformable Model Guided by Partial Active Shape Model for TRUS Image Segmentation. IEEE Transactions on Biomedical Engineering 57, 1158–1166 (2010)
16. Zhan, Y., Shen, D.: Deformable Segmentation of 3D Ultrasound Prostate Images Using Statistical Texture Matching Method. IEEE Transactions on Medical Imaging 25, 256–272 (2006)

Facilitating 3D Spectroscopic Imaging through Automatic Prostate Localization in MR Images Using Random Walker Segmentation Initialized via Boosted Classifiers

Parmeshwar Khurd[1], Leo Grady[1], Kalpitkumar Gajera[1],
Mamadou Diallo[1], Peter Gall[2], Martin Requardt[2], Berthold Kiefer[2],
Clifford Weiss[3], and Ali Kamen[1]

[1] Siemens Corporation, Corporate Research, Princeton, NJ, USA
[2] Siemens Healthcare, MR Oncology, Erlangen, Germany
[3] Johns Hopkins Medical Institutions, Baltimore, MD, USA

Abstract. Magnetic resonance imaging (MRI) plays a key role in the diagnosis, staging and treatment monitoring for prostate cancer. Automatic prostate localization in T2-weighted MR images could facilitate labor-intensive cancer imaging techniques such as 3D chemical shift MR spectroscopic imaging as well as advanced analysis techniques for diagnosis and treatment monitoring. We present a novel method for automatic segmentation of the prostate gland in MR images. Accurate prostate segmentation in MR imagery poses unique challenges. These include large variations in prostate anatomy and disease, intensity inhomogeneities, and near-field artifacts induced by endorectal coils. Our system meets these challenges with two key components. First is the automatic center detection of the prostate with a boosted classifier trained on intensity-based multi-level Gaussian Mixture Model Expectation Maximization (GMM-EM) segmentations of the raw MR images. The second is the use of a shape model in conjunction with Multi-Label Random Walker (MLRW) to constrain the seeding process within MLRW. Our system has been validated on a large database of non-isotropic T2-TSE (Turbo Spin Echo) and isotropic T2-SPACE (Sampling Perfection with Application Optimized Contrasts) images.

1 Introduction and Background

MRI plays a key role in the diagnosis, staging and treatment monitoring for prostate cancer. Various MR modalities such as T2 MRI using endorectal (ER) coils, dynamic contrast enhanced (DCE) MRI, diffusion-weighted imaging and 3D chemical shift spectroscopy imaging contribute complementary forms of information during these processes [19]. Prostate localization is a pre-requisite for optimal positioning of radio-frequency (RF) saturation bands to prevent fat contamination in 3D MR chemical shift spectroscopy [14] by the fat surrounding the prostate. Automatic prostate localization is thus a key enabler for this application making it significantly less labor-intensive. It is best to pre-segment

A. Madabhushi et al. (Eds.): Prostate Cancer Imaging 2011, LNCS 6963, pp. 47–56, 2011.
© Springer-Verlag Berlin Heidelberg 2011

the prostate from T2 images since they are the "workhorse" images for prostate cancer [19] and clearly show the zonal anatomy and the cancerous tumors.

Automatic segmentation of the prostate gland in medical images is an especially challenging task on account of the large anatomical variability observed across patients and the wide range of pathologies affecting this gland, e.g., benign prostatic hyperplasia, prostate cancer and chronic prostatitis [5]. This problem is compounded in MR images on account of the intensity inhomogeneity artifacts and the near-field artifacts induced by the occasional use of ER coils. The latter causes accuracy problems in including the peripheral zone (PZ) of the prostate within the overall segmentation. Since the PZ is widely affected by prostate pathologies, it must be included within the segmentation. Our method copes with the above challenges using several innovations described in Sec. 2. A typical result for the positioning of the RF saturation bands is displayed in Fig. 1(a). The remainder of this document is organized as follows: In Sec. 2, we describe our system in detail and use it to segment non-isotropic T2-TSE and T2-SPACE images in Sec. 3. We conclude with some final remarks in Sec. 4.

Related Work: The prostate segmentation problem in CT and ultrasound images has received a lot of attention, e.g., [12], [7], but the MR prostate segmentation problem poses some unique problems as noted earlier, some of which have been addressed in [15,16,11,13,4,1,17,9]. However, [11,13,4,1] only provide anecdotal results and do not include an evaluation on a database of images, whereas [15,16] evaluate their technique on 2D slices and [16] uses 3D spectroscopy to initialize segmentation on T2 images. Moreover, none of these methods address the unique problems (related to the PZ and the ER coil) addressed by us. The work in [17] uses T1 images and it is not clear if they capture the PZ. They also show anecdotal results and do not report error metrics on their database. More importantly, we note that unlike previous studies on MR prostate segmentation, our problem is extremely challenging because apart from the various pathologies affecting our patient data, it was obtained via different acquisition protocols from multiple clinical sites using variable scan parameters. The frequent use of ER coils increased prostate shape variability. Our system is the only 3D segmentation method capable of dealing with all this variability, while capturing the peripheral zone. The 3D atlas-based segmentation method developed in [9] does capture the PZ, but they only work with data obtained from a single clinical site using identical optimized scan parameters. Note also that the method in [9] includes the seminal vesicles within the prostate segmentation, whereas we exclude them.

2   Methods

The workflow of our entire system is displayed in Fig. 1(b) and consists of the following steps: (1) We first find the center of the prostate gland with a boosted classifier [20] trained on intensity-based multi-level GMM-EM segmentations of the raw MR images, thus rendering our center-point localization robust to intensity changes both within and across patients. If a rough point close to the

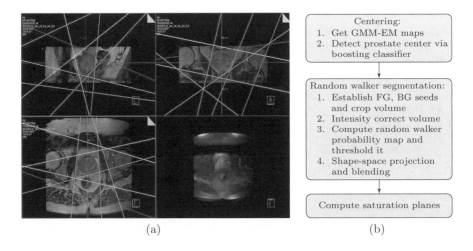

Centering:
1. Get GMM-EM maps
2. Detect prostate center via
   boosting classifier

Random walker segmentation:
1. Establish FG, BG seeds
   and crop volume
2. Intensity correct volume
3. Compute random walker
   probability map and
   threshold it
4. Shape-space projection
   and blending

Compute saturation planes

(a)   (b)

Fig. 1. (a) Typical prostate segmentation output with computation of saturation bands for spectroscopic imaging (b) Stages of evaluation within our system

center of the prostate gland is already available to the segmentation, then we use it to limit the search range of the boosted classifier. In case the boosted classifier encounters a prostate shape or appearance significantly different from one encountered during training and reports a very low detection probability, then we use the rough center to bias the location of the detected center towards it. (2) We then use a shape model guided by prostate muscle and rectum detectors to initialize the foreground (FG) and background (BG) seeds for the RW segmentation algorithm [8]. The muscle and rectum boundaries are detected from the GMM-EM segmentation as described below. (3) Prior to the use of the RW algorithm, we use a novel intensity correction technique to deal with the near-field artifacts induced by ER coils. (4) Finally, in order to detect the peripheral zone of the prostate gland, we have devised a novel technique for computing the threshold of the RW probability map. (5) As a post-processing step for smoothing the RW segmentation, we use shape-space projections. We now describe the system components in detail.

2.1 Multi-level GMM-EM Intensity Clustering

The well-known GMM-EM algorithm [2] is a clustering algorithm that can identify and fit Gaussian clusters within a sample dataset. We initialize the EM algorithm using the output of k-means clustering, which in turn is initialized using a set of randomly selected samples as cluster centers (The same random seed is used to guarantee reproducible results although we have observed extremely minimal dependence of the GMM-EM clustering output on this initialization in separate experiments on our MR database presented in Sec. 3). Variants of this GMM-EM algorithm have been routinely used in MR brain intensity segmentation to label 3 components: cerebrospinal fluid, white matter and gray matter

[10]. An example of 3-intensity GMM-EM prostate MR segmentation is shown in Fig. 2. We refer to the 3 components as the low-intensity, middle-intensity and high-intensity clusters. However, we do not necessarily use GMM-EM to identify meaningful regions. It serves three purposes in our system. Firstly, it reduces the effects of intensity inhomogeneities across patients in order to train our classifier in Sec. 2.2. Second, it helps us in identifying the boundaries for the left and right prostate muscles and the rectum in Sec. 2.3. Thirdly, it identifies the high-intensity voxels affected by the ER coil in Sec. 2.3.

2.2   Boosted Hierarchical Classifiers with Haar Features

Boosting is a classification technique that linearly combines a series of weak classifier outputs in order to obtain a strong classifier. We use a boosting classifier in a sliding-window fashion [20] in order to locate the center of the prostate gland. Our weak classifiers are decision stumps, each trained on a Haar-like feature computed from the 3-component intensity segmentation maps obtained with the GMM-EM algorithm in Sec. 2.1. We use the set of 3D Haar-like features defined in [18] and train separate classifiers for different types of MR acquisitions in an offline training phase as described in Sec. 3. Using the GMM-EM maps reduces classifier complexity by decreasing the effect of inter-patient intensity inhomogeneities and thus reduces classifier over-fitting. For increased speed, we first apply a low-resolution boosting classifier followed by a high-resolution classifier on the high-probability regions identified by the low-resolution classifier.

2.3   Random Walker Segmentation

Given a set of FG and BG seeds and weights corresponding to intensity similarities between neighboring voxels, the RW segmentation algorithm [8] computes a map indicating the probability that a RW starting from each voxel would encounter an FG seed first. By thresholding this probability map, we can obtain the foreground segmentation. We compute the neighborhood similarities using the intensity-corrected MR image rather than the original. Details regarding these steps are given below:

Seeding. In an offline training phase, we build a mean prostate shape from our database as described in Sec. 3 in the form of a signed distance map. Based upon the maximum and minimum prostate volumes mentioned in Sec. 3, we derive inner and outer thresholds on this distance map and the corresponding inner and outer masks so that these mask volumes are greater or smaller than the maximum and minimum volumes by about 10%, respectively. We then center these inner and outer masks obtained in the offline phase at the previously detected prostate center in order to obtain an initial estimate of the FG and BG seeds. For SPACE images, in conjunction with the probability threshold computation described below, these initial FG/BG estimates lead to sufficient accuracy. However, for the more challenging case of non-isotropic TSE images, we refine it using the

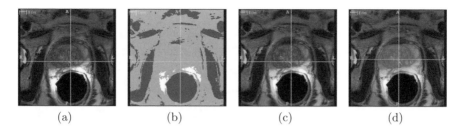

(a)   (b)   (c)   (d)

Fig. 2. (a) Raw image (b) 3-component segmentation with left/right muscles and rectum in low-intensity cluster and ER-voxels in high-intensity cluster (c) Intensity-corrected image input to the RW (d) Final shape-constrained segmentation output

boundaries of the left/right muscles and rectum identified by GMM-EM. We first expand the FG seeds towards these boundaries on each slice simply by adding seeds on each horizontal scan-line intersecting the left/right muscles and each vertical scan-line intersecting the rectum. There may be fat layers around the prostate, e. g., between the outer PZ boundary and the left muscle. Therefore, we keep a 20% offset between the FG seeds and the left/right muscle boundaries and a 40% offset between the FG seeds and the rectum boundary. Then we compute the convex hull of all FG seeds. The volume enclosed by the hull is computed [3] and forms the new FG seeds estimate. Since the ER coil can introduce a concavity, we remove any FG seeds intersecting the low-intensity rectum. The BG seeds are then refined using this new estimate of the FG seeds as follows: We re-consider the mean distance map and compute the smallest value for the FG seeds. We add new BG seeds when the distance is lower than this smallest value by a $4mm$ offset.

Intensity Correction. The voxels affected by the ER-coil near-field effect (ER-voxels) are spatially close and belong to the high-intensity cluster in the 3-component map found by GMM-EM. Unless these high-intensities are corrected, RW is often unable to cross the high-intensity barrier and capture the entire PZ. Occasionally, the bladder also belongs to this high-intensity component, but it can be easily separated from this cluster by spatial connected component analysis. Given the mean μ_h and std. dev. σ_h for these ER-voxels, we make their std. dev. equal to that of the middle-intensity component (σ_m) and the mean equal to the small middle-intensity mean (μ_m) plus a small constant ϵ (proportional to σ_h). If v_{old} and v_{new} denote the un-corrected and corrected intensities for an ER-voxel, then the corresponding linear intensity transformation can be expressed as:

$$v_{new} = \mu_m + \epsilon + \frac{\sigma_m}{\sigma_h}(v_{old} - \mu_h). \tag{1}$$

The effect of this correction is shown in Fig. 2. Adding ϵ leads to visually pleasing intensity correction, but we observed that setting this constant to zero led to improved segmentation metrics in Sec. 3.

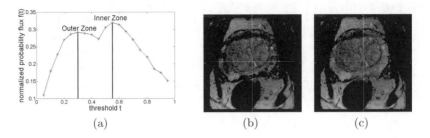

(a)   (b)   (c)

Fig. 3. RW probability threshold computation for SPACE images: (a) Normalized flux profile (b) Inner zone (0.55 threshold) (c) Outer zone (0.3 threshold)

Probability Threshold Computation. The conventional RW algorithm uses a probability threshold of 0.5, but we use two different techniques for threshold computation in the SPACE and TSE images in order to capture the PZ. We compute the normalized flux of the probability maps gradient (using the divergence theorem) as a function of the threshold. If $p(x, y, z)$ denotes the probability map and $S_A(t)$ denotes the surface area of the binary mask obtained at threshold t, then the normalized flux is given by:

$$f(t) = \frac{1}{S_A(t)} \int_{p(x,y,z) \geq t} \nabla^2 p(x, y, z) \, \mathrm{d}x \, \mathrm{d}y \, \mathrm{d}z. \qquad (2)$$

A local maximum of this flux corresponds to a sharp boundary. For SPACE images, on account of the isotropic voxels and optimized contrast, we see two clear peaks corresponding to the inner and outer boundary of the peripheral zone as seen in Fig. 3 when a clear PZ is present. We note that in (2), normalizing by the surface area in the denominator, and not the volume, gives the average probability gradient over the surface. Note that the numerator is a surface integral over the probability gradient converted into a volume integral over the probability Laplacian. Normalizing by the volume actually gives worse results since the local maxima of this alternative normalized flux do not correspond to the inner and outer zones. However, for non-isotropic TSE images, even with our surface area normalization, we occasionally see a single normalized flux peak corresponding to a boundary that shifts between the inner and outer zone. Therefore, we set the probability threshold equal to the maximum of the product of the normalized flux and volume in order to shift the peak towards the outer zone.

Shape Model Constraints. Since the RW algorithm might result in small undesirable wiggles in the segmentation output (please see Fig. 3), we project the RW segmentations distance map into shape-space as described in [17]. However, this projection might over-constrain the segmentation result. So we blend the original distance map (compute using the fast marching method, as in [17]) with its projected version by convex linear combination using a blending factor of 0.25 weighting the projected version. Although this convex linear combination is not guaranteed to yield a valid binary segmentation, we have obtained excellent results with this technique. Imposing these shape model constraints does not significantly affect our segmentation error metrics in Sec. 3, but merely serves to improve the visual appearance of our segmentation.

2.4   Saturation Band Computation for Chemical Shift Spectroscopy

Given the segmentation output, we first compute its triangulated convex hull [3]. Since 8 or 16 planes for the saturation bands are required, we obtain intersections of 8 or 16 spherically symmetric direction vectors with the convex hull and then pick saturation bands corresponding to the triangles of intersection.

3   Results and Discussion

The proposed system has been evaluated on a set of 23 3T T2-SPACE (typical dimensions: $320 \times 320 \times 88$, resolution: $0.75mm \times 0.75mm \times 0.9mm$) patient images, 53 axially oriented 3T T2-TSE (typical dimensions: $320 \times 320 \times 28$, resolution: $0.7mm \times 0.7mm \times 3.3mm$) non-isotropic acquisitions (which included the 23 SPACE patients but with slightly different segmentations on account of bladder movement) and 58 1.5T axially oriented T2-TSE non-isotropic acquisitions. These three acquisitions are characterized by unique contrasts and we have hence trained 3 separate prostate-center classifiers. ER coils were used in about 90% of the total acquisitions. The shape model was obtained using principal component analysis [17] from the SPACE images since they adequately capture the spatial variation needed to eliminate the wiggles as described in Sec. 2.3. The minimum and maximum prostate volumes in our database were $18ml$ and $158ml$ (a case of benign prostatic hyperplasia) respectively. The segmentation error metrics are given in Table 1. The center-point error represents the error from boosting-based center detection and volumetric difference is the absolute difference between volumes corresponding to the expert-labelled ground truth G and the automatic segmentation S. The inner (outer) surface error is the average distance from the border voxels of S inside (outside) G to the closest border voxel in G. The last column is the average symmetric surface error defined in [6]. We note that of the error metrics considered in Table 1, the average symmetric surface error [6] is the most commonly employed segmentation evaluation measure. However, we report internal and external surface errors as minimizing internal error is more important in our application of placing saturation bands. The volumetric difference in milliliters is an important segmentation error metric for other applications such as pharmacokinetic modeling [5]. The 3T non-isotropic TSE dataset was divided into two sets of 33 and 20 images. The first three rows correspond to training sets used with the boosting classifiers for the 3 acquisition types and hence represent the segmentation outputs using near-perfect center initializations. Moreover, the various parameters in the algorithm (center detection: parameters for low-resolution and high-resolution classifiers, probability threshold use to select region for high-resolution classifier,

Table 1. Segmentation errors (Results in rows 1-3 present errors on training sets used for the boosting classifiers and the result in row 4 presents errors on an independent unseen test set. Please refer to text for explanation.)

Acquisition Type	Center point error (mm)	Volumetric difference (ml)	Inner surface error (mm)	Outer surface error (mm)	Symmetric surface error (mm)
3T SPACE (23 patients)	0.4 ± 0.4	9.7 ± 6.9	0.87 ± 0.5	2.4 ± 0.8	1.6 ± 0.5
3T TSE (33 patients)	0.6 ± 0.7	15.5 ± 12.9	0.77 ± 0.5	3.6 ± 1.6	2.3 ± 1.2
1.5T TSE (58 patients)	1.1 ± 2.0	17.6 ± 12.2	0.93 ± 0.8	3.4 ± 1.5	2.4 ± 1.1
3T TSE (20 unseen)	6.3 ± 3.9	21.5 ± 19.0	0.60 ± 0.7	3.9 ± 3.0	2.5 ± 2.1

seeding: initial shrinking/expansion parameters and offsets to left muscle, etc., intensity correction: constant added to mean, shape-space projection: number of modes, blending factor) were optimized to obtain good results in rows 1 and 2. Hence, we regard the results in rows 1-3 as results on training sets and therefore, an independent evaluation on a test set is essential. The fourth row represents the error on an unseen test set of 20 3T TSE non-isotropic acquisitions with the center of the image selected as the initial prostate center estimate (the results in the first three rows are unaffected by this initial seed estimate). Note that the symmetric surface error on this test set is only marginally higher than that of the training set although the center-point error is much higher.

Although unimportant in our application, we also note that the Dice coefficients (a commonly used segmentation error metric employed for MR prostate segmentation evaluation in [9]) corresponding to rows 1-4 had the mean and standard deviation values: 0.86 ± 0.04, 0.82 ± 0.09, 0.82 ± 0.07 and 0.82 ± 0.12, respectively. These values are comparable to those reported in [9], although our dataset has considerably greater variablity on account of the reasons discussed in Sec. 1.

4   Conclusion

We have presented an accurate automatic prostate segmentation technique for T2 MR images and shown how it can facilitate improved 3D chemical shift spectroscopic imaging with accurate saturation band placement [14]. The current process of placing saturation bands is manual, time-consuming and can lead to sub-optimal images for inexperienced operators. Our automatic segmentation algorithm serves an important clinical need by automating this process and thus reducing the burden on the operator. It could also enable advanced analysis techniques such as pharmacokinetic modelling from DCE-MRI [5]. Besides enabling advanced cancer imaging and computer-aided diagnosis techniques, our automated system could pave the way for other applications such as radiotherapy planning and drug therapy assessment. Note that some of our contributions in order to capture the PZ via the RW algorithm, viz., boosting-based centering, initialization via left/right muscle detection and intensity correction can be readily incorporated into level set segmentation techniques employing a shape model [17] as well.

References

1. Betrouni, N., Puech, P., Dewalle, A., Lopes, R., Dubois, P., Vermandel, M.: 3D automatic segmentation and reconstruction of prostate on MR images. In: IEEE EMBS Conf. (2007)
2. Bishop, C.: Pattern Recognition and Machine Learning. Springer, Heidelberg (2006)
3. Dobkin, D., Kirkpatrick, D.: Determining the separation of preprocessed polyhedra - a unified approach. Automata, Languages and Programming 443, 400–413 (1990)
4. Flores-Tapia, D., Thomas, G., Venugopal, N., McCurdy, B., Pistorius, S.: Semi-automatic MRI prostate segmentation based on wavelet multiscale products. In: IEEE EMBS Conf. (2008)
5. Franiel, T., Ludemann, L., Rudolph, B., Rehbein, H., Stephan, C., Taupitz, M., Beyersdorff, D.: Prostate MR imaging: Tissue characterization with pharmacokinetic volume and blood flow parameters and correlation with histologic parameters. Radiology 252(1), 101–108 (2009)
6. van Ginneken, B., Heimann, T., Styner, M.: 3D segmentation in the clinic: A grand challenge. In: MICCAI Wshp. 3D Segmentation in the Clinic (2007)
7. Gong, L., Pathak, S., Haynor, D., Cho, P., Kim, Y.: Parametric shape modeling using deformable superellipses for prostate segmentation. TMI 23(3) (2004)
8. Grady, L.: Random walks for image segmentation. IEEE Pattern Analysis and Machine Intelligence 28(11), 1768–1783 (2006)
9. Klein, S., van der Heide, U.A., Lips, I., van Vulpen, M., Maes, F., Staring, M., Pluim, J.: Automatic segmentation of the prostate in 3D MR images by atlas matching using localized mutual information. Medical Physics 35(4), 1407–1417 (2008)
10. Leemput, K.V., Maes, F., Vandermeulen, D., Suetens, P.: Automated model-based bias field correction of MR images of the brain. TMI 18(10), 885–896 (2003)
11. Liu, X., Langer, D.L., Haider, M.A., der Kwast, T.H.V., Evans, A.J., Wernick, M.N., Yetik, I.S.: Unsupervised segmentation of the prostate using MR images based on level set with a shape prior. In: IEEE EMBS Conf. (2009)
12. Rousson, M., Khamene, A., Diallo, M.H., Celi, J.C., Sauer, F.: Constrained surface evolutions for prostate and bladder segmentation in CT images. In: Liu, Y., Jiang, T.-Z., Zhang, C. (eds.) CVBIA 2005. LNCS, vol. 3765, pp. 251–260. Springer, Heidelberg (2005)
13. Samiee, M., Thomas, G., Fazel-Rezai, R.: Semi-automatic prostate segmentation of MR images based on flow orientation. In: IEEE International Symposium on Signal Processing and Information Technology (2006)
14. Scheenen, T., Heijmink, S., Roell, S., de Kaa, C.H., Knipscheer, B., Witjes, J., Barentsz, J., Heerschap, A.: Three-dimensional proton MR spectroscopy of human prostate at 3 T without endorectal coil. Radiology 245(2), 507–516 (2007)
15. Toth, R., Chappelow, J., Rosen, M.A., Pungavkar, S., Kalyanpur, A., Madabhushi, A.: Multi-attribute non-initializing texture reconstruction based active shape model (MANTRA). In: Metaxas, D., Axel, L., Fichtinger, G., Székely, G. (eds.) MICCAI 2008, Part I. LNCS, vol. 5241, pp. 653–661. Springer, Heidelberg (2008)
16. Toth, R., Tiwari, P., Rosen, M., Reed, G., Kurhanewicz, J., Kalyanpur, A., Pungavkar, S., Madabhushi, A.: A magnetic resonance spectroscopy driven initialization scheme for active shape model based prostate segmentation. Medical Image Analysis 15, 214–225 (2011)

17. Tsai, A., Yezzi, A., Wells, W., Tempany, C., Tucker, D., Fan, A., Grimson, W., Willsky, A.: A shape-based approach to the segmentation of medical imagery using level sets. TMI 22(2), 137–154 (2003)
18. Tu, Z., Zhou, X., Barbu, A., Bogoni, L., Comaniciu, D.: Probabilistic 3D polyp detection in CT images: The role of sample alignment. In: CVPR (2006)
19. Turkbey, B., Pinto, P., Choyke, P.L.: Imaging techniques for prostate cancer: implications for focal therapy. Nature Reviews: Urology 6, 191–203 (2009)
20. Viola, P., Jones, M.: Robust real-time face detection. Int. J. Comp. Vision 57(2), 137–154 (2004)

Intrafraction Prostate Motion Correction Using a Non-rectilinear Image Frame

Rupert Brooks

Elekta Ltd.,
2050 Bleury St., Suite 200, Montreal, QC, Canada
rupert.brooks@elekta.com
http://www.elekta.com

Abstract. Ultrasound data collected using a mechanical scanning probe naturally fits on a non-rectilinear coordinate frame. We report on the direct use of this non-rectilinear coordinate frame in a registration algorithm in the context of tracking intrafraction prostate motion during radiotherapy. Registration on the non-rectilinear frame performs as well as registration after reconstruction, and avoids the time demands and numerical noise introduced in a reconstruction process.

Keywords: ultrasound, registration, tracking, non-rectilinear image, cylindrical image, intrafraction, prostate cancer, organ motion, radiotherapy.

1   Introduction

Prostate cancer is the most common cancer affecting men, with one in seven men receiving this diagnosis in their lifetimes[2]. Radiation therapy is frequently used as treatment. Key to its success is that the radiation dose covers the entire prostate, but exposure of organs outside the prostate is minimized. Despite careful patient positioning, due to physiological effects such as bladder filling, the prostate may shift during dose delivery. Thus, there is a need for *intrafraction* monitoring of prostate position during treatment. This presents particular challenges as both rapid response time and a low false alarm rate are necessary.

Several approaches have been examined for intrafraction prostate position monitoring including fluoroscopic tracking of implanted markers[1], magnetically tracked implants[3] and ultrasound. Ultrasound provides a useful image guidance technique, as it is rapid, non-invasive, and does not increase the radiation dose. We explore one aspect of the use of TPUS (Trans-Perineal UltraSound) data gathered with a robotically swept probe to monitor prostate motion during treatment. In particular, we compare the effectiveness of registration using a traditional reconstruct and register approach with an approach that treats the data collected from the swept probe as an image sampled on a non-rectilinear grid and registers the data collected directly.

A. Madabhushi et al. (Eds.): Prostate Cancer Imaging 2011, LNCS 6963, pp. 57–59, 2011.

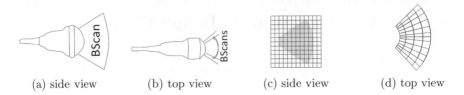

(a) side view	(b) top view	(c) side view	(d) top view

Fig. 1. a,b) Mechanically swept probe; c,d) Cylindrical coordinates

2   Non-rectilinear Coordinate Frame

One method for obtaining a 3D ultrasound scan is to use a mechanically swept probe, such as the Ultrasonix m4DC7-3/40 used in this work. This probe consists of a sensor array that is mechanically swept through an arc. Two dimensional ultrasound B-scans are taken at regular positions along this arc. This gives rise to a set of scans in space as shown in Fig. 1. The usual method for dealing with these scans is to resample them into a rectilinear grid with a reconstruction algorithm. However, this has the disadvantage of requiring calculation time, and introducing some numerical noise due to resampling.

The swath of images captured by the probe can be considered as an image sampled in a cylindrical coordinate system. Use in a registration context, requires the image frame to support transforming to and from voxel and world spaces, interpolation, and calculating oriented image derivatives.

The relationships between voxel coordinates $X_p = i, j, k$, and world coordinates X_w are defined in Eq. 1-3, where s_i, s_j are the pixel scalings, α is the rotational step, r is the radial offset from the voxel origin (X_o) to the axis of rotation, and D is the matrix of direction cosines.

$$X_w = X_o + D\left(\begin{bmatrix} i \cdot s_i \\ (j \cdot s_j + r)\cos(\alpha k) - r \\ (j \cdot s_j + r)\sin(\alpha k) \end{bmatrix}\right) \quad (1) \qquad X_p = \begin{bmatrix} u \\ \sqrt{v^2 + w^2} \\ \tan^{-1}(v, w) \end{bmatrix} \quad (2)$$

$$\begin{bmatrix} u \ v \ w \end{bmatrix} = \mathrm{diag}(s_i, s_j, s_j)^{-1} \cdot D^{-1}(X_w - X_o) \quad (3)$$

Interpolation of non integer voxel values may be done using a rectilinear interpolation technique on the non-integer voxel coordinates with only a minor amount of error. Image derivatives in spatial coordinates, however, must take the curved nature of the coordinate system into account using $\frac{\partial F}{\partial X_w} = \frac{\partial F}{\partial X_p} \cdot \frac{\partial X_p}{\partial X_w}$

3   Evaluation

We use a parametric intensity based registration technique for tracking prostate motion[4]. In this type of approach, a similarity measure is defined between two images to be registered, one of which is transformed to fit the other. The transformation parameters that maximize the image similarity are deemed to be

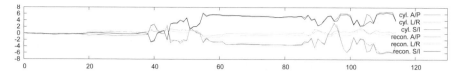

Fig. 2. Prostate displacement (mm) vs time (s) on a typical series

the correct registration. We used the normalized correlation similarity measure, and a rigid transformation limited to a zone around the prostate. The system was implemented using the ITK library and was applied directly to the cylindrically structured data, and to the data after reconstruction on a rectilinear grid.

Tracking was performed on 6 sequences of 3D TPUS scans collected from healthy volunteers. Prostate segmentation was performed on the first scan, and used to initialize the algorithm. Registration results using each method were compared and found to be extremely similar (mean registration difference 0.30mm ±0.73), as shown in the typical result in Fig. 2. The self consistency of each registration was explored by measuring the difference between the transformations found considering the series in the forward direction, and those found considering the series in the reverse direction. No statistically significant difference could be found between the two approaches.

Timing results were collected for the processed sequences on an Intel Core i7 under Windows XP. Calculations for both approaches were limited to using 30000 voxels (which gave results of equivalent accuracy). Registration with the cylindrical structure required 0.66s (±0.30) per volume while using the rectilinear image averaged 0.23s (±0.12). The number of cost function evaluations was not significantly different; thus we suggest the additional time is due to the additional operations in Eqs. 1 and 2. As reconstruction requires approximately 2 s per volume the approach remains interesting in terms of time savings.

Data from a mechanically swept US probe naturally falls on a cylindrical coordinate system. Using this coordinate system directly in the intensity based tracking problem which arises when monitoring intrafraction prostate motion using TPUS volume scanning gives equivalent results to using a reconstruction based approach. It has the advantage of saving the reconstruction time and computational resources, at a small additional cost in the registration calculation.

References

1. Adamson, J., Wu, Q.: Prostate Intrafraction Motion Assessed by Simultaneous Kilovoltage Fluoroscopy at Megavoltage Delivery I: Clinical Observations and Pattern Analysis. Int. J. Radiation Oncology, Biology, Physics 78(5), 1563–1570 (2010)
2. Canadian Cancer Society: Prostate cancer statistics at a glance (2011), http://tinyurl.com/6cmyvd9
3. Langen, K., et al.: Observations on real-time prostate gland motion using electromagnetic tracking.. Int. J. Rad. Oncology, Biology, Physics 71(4), 1084–1090 (2008)
4. Modersitzki, J.: Numerical Methods for Image Registration. Numerical Mathematics and Scientific Computation. Oxford University Press, Oxford (2004)

Spatial Characterization and Classification of Rectal Bleeding in Prostate Cancer Radiotherapy with a Voxel-Based Principal Components Analysis Model for 3D Dose Distribution

Baiyang Chen[1,2], Oscar Acosta[1,2], Amar Kachenoura[1,2], Juan David Ospina[1,2,4],
Gaël Dréan[1,2], Antoine Simon[1,2], Jean-Jacques Bellanger[1,2], and Pascal Haigron[1,2],
and Renaud de Crevoisier[1,2,3]

[1] INSERM, U 642, Rennes, F-35000, France
[2] Université de Rennes 1, LTSI, F-35000, France
Baiyang.Chen@etudiant.univ.renes1.fr,
{Oscar.Acosta,Amar.Kachenoura,Gael.Drean,Antoine.Simon,
jean-jacques.bellanger,Pascal.Haigron}@univ-rennes1.fr
[3] Département de Radiothérapie, Centre Eugène Marquis, Rennes, F-35000, France
r.de-crevoisier@rennes.fnclcc.fr
[4] School of Statistics, Universidad Nacional de Colombia, Campus Medellin, Colombia
jdospina@unal.edu.co

Abstract. Although external beam radiotherapy is one of the most commonly prescribed treatments for prostate cancer, severe complications may arise as a result of high delivered doses to the neighboring organs at risk, namely the bladder and the rectum. The prediction of this toxicity events are commonly based on the planned dose distribution using the dose-volume histograms within predictive models. However, as different spatial dose distributions may produce similar dose-volume histograms, these models may not be accurate in revealing the subtleties of the dose-effect relationships. Using the prescribed dose, we propose a voxel-based principal component analysis method for characterizing and classifying those individuals at risk of rectal bleeding. Sixty-five cases of patients treated for prostate cancer were reviewed; fifteen of them presented rectal bleeding within two years after the treatment. The method was able to classify rectal bleeding with 0.8 specificity and 0.73 sensitivity. In addition, eigenimages with the most discriminant features suggest that some specific dose patterns are related to rectal bleeding.

1 Introduction

In prostate cancer radiotherapy (RT), the challenge is to deliver high doses of radiation to the prostate and seminal vesicles (SV), while sparing the adjacent Organs At Risk (OAR). The prediction of complications due to the delivered dose is crucial in improving patient outcome [1, 2]. The risk of toxicity for the OAR, like the rectum and bladder, related to the prescribed dose has been classically assessed using Dose Volume Histograms (DVH) [3] or Dose Surface Histograms (DSH). Although many studies

A. Madabhushi et al. (Eds.): Prostate Cancer Imaging 2011, LNCS 6963, pp. 60–69, 2011.

have shown a correlation between dose, volume and rectal toxicity [4,5,6,7,8,9], they lack spatial accuracy and are not able to correlate the treatment outcome with the specific dose pattern. While reducing the rich three-dimensional information of the dose to a two-dimensional pattern such as the DVH, the potential correlation that may exist between toxicity and irradiation at small portions of the rectum may not be detected. Some attempts have been made to introduce the notion of spatiality [10] but still within the dose-volume space. In [11] Buettner et al. have shown that late complications in the rectum are not only related to volumetric aspects of the dose, but particularly to the shape of the dose distribution. More recently, in [12] spatial considerations were incorporated by parameterizing the 3D patterns of dose. In this way, by selecting a limited set of predictive features, their method outperforms the classical models based on DVH/DSH. This approach still lies in the reduction of feature dimensionality by fitting analytic functions to each dose shape. Nevertheless, subtle underlying correlations may exist between the toxicity and the dose spatial distribution at a voxel level. Producing voxel-wise statistical models of toxicity might therefore help to reveal these relationships in an accurate manner and would allow the highlighting of heterogeneous intra-organ sensitivity.

The value of the dose at each voxel can be seen as a single feature of an individual, rising in thousands of features per individual. Then, following a pattern recognition methodology [13], an analysis of all the features may be performed aimed at characterizing and classifying the whole population. Alternatively, undertaking a voxel-based morphometry (VBM) methodology [14], as voxel-wise comparisons allow assessing significant differences of dose between two groups (toxicity and non-toxicity). Examples of the latter, explaining urinary tract toxicity [15] and tumor control in the prostate, were recently published [16]. Those methods map the doses to a single template based on the radially-computed distances from the organ delineations and are therefore approximated in terms of spatial location in cases where inter-individual variability is important. In order for these voxel-wise comparisons to be meaningful in terms of features, the doses have to be perfectly mapped beforehand to a common coordinate system, which is a challenging task due to the difficulties lying on the high inter-individual variability. Thus, efficient ways of statistically dealing with high dimensional data must be devised.

Principal component analysis (PCA) is a methodology that identifies the underlying structure of data across a population by computing the significant modes of variation as a set of orthogonal directions (eigenvectors), and the amount of variation, encoded in the eigenvalues, computed from the covariance matrix of the data. PCA has been used before for characterizing voxel data with ^{11}C PiB PET images on Alzheimer's disease (AD) patients [17], or with Fluorodeoxyglucose (^{18}F) PET images to classify fronto temporal dementia and AD [18].

In this paper, we propose characterizing rectal bleeding using voxel-based PCA on a group of patients treated for prostate cancer with RT, and using the more discriminant features to classify the individuals' toxicity. As opposed to [12], the proposed method initially considers each single voxel as a feature. Subsequently, the PCA analysis is applied in extracting the most discriminant features, reducing the data dimensionality across the whole population.

2   Materials and Methods

The two-level method, namely training and validation, are depicted in figure 1. After a preprocessing step where the individuals' CT scans were non-rigidly registered towards a common template, each individual's dose was propagated on the same coordinate system. With regards to the training step Voxel-based PCA was used to extract the main modes of variations for the whole population. Finally, a feature selection step was performed to select the most discriminant principal components (PCs) followed by a leave-one-out cross-validation scheme to validate the classification.

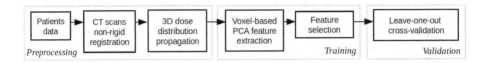

Fig. 1. Proposed methodology

2.1   Data

Sixty-five individuals treated for prostate cancer with external radiotherapy and a two-years follow-up were selected. Fifteen of them presented rectal bleeding. The patients underwent a planning CT scan before the treatment. The size of the images in the axial plane was 512×512 with 1 mm pixels and 2 mm thick slices. For each patient, the bladder, rectum, prostate and seminal vesicles (SV) were manually contoured following the same protocol. For each patient, the prescribed dose was computed in a standard Treatment Planning System (TPS) step and then resampled into the CT native space.

2.2   Registration

As illustrated in Fig. 2, the individuals' 3D CT scans and planned doses were non-rigidly registered towards a single template using a two step process. The template was chosen as a representative individual external to this database.

Firstly, CT scans were rigidly registered towards the template using the cross correlation as a similarity measure. Secondly, a non-rigid hybrid organ/intensity registration based on the demons algorithm [19] was implemented to eventually align the considered organs. In this non-rigid registration step, the manually-segmented organs (prostate, bladder and rectum) in the CT scan were replaced by a set of Normalized Distance Maps (NDMAPS) obtained as follows: for each individual's organ i) an euclidean distance map was computed, ii) the distance map of the individual's organ was multiplied by the maximum of the distance map in the template, likewise for the distance map of the template, which was multiplied by the maximum of the individual's distance map. Combining the NDMAPS with the CT scans within the registration step allowed the alignment of organ barycentres and helped to overcome the problems of contrast distribution within the organs.

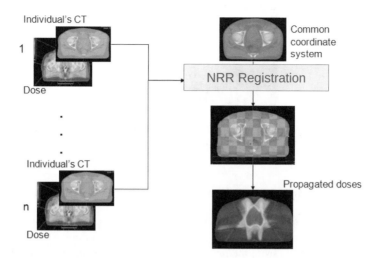

Fig. 2. Non-rigid mapping of doses towards a single template. In this paper $n = 65$.

The first row of Fig. 3 shows the CT scan of the template (Fig. 3(a)), the manual segmentations (Fig. 3(b)) and the NDMAP (Fig. 3(c)). The second row shows an example of an individual's CT scan (Fig. 3(d)) registered towards the template. In this example, the individual's NDMAP fits with the template NDMAP (Fig. 3(f)). The resulting warped dose on the template space for this individual appears in Fig. 3(g). It is interesting to show the organ coincidence rate map computed over the 65 patients in the template coordinate system as illustrated in Fig. 4. Further, we obtained an average dice overlap of 0.78, 0.87 and 0.71 for the prostate, bladder and rectum, respectively.

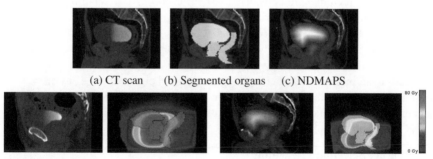

(a) CT scan   (b) Segmented organs   (c) NDMAPS

(d) Individual's CT   (e) TPS Planned Dose   (f) Registered NDMAP   (g) Warped dose

Fig. 3. (a) Sagittal cut plane of the CT Image which serves as the template; (b) Manually Segmented organs; (c) Normalized Distance Map (NDMAP) of each organ combined with the CT scan; d) A typical individual's CT; e) the corresponding TPS planned dose; f) Normalized Distance Map (NDMAP), g) warped dose, using the computed transformation

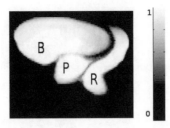

Fig. 4. Organ coincidence rate maps after the sixty-five individuals' organs were registered on the template. (B) Bladder; (P) Prostate; (R) Rectum.

2.3 Voxel-Based Principal Component Analysis

The purpose of PCA is to derive a relatively small number of decorrelated linear combinations (principal components) of a set of random zero-mean variables while retaining as much of the information from the original variables as possible. Typically, the PCA for the random vector $x^m = [x_1^m, \cdots, x_N^m]^\mathsf{T}$ consists in looking for an overdetermined $(N \times P)$ (i.e. $P \leq N$) orthonormal linear transform W such that the P components of the vector $z^m = [z_1^m, \cdots, z_P^m]^\mathsf{T} = W^\mathsf{T} x^m$ are mutually uncorrelated. Thus, if we denote $[e_1 \ldots e_P]^\mathsf{T}$ as the eigenvectors of R_x (the covariance matrix of x^m), corresponding to the eigenvalues $(\lambda_1, \ldots \lambda_P)$ where $\lambda_1 \geq \ldots \geq \lambda_P$, the first principal component of x^m is $z_1^m = e_1^\mathsf{T} x^m$. Likewise, the P-th principal component is obtained as $z_P^m = e_P^\mathsf{T} x^m$.

In our case, each individual's 3D dose image can be represented as a 1D vector by concatenating the rows of all the slices. Thus, we obtained a $N \times M$ matrix $\mathbf{X}$ for all the individuals, where $N = 65$ represents the number of individuals (the number of observations carried out) and M the number of voxels (the variables). Only the voxels lying within the rectum were considered ($M = 12000$). After centering the data, the eigen-decomposition of the covariance matrix $R_x = \mathbf{X}^\mathsf{T} \mathbf{X}$ must be performed. However, because of the huge size of R_x (about 12000×12000), it is computationally expensive to find it directly. A common procedure is to perform the eigen-decomposition of a $N \times N$ covariance matrix $C_x = \mathbf{X}\mathbf{X}^\mathsf{T}$, yielding new P eigenvectors $[y_1 \ldots y_P]^\mathsf{T}$. This leads to an indirect way of computing the original eigenvectors e_p as $e_p = \mathbf{X}^\mathsf{T} y_p$. We note that because the rank of R_x can not exceed N, the maximum number P of meaningful eigenvectors must be less or equal to N.

2.4 Feature Selection - Learning

A key point in PCA classification is the choice of the more discriminant features (eigenvectors). We used the Receiver Operating Characteristic (ROC) curve as the main criterion to select the features that better divide the population to rectal and non-rectal bleeding categories. For each axis, the probability density functions of each class is computed. Figure 5(a) illustrates the overlapping probability density function of the two classes for one principal axis. Figure 5(b) depicts the corresponding ROC curve, after computing the True Positive Rate (TPR) and False Positive Rate (FPR) at each separation level. Thus, the most discriminant axis was selected as the one with the highest distance to the random guess line (RGL). Then, the "Sequential Forward Selection (SFS)" [13] strategy was used to select the optimum feature set as the top n-ranked axis (the top five obtained features were the 21st, 44th, 50th, 37th and 4th axis). Figure 6 shows the result of the feature-selection procedure using the SFS method. It can be observed that, with only two features (axis 21st and 44th), the achieved accuracy, sensitivity and specificity were 0.89, 0.80 and 0.92, respectively.

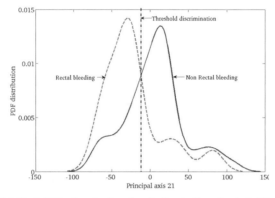

(a) Probability density function (estimated) on the Axis 21

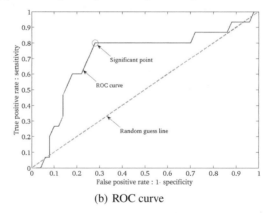

(b) ROC curve

Fig. 5. (a) Probability density functions (estimated) of rectal bleeding and non-bleeding for the principal axis 21 and (b) the corresponding ROC curve with the distance to the random guess line (RGL)

2.5 Validation

Because of the reduced number of patients, a leave-one-out cross-validation was performed to evaluate the performance of the classifier by using different combinations of features (the top n-ranked) $n = 1, .., 5$. Thus, at each iteration a single individual was extracted from the training data and used as a test sample. Figure 7 displays the results

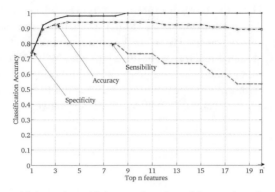

Fig. 6. Accuracy, sensitivity and specificity as a function of the number of exploited features

of the classification. When using just the bestfeatures (namely the 21st), one can observe that, although most of the rectal bleeding patients were well classified (0.73 sensitivity), we also misclassified the non-rectal bleeding (0.62 specificity). On the contrary, when using more than three features, the performance drops down in terms of sensitivity (0.26), with 0.86 specificity. The best classifier was obtained when using the two best features (21 , 44) with 0.8 specificity and 0.73 sensitivity.

Fig. 8, shows the two most discriminant eigenvectors (21st, 44th) reshaped as 3D eigenimages (that we can also call eigendoses). These results suggest that spatial patterns discriminating between the two groups may be identified. As it can be seen, particularly in the 21st eigenimage, two different patterns showed up. The first one (a) in the anterior rectal wall (close to the prostate), where the irradiated dose is likely to be high, and the second one (b) in the upper part of the rectum close to the sigmoid where the delivered dose is supposed to be very low. This may suggest, that the differences in prescribed dose in those areas are related to rectal bleeding.

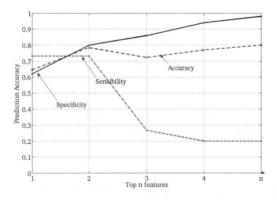

Fig. 7. Learning accuracies distribution (left) and Prediction accuracies (right) vs the number of features used

Fig. 8. Sagittal view of the template, overlaid with the reshaped eigenvectors 21 (left) and 44 (right)

3   Discussion and Conclusion

In this paper, we have presented a preliminary study aimed at the creation of appearance models of dose distribution focused on the rectum in order to produce predictive models of toxicity. The proposed PCA method allows the decomposition of dose distributions and the identification of the most meaningful features in further classifying of individuals with/without rectal bleeding. Moreover, as opposed to voxel-wise comparisons, the proposed method may be more robust to misregistrations as it finds underlying spatial patterns (sets of voxels) related to the variation of dose across the population.

Although the experiments were performed on a reduced data set, the results are promising in studying the dose-effect relationship, as a good classification was reached by using only two main features (0.8 specificity and 0.73 sensitivity). When more than three features were included a lower performance was obtained indicating a great sensitivity above the 3rd axis. However, for the sake of feasibility we used just a non-linear, feature by feature, classification method. It is expected that better classifiers would produce better results.

Using the resultant eigenimages (eigendoses), allowed the highlighting of some regions where rectal bleeding may be related to different dose patterns. It is important to note that the meaningful eigenvectors were not necessarily those related to the highest eigenvalues. The top axis were the 21st and 44th, which explains a low portion of the variability across the whole population. This suggests, however, that subtle differences in spatial patterns may appear to be more informative and related to rectal bleeding. These regions may therefore guide the planning of dose distribution for patients, mainly at the inverse planning systems of Intensity-Modulated Radiotherapy (IMRT).

The robustness of the proposed method will be further studied in future work on a larger database with different toxicity groups and with numerical phantoms. In addition, as the toxicity is also related to specific factors of an individual, such as radio-sensitivity or personal medical history, other parameters may also help to guide the training step, such as age, etc. Further validation with the toxicity of other organs, as the bladder, is in progress as well as the implementation of better classifiers and non-rigid registration methods to improve specificity. The proposed method opens the way to larger studies aimed at unravelling the spatial relationship between the dose and the treatment outcome.

References

1. Fiorino, C., Rancati, T., Valdagni, R.: Predictive models of toxicity in external radiotherapy: dosimetric issues. Cancer 115 (suppl. 13), 3135–3140 (2009)
2. de Crevoisier, R., Tucker, S.L., Dong, L., Mohan, R., Cheung, R., Cox, J.D., Kuban, D.A.: Increased risk of biochemical and local failure in patients with distended rectum on the planning ct for prostate cancer radiotherapy. Int. J. Radiat. Oncol. Biol. Phys. 62(4), 965–973 (2005)
3. Ting, J.Y., Wu, X., Fiedler, J.A., Yang, C., Watzich, M.L., Markoe, A.: Dose-volume histograms for bladder and rectum. Int. J. Radiat. Oncol. Biol. Phys. 38(5), 1105–1111 (1997)
4. Sohn, M., Alber, M., Yan, D.: Principal component analysis-based pattern analysis of dose-volume histograms and influence on rectal toxicity. Int. J. Radiat. Oncol. Biol. Phys. 69(1), 230–239 (2007)
5. Fiorino, C., Vavassori, V., Sanguineti, G., Bianchi, C., Cattaneo, G.M., Piazzolla, A., Cozzarini, C.: Rectum contouring variability in patients treated for prostate cancer: impact on rectum dose-volume histograms and normal tissue complication probability. Radiother Oncol. 63(3), 249–255 (2002)
6. Fiorino, C., Cozzarini, C., Vavassori, V., Sanguineti, G., Bianchi, C., Cattaneo, G.M., Foppiano, F., Magli, A., Piazzolla, A.: Relationships between dvhs and late rectal bleeding after radiotherapy for prostate cancer: analysis of a large group of patients pooled from three institutions. Radiother Oncol. 64(1), 1–12 (2002)
7. Marzi, S., Arcangeli, G., Saracino, B., Petrongari, M.G., Bruzzaniti, V., Iaccarino, G., Landoni, V., Soriani, A., Benassi, M.: Relationships between rectal wall dose-volume constraints and radiobiologic indices of toxicity for patients with prostate cancer. Int. J. Radiat. Oncol. Biol. Phys. 68(1), 41–49 (2007)
8. Benk, V.A., Adams, J.A., Shipley, W.U., Urie, M.M., McManus, P.L., Efird, J.T., Willett, C.G., Goitein, M.: Late rectal bleeding following combined x-ray and proton high dose irradiation for patients with stages t3-t4 prostate carcinoma. Int. J. Radiat. Oncol. Biol. Phys. 26(3), 551–557 (1993)
9. Rancati, T., Fiorino, C., Gagliardi, G., Cattaneo, G.M., Sanguineti, G., Borca, V.C., Cozzarini, C., Fellin, G., Foppiano, F., Girelli, G., Menegotti, L., Piazzolla, A., Vavassori, V., Valdagni, R.: Fitting late rectal bleeding data using different ntcp models: results from an italian multi-centric study (airopros0101). Radiother Oncol. 73(1), 21–32 (2004)
10. Kupchak, C., Battista, J., Dyk, J.V.: Experience-driven dose-volume histogram maps of NTCP risk as an aid for radiation treatment plan selection and optimization. Med. Phys. 35, 333–343 (2008)
11. Buettner, F., Gulliford, S.L., Webb, S., Sydes, M.R., Dearnaley, D.P., Partridge, M.: Assessing correlations between the spatial distribution of the dose to the rectal wall and late rectal toxicity after prostate radiotherapy: an analysis of data from the mrc rt01 trial (isrctn 47772397). Physics in Medicine and Biology 54(21), 6535 (2009)
12. Buettner, F., Gulliford, S.L., Webb, S., Partridge, M.: Modeling late rectal toxicities based on a parameterized representation of the 3d dose distribution. Physics in Medicine and Biology 56(7), 2103 (2011)
13. Jain, A.K., Duin, R.P., Mao, J.: Statistical pattern recognition: A review. IEEE Transactions on pattern analysis and machine intelligence 22(1), 4–37 (2000)
14. Friston, K.J., Holmes, A.P., Worsley, K.J., Poline, J.P., Frith, C.D., Frackowiak, R.S.J.: Statistical Parametric Maps in Functional Imaging: A General LInear Approach. In: Human Brain Mapping, pp. 189–210 (1995)

15. Heemsbergen, W.D., Al-Mamgani, A., Witte, M.G., van Herk, M., Pos, F.J., Lebesque, J.V.: Urinary obstruction in prostate cancer patients from the dutch trial (68 gy vs. 78 gy): Relationships with local dose, acute effects, and baseline characteristics. Int. J. Radiat. Oncol. Biol. Phys. (January 2010)
16. Witte, M.G., Heemsbergen, W.D., Bohoslavsky, R., Pos, F.J., Al-Mamgani, A., Lebesque, J.V., van Herk, M.: Relating dose outside the prostate with freedom from failure in the dutch trial 68 gy vs. 78 gy. Int. J. Radiat. Oncol. Biol. Phys. 77(1), 131–138 (2010)
17. Fripp, J., Bourgeat, P., Acosta, O., Raniga, P., Modat, M., Pike, K.E., Jones, G., O'Keefe, G., Masters, C.L., Ames, D., Ellis, K.A., Maruff, P., Currie, J., Villemagne, V.L., Rowe, C.C., Salvado, O., Ourselin, S.: Appearance modeling of (11)c pib pet images: Characterizing amyloid deposition in alzheimer's disease, mild cognitive impairment and healthy aging. NeuroImage (August 2008)
18. Higdon, R., Foster, N., Koeppe, R., DeCarli, C., Jagust, W., Clark, C., Barbas, N., Arnold, S., Turner, R., Heidebrink, J., Minoshima, S.: A comparison of classification methods for differentiating fronto-temporal dementia from alzheimer's disease using fdg-pet imaging. Statistical Medicine 23(2), 315–326 (2004)
19. Vercauteren, T., Pennec, X., Perchant, A., Ayache, N.: Non-parametric diffeomorphic image registration with the demons algorithm. In: Ayache, N., Ourselin, S., Maeder, A. (eds.) MICCAI 2007, Part II. LNCS, vol. 4792, pp. 319–326. Springer, Heidelberg (2007)

Dose Monitoring in Prostate Cancer Radiotherapy Using CBCT to CT Constrained Elastic Image Registration

Guillaume Cazoulat[1,2], Antoine Simon[1,2], Oscar Acosta[1,2], Juan David Ospina[1,2], Khemara Gnep[3], Romain Viard[4], Renaud de Crevoisier[1,2,3], and Pascal Haigron[1,2]

[1] INSERM, U 642, Rennes, F-35000, France
[2] Université de Rennes 1, LTSI, F-35000, France
{guillaume.cazoulat,antoine.simon,oscar.acosta,juan.ospina,
pascal.haigron}@univ-rennes1.fr
[3] Département de Radiothérapie, Centre Eugène Marquis, Rennes, F-35000, France
{k.gnep,r.de-crevoisier}@rennes.fnclcc.fr
[4] Aquilab, Loos Les Lille, F-59120, France
romain.viard@aquilab.com

Abstract. The recent concept of Dose Guided Radiotherapy (DGRT) consists in computing a cumulative dose distribution at each treatment fraction to decide if a treatment replanning is necessary. These cumulative dose distributions are obtained by mapping the daily dose distributions with the results of a non-rigid registration between the planning CT scan and daily CBCT images. But, mainly because of large deformations and of the scatter effect of CBCT, the application of this methodology to prostate cancer radiotherapy is very challenging. In this paper, we adapt a nonparametric non-rigid registration algorithm based on Mutual Information to register the daily CBCT scan to the planning CT scan in the context of prostate cancer DGRT. In order to improve registration accuracy, we then propose a modification of the registration framework to introduce landmark constraints. We show that this constrained non-rigid registration algorithm was able to significantly increase the accuracy of the cumulative dose estimation.

1 Introduction

Radiotherapy is used to treat all stages of localized prostate cancer with proven efficacy. The main challenge in radiotherapy is to deliver the prescribed dose to the clinical target (for local control), while limiting the irradiation of the organs at risk (OAR), thus avoiding subsequent toxicity-related events. One of the major innovations of the last years is the evolution of imaging devices integrated to the treatment device to perform an Image-Guided RadioTherapy (IGRT). Today, the most widespread imaging device for IGRT is the cone beam computed tomography (CBCT) which allows the visualization of the soft tissues under the treatment device, and if needed to reposition the patient according to the tumor position [1]. In case of prostate cancer irradiation, typically fractionated into 39 daily treatment sessions, this approach is particularly interesting in correcting the prostate motion relative to the pelvic bone. However, rigid registration of

A. Madabhushi et al. (Eds.): Prostate Cancer Imaging 2011, LNCS 6963, pp. 70–79, 2011.

the prostate does not allow for the compensation of anatomical deformations that may expose the patient to an overdosage of the organs at risk and/or an underdosage of the tumor. In this context, only a replanning of the treatment before a new fraction deliverance can compensate for these anatomical deformations. To determine if a replanning is necessary, the effective dose distribution on the planning CT scan, taking anatomical variations into account, has to be estimated between each treatment fraction. This recent concept of Dose-Guided RadioTherapy (DGRT) [2,3] relies on the capability of tracking the planning CT voxels on each CBCT scan. Voxel tracking is typically performed by non-rigid image registration (NRR) and the computed deformations are used to map the daily dose on the planning CT [4,5], which is the spatial reference for the clinician. Mapped daily dose distributions can then be summed to provide an estimation of the current cumulative dose at any fraction and so indicate a possible deviation from the prescribed dose. The calculation of the cumulative dose may be prone to errors caused by: (i) the registration errors; (ii) the dose mapping method that does not take into account tissue inhomogeneities [6]. In this paper, we focus on the impact of registration errors on cumulative dose estimation, and particularly in the benefits of incorporating landmark-based constraints in the registration method.

A small number of solutions have been proposed to register CT to CBCT for the purpose of prostate cancer DGRT. Registration of pelvic CT and CBCT is very challenging because of various problems: (i) a poor soft tissue contrast in CBCT; (ii) the scatter effect in CBCT acquisition; (iii) important deformations encountered in this anatomical area, especially the bladder and the rectum; (iv) the apparition/disparition of bowel gas. In this context, Greene et al [7] proposed Constrained non-rigid registration (CNRR) with Free-Form Deformations (FFD). This work showed improvements at aligning soft organs and bones, by adding constraints to the control points of the deformations lying in these structures. In [8], Lu et al proposed a Hard-constrained non-rigid registration using the Lagrange multiplier method, and also showed an improvement in the results. Both authors adopted a Normalized Cross Correlation metric. In the family of nonparametric registration algorithms, the only solution investigated to our knowledge was an implementation of the Demons algorithm [9]. This type of approach exhibits two interesting properties in the context of radiotherapy: speed and easy parameterization. However, because the Demons require perfect correspondences between voxel intensities to succeed, these methods faced the challenging problem of converting CBCT units to Hounsfield Units [10]. A more straightforward approach is to keep the Demons registration framework but to change the force computation formula to consider another metric different to Sum of Squared Differences (SSD) [11,12]. Moreover, the integration of constraints in this kind of registration algorithm is simple and intuitive.

The goal of this work is: (i) to adapt a nonparametric registration algorithm based on a mutual information similarity measure; (ii) to integrate constraints related to organ delineations; (iii) to determine if the integration of these constraints will improve the registration and the cumulative dose accuracy.

2   Methods

2.1   Patient Data

One patient treated for prostate cancer received a radiotherapy fixed to 80Gy with a Volumetric Arc Modulated Therapy (VMAT) technique. At each of the 39 daily treatment fractions, a CBCT was acquired for repositioning purposes. For the needs of this study, the same radiation oncologist manually contoured the prostate, the seminal vesicles, the rectum and the bladder on the planning CT and on a total of 30 CBCTs. These delineations were validated by a second expert. In this study, we simulated the patient repositioning under the treatment device with a registration algorithm that finds the translation between the CBCT and the planning CT maximizing Mutual Information between the two images. A ROI is defined on the planning CT, and all the CBCTs are resampled to this ROI after the rigid registration. This ROI on the planning CT with delineation and an example of daily CBCT are presented in Fig. 1.

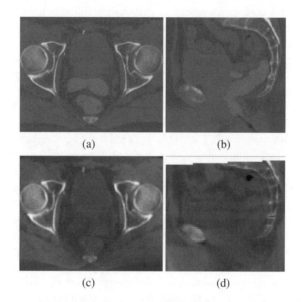

(a) (b)

(c) (d)

Fig. 1. (a) and (b): axial and coronal slices of the ROI defined on the planning CT with overlaid planning delineation. (c) and (d): axial and coronal slices of a rigidly registered CBCT scan

2.2   Nonparametric Elastic Registration Algorithm

The NRR algorithm we adopted aims to maximize mutual information. It is an implementation of a method described by Rogelj et al [12]. Mutual Information is a global measure for the whole image that can be seen as the sum of local point similarity measures S_L. We then define a global measure S_G between the fixed image F and the moving image M as:

$$S_G = \sum_x S_L(x) \tag{1}$$

with

$$S_L(x) = \log \frac{p(i_F(x), i_M(x))}{p(i_F(x)).p(i_M(x))} \qquad (2)$$

with $i_F(x)$ and $i_M(x)$ the voxel intensities at coordinate x in images F and M respectively.

A gradient descent of this similarity measure can then be achieved by the following iterative process:

1. Deform M with the current global deformation field U (first iteration: no deformation) to obtain M'
2. For each voxel, a forward force $\overrightarrow{F_f}$ corresponding with the point similarity gradient is computed:

$$\overrightarrow{F_f}(x) = \left.\frac{\partial}{\partial \epsilon}\right|_{\epsilon=0} S_L(i_F(x+\epsilon), i_{M'}(x)) \qquad (3)$$

as well as a reverse force $\overrightarrow{F_r}$:

$$\overrightarrow{F_r}(x) = \left.\frac{\partial}{\partial \epsilon}\right|_{\epsilon=0} S_L(i_F(x), i_{M'}(x+\epsilon)) \qquad (4)$$

The consistent force at this voxel coordinate x is then:

$$\overrightarrow{F} = \overrightarrow{F_f} - \overrightarrow{F_r} \qquad (5)$$

3. An update deformation field u is then obtained. In our implementation, we normalized u in order that the maximum vector amplitude has the value of the voxel spacing at the current multiresolution level.
4. Compose the global deformation field U with u: $U \leftarrow U \circ u$
5. The global deformation field is regularized by convolution with a gaussian kernel G, simulating an elastic behavior [13]: $U \leftarrow U \otimes G$. We fixed the standard deviation σ of the gaussian kernel G to the voxel diameter of the current multiresolution level.

We introduce exceptions in voxel forces computation: if the voxel intensity I is under a threshold T specific to bowel gas ($I < -500$ for the CT and $I < 100$ for the considered CBCT), the force is fixed to zero to avoid large registration errors. Also, if the voxel intensity corresponds to a bone tissue ($I > 100$ for the CT and $I > 500$ for the considered CBCT), the force is fixed to zero. Finally, the registration follows a three-level multiresolution scheme.

2.3   Prior Surface Matching

To automatically determine landmarks correspondences between the CT scan and any daily CBCT we used a simple organ surface matching method. First, signed Euclidean distance maps are computed from the binary images representing the organs. Then a three-resolution-level Demons algorithm [14] implemented in the Insight ToolKit (ITK) is applied between the distance maps. This method generally performs well to align the zero isoline of the distance maps or in other words, to match the organ surfaces. Finally, in the computed deformation fields, we only consider the vectors lying on the organ surfaces.

The results of this surface matching are considered accurate enough to serve as force constraints in the registration process but also as elements of comparison for the registration evaluation.

2.4   Constrained Non-rigid Registration Algorithm (CNRR)

In order to handle large deformations of the organs, but also to consider the intensity information, forces constraints are integrated into the nonparametric elastic registration algorithm previously exposed. These force constraints $\{\vec{c}\}$ can be determined, for example as explained in section 2.3. They have to be applied progressively, iteration by iteration, in order not to violate the deformation field regularization scheme. We keep the same registration process as exposed in section 2.2, except that a new step is inserted just before the regularization step. This new step locally removes the computed force where a force constraint is specified, and replaces it by the time-weighted force constraint. Our iterative registration process then becomes:

1. Deform M with the current global deformation field U to obtain M'
2. For each voxel, $\vec{F} = \vec{F_f} - \vec{F_r}$
3. u is normalized
4. $U \leftarrow U \circ u$
5. For all voxels of the image where a constrain vector $\vec{c}$ exists, the computed local force is replaced by:

$$\vec{F} = \max\left(\|\overrightarrow{F_{k-1}}\|, \min\left(\|\vec{c}\|, k \cdot \Delta l\right)\right) \cdot \vec{c} \tag{6}$$

where k is the iteration number, $\overrightarrow{F_{k-1}}$ is the force computed at the previous iteration and Δl is the maximum vector length update step (equal to the voxel spacing in our implementation).
6. $U \leftarrow U \otimes G$

3   Results

All the 30 CBCTs were registered to the planning CT: (i) rigidly as mentioned in section 2.1, (ii) with NRR based on mutual information and (iii) with CNRR based on mutual information and with landmark constraints obtained from a prior organ surface matching.

3.1   Dice Scores and Normalized Mutual Information

To evaluate our methods, for each kind of registration, the manual delineation of the prostate, the seminal vesicles, the rectum and the bladder have been propagated from the 30 CBCTs to the planning CT. Each time a Dice score has been computed between the propagated delineation and the planning delineation ($DSC = 2(|A \cap B|/(|A| \cup |B|))$).

Resulting Dice scores are presented in Fig. 2. The proposed NRR method succeeded improving prostate, seminal vesicles and bladder correspondences. However, it failed to improve rectum alignment. This was expected, considering the large deformations due to rectum filling and to the presence of bowel gas. The CNNR outperformed the previous NRR for all the organs thanks to the use of constraints based on surface matching.

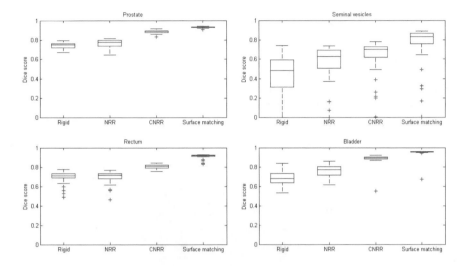

Fig. 2. Dice scores obtained after delineation propagation for different registration strategies

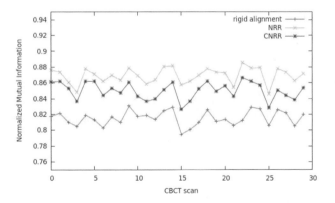

Fig. 3. Normalized Mutual Information (NMI) computed after registration between the warped CBCT and the planning CT

In order to evaluate the efficiency of the proposed mutual information maximization process, Normalized Mutual Information (NMI) has also been computed after registration between the warped CBCT and the planning CT. Fig. 3 shows that we obtained a slightly lower mutual information with the CNRR than with the CRR. However, the CNRR leaded to a good compromise between organ correspondences and mutual information.

3.2   Localization of Registration Errors

Fig. 4 represents the mean registration difference $d(x) = |\overrightarrow{F_{SM}}(x) - \overrightarrow{F_{NRR}}(x)|$ obtained for each point of the organ surfaces. Considering the surface matching as being the most reliable registration method for organ surfaces, this figure provides information on the registration accuracy. These registrations errors are mainly observed in the base of bladder.

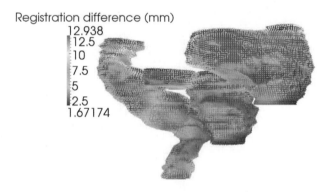

Fig. 4. Mean registration error computed on each point of the organ surfaces

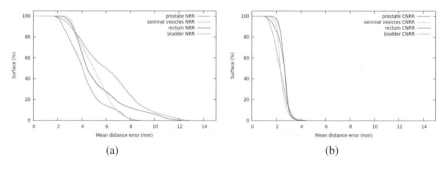

Fig. 5. Error surface histograms (a): In case of NRR, (b): In case of CNRR

A more synthetic representation of the registration accuracy is given by Error Surface Histograms (Fig.5). While the NRR yielded to the largest registration errors especially for the bladder, CNRR appears to considerably reduce the error values and to homogenize it on all the organ surfaces.

3.3 Dosimetric Impact of Registration Errors - Comparison between NRR and CNRR

The 30 daily dose distributions were all mapped to the planning CT according to the tranformation computed by NRR or CNRR. In this way, 30 cumulative dose distributions were obtained for each registration strategy. Thanks to the previous surface matching, a good approximation of the true cumulative dose distributions on the organ surfaces were available. We are therefore able to represent the Cumulated Dose Surface Histogram (DSH). To measure the dosimetric impact of registration errors, we also computed the cumulated dose surfaces histograms after NRR and CNRR. Fig. 6 shows that the CNRR gives a significant better estimation of the cumulative dose than the initial NRR at least on organ surfaces. However, from a clinician point of view, only Dose Volume Histograms (DVH) constitute a reference to evaluate and compare treatment plans. Fig. 7 shows large differences between the cumulated DVHs obtained with the first NRR explained methodology and our proposed CNRR methodology. These results suggest that, without using the landmark constraints, the CBCT to CT registration is not accurate enough for dose accumulation.

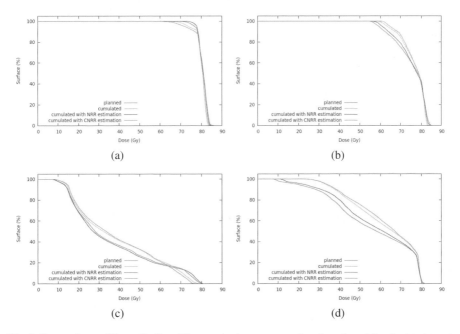

Fig. 6. Comparison of Dose Surface Histograms (percentage of surface (y-axis) submitted to, at least, a given mean error (x-axis)). (a): prostate, (b): seminal vesicles, (c): rectum and (d): bladder.

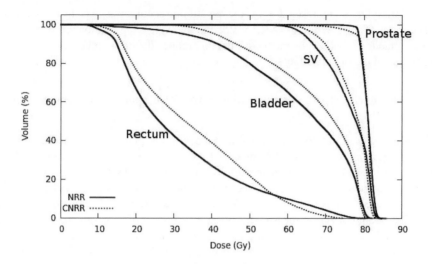

Fig. 7. Comparison of the cumulative DVH obtained by NRR or by CNRR

4 Conclusion and Discussion

In this paper, we presented an original constrained non-rigid registration (CNRR) method in the context of prostate DGRT. Thanks to a surface matching of the manual delineation, we automatically defined a set of landmarks correspondences that served as constraints in our CNRR algorithm. Results show that this CNRR algorithm outperformed the initial NRR algorithm at aligning critical structures, and at the same time registered the whole image where no constraints were specified. Without the use of the landmark constraints from the organ delineations, large errors on the cumulative dose estimation were observed on the organ surfaces. It appears that, in case of prostate cancer treatment, accurate cumulative dose estimation based on CBCT to CT image registration requires the integration of landmark constraints on prostate and OARs. However, the manual delineation of CBCT images is very time consuming. Therefore, in future work, we will evaluate the performance of this CNRR algorithm with just a reduced number of well-chosen landmark constraints.

Acknowledgments. This work was partially funded by the french research agency (ANR): TIGRE project.

References

1. Thilmann, C., Nill, S., Tucking, T., Hoss, A., Hesse, B., Dietrich, L., Bendl, R., Rhein, B., Haring, P., Thieke, C., et al.: Correction of patient positioning errors based on in-line cone beam CTs: clinical implementation and first experiences. Radiation Oncology 1(1), 16 (2006)
2. Chen, J., Morin, O., Aubin, M., Bucci, M., Chuang, C., Pouliot, J.: Dose-guided radiation therapy with megavoltage cone-beam CT. Br. J. Radiol. 79, S87–S98 (2006)

3. Pouliot, J.: Megavoltage imaging, megavoltage cone beam CT and dose-guided radiation therapy. Front. Radiat. Ther. Oncol. 40, 132–142 (2007)
4. Schaly, B., Kempe, J., Bauman, G., Battista, J., Dyk, J.: Tracking the dose distribution in radiation therapy by accounting for variable anatomy. Physics in Medicine and Biology 49, 791 (2004)
5. Foskey, M., Davis, B., Goyal, L., Chang, S., Chaney, E., Strehl, N., Tomei, S., Rosenman, J., Joshi, S.: Large deformation three-dimensional image registration in image-guided radiation therapy. Physics in Medicine and Biology 50, 5869 (2005)
6. Zhong, H., Siebers, J.V.: Monte Carlo dose mapping on deforming anatomy. Physics in medicine and biology 54, 5815 (2009)
7. Greene, W.H., Chelikani, S., Purushothaman, K., Chen, Z., Knisely, J.P.S., Staib, L.H., Papademetris, X., Duncan, J.: A constrained non-rigid registration algorithm for use in prostate image-guided radiotherapy. In: Metaxas, D., Axel, L., Fichtinger, G., Székely, G. (eds.) MICCAI 2008, Part I. LNCS, vol. 5241, pp. 780–788. Springer, Heidelberg (2008)
8. Lu, C., Chelikani, S., Papademetris, X., Staib, L., Duncan, J.: Constrained non-rigid registration using lagrange multipliers for application in prostate radiotherapy. In: 2010 IEEE Computer Society Conference on Computer Vision and Pattern Recognition Workshops (CVPRW), pp. 133–138. IEEE, Los Alamitos (2010)
9. Nithiananthan, S., Brock, K., Daly, M., Chan, H., Irish, J.C., Siewerdsen, J.H.: Demons deformable registration for CBCT-guided procedures in the head and neck: Convergence and accuracy. Medical physics 36, 4755 (2009)
10. Nithiananthan, S., Schafer, S., Uneri, A., Mirota, D., Stayman, J., Zbijewski, W., Brock, K., Daly, M., Chan, H., Irish, J., Siewerdsen, J.: Demons deformable registration of CT and cone-beam CT using an iterative intensity matching approach. Medical physics 38, 1785–1798 (2011)
11. Modat, M., Vercauteren, T., Ridgway, G., Hawkes, D., Fox, N., Ourselin, S.: Diffeomorphic demons using normalized mutual information, evaluation on multimodal brain MR images (proceedings paper) (2010)
12. Rogelj, P., Kovai, S., Gee, J.: Point similarity measures for non-rigid registration of multimodal data. Computer vision and image understanding 92(1), 112–140 (2003)
13. Pennec, X., Cachier, P., Ayache, N.: Understanding the demon's algorithm: 3D non-rigid registration by gradient descent. In: Taylor, C., Colchester, A. (eds.) MICCAI 1999. LNCS, vol. 1679, pp. 597–605. Springer, Heidelberg (1999)
14. Thirion, J.P.: Image matching as a diffusion process: an analogy with Maxwell's demons. Medical image analysis 2(3), 243–260 (1998)

Weighted Combination of Multi-Parametric MR Imaging Markers for Evaluating Radiation Therapy Related Changes in the Prostate*

Pallavi Tiwari[1], Satish Viswanath[1], John Kurhanewicz[2], and Anant Madabhushi[1]

[1] Department of Biomedical Engineering, Rutgers University, USA
pallavit@eden.rutgers.edu, anantm@rci.rutgers.edu
[2] Department of Radiology, University of California, San Francisco, USA

Abstract. Recently, multi-parametric (MP) Magnetic Resonance (MR) Imaging (T2-weighted, MR Spectroscopy (MRS), Diffusion-weighted (DWI)) has shown great potential for evaluating the early effects of radiotherapy (RT) in the prostate. In this work we present a framework for quantitatively combining MP-MRI markers in order to assess RT changes on a voxel-by-voxel basis. The suite of segmentation, registration, feature extraction, and classifier tools presented in this work will allow for identification of (a) residual disease, and (b) new foci of cancer (local recurrence) within the prostate. Our scheme involves, (a) simultaneously evaluating differences in pre-, post-RT MR imaging markers, and (b) intelligently integrating and weighting the imaging marker changes obtained in (a) to generate a combined MP-MRI difference map that can better quantify treatment specific changes in the prostate. We demonstrate the applicability of our scheme in studying intensity-modulated radiation therapy (IMRT)-related changes for a cohort of 14 MP (T2w, MRS, DWI) prostate MRI patient datasets. In the first step, the different MRI protocols from pre- and post-IMRT MRI scans are affinely registered (accounting for gland shrinkage), followed by automated segmentation of the prostate capsule using an active shape model. Individual imaging marker difference maps are generated by calculating the differences of textural, metabolic, and functional MRI marker attributes, pre- and post-RT, on a per-voxel basis. These difference maps are then combined via an intelligent optimization scheme to generate a combined weighted difference map, where higher difference values on the map signify larger change (new foci of cancer), and low difference values signify no/small change post-RT. In the absence of histological ground truth (surgical or biopsy), radiologist delineated CaP extent on pre-, and post-RT MRI was employed as the ground truth for evaluating the accuracy of our scheme in successfully identifying MP-MRI related disease changes post-RT. A mean area under the receiver operating curve (AUC) of 73.2% was obtained via the weighted MP-MRI map, when evaluated against expert delineated CaP extent on pre-, post-RT MRI. The difference maps corresponding to the individual structural (T2w intensities), functional (ADC intensities) and metabolic (choline, creatine) markers yielded a corresponding mean AUC of 54.4%, 68.6% and 70.8%.

* This work was supported by the Wallace H. Coulter Foundation, the National Cancer Institute under Grants R01CA136535, R21CA127186, R03CA128081, and R03CA143991, the Cancer Institute of New Jersey, and the Department of Defense (W81XWH-09).

A. Madabhushi et al. (Eds.): Prostate Cancer Imaging 2011, LNCS 6963, pp. 80–91, 2011.

1   Introduction

Prostate cancer (CaP) is the second leading cause of cancer related deaths amongst men in United States with an estimated 217,730 new cases in 2010. Upto 25% of all CaP patients undergo some form of radiation therapy (RT) (e.g. intensity-modulated radiation therapy (IMRT), proton beam therapy, brachytherapy) as treatment for clinically localized disease[1] Currently, differentiation between local or systemic recurrence of CaP (which have radically different prognoses and treatment regimens) is only appreciable on trans-rectal ultrasound, that too at a relatively advanced stage [1]. Early identification of non-responders via the use of imaging will allow for modification of the therapy [1], as well as provide clues about long-term patient outcome.

Recently, *in-vivo* multi-parametric (MP) Magnetic Resonance (MR) Imaging (MRI) (T2-weighted, MR Spectroscopy (MRS), and Diffusion-weighted (DWI)) has shown great potential in early identification of RT related changes in the prostate [2] (Figure 1). Pucar et al. [1] showed that MP-MRI significantly improves identification of CaP regions pre-, post-RT, compared to sextant biopsy and digital rectal examination. Similarly, in [3] an area under the receiver operating curve (AUC) of 0.79 was obtained via qualitative examination of MP-MRI (T2w, MRS) in accurately identifying new and recurrent disease post-RT. In another similar study [4], DWI when combined with T2-w MRI was shown to significantly outperform T2w MRI alone, for accurately predicting locally recurrent CaP post-RT. Successful treatment of CaP on T2w MRI, post RT, is characterized by uniform T2w signal intensity without focal abnormalities, while new or locally recurrent CaP is characterized by hypo-intense regions of smooth texture [5] (Figure 1(d)). MRS shows an absence of citrate, as well as low metabolic activity in cases of successful treatment (Figure 1(e), outlined in blue). New foci and locally recurrent CaP on post-RT MRS is characterized by elevated levels of choline [5] (Figure 1(e), outlined in red). Similarly, post-RT, DWI shows an overall increase in apparent diffusion coefficient (ADC) values within the entire prostate when CaP is successfully treated. Unchanged or decreased ADC values correspond to locally recurrent CaP [6] (Figure 1(f)).

Visual examination of post-RT MRI for evaluating treatment related changes and residual disease is usually associated with poor detection rates due to (a) diffuse T2w signal intensity and indistinct zonal anatomy on T2w MRI [7], (b) adverse effects of post-biopsy hemorrhage and hormonal therapy which in turn adversely affects identification of metabolic peaks [8], and (c) significant gland shrinkage and distortion post-RT [1]. Automated quantitative assessment of RT changes on a per voxel basis may thus allow accurate and precise identification of (a) residual disease, and (b) new foci of cancer (local recurrence) within the prostate. Additionally, since each of the individual MR imaging markers provide orthogonal information (structural, functional, metabolic), a MP-MRI approach that can leverage multiple imaging channels could significantly improve detection specificity and sensitivity.

While a number of sophisticated quantitative data integration strategies on pre-RT MP-MRI have been proposed [9,10,11], one of the limitations of these strategies [9,10,11] is that they naïvely concatenate/combine original feature representations to obtain the

---

[1] American Cancer Society.

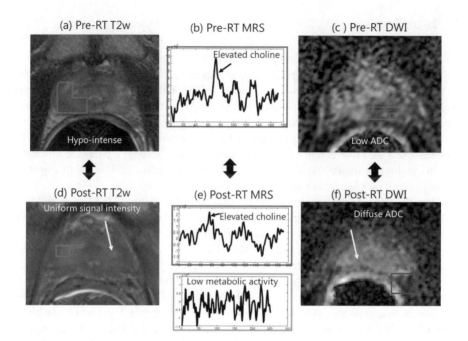

Fig. 1. (a), (b), (c) show the pre-treatment imaging markers for T2w MRI, MRS and DWI respectively, where (a) shows hypointense T2w MRI intensity regions (outlined in red) on a single T2w MRI slice, (b) shows a typical MRS CaP spectrum characterized with elevated choline peak, and (c) shows a DWI image with CaP outlined in red, defined by low ADC values. Figures 1(d), (e), and (f) show the T2w MRI, MRS and DWI scenes post-RT where, (d) shows the corresponding post RT T2w MRI slice with uniform signal intensities characterizing successful treatment, while hypo intense CaP region is outlined in red, reflecting local disease recurrence, Similarly in (e) the elevated choline peak appears to suggest local CaP recurrence within a single MR spectrum (outlined in red), along with a spectrum showing low metabolic activity (outlined in blue) reflecting disappearance of disease. (f) shows CaP recurrence defined by low ADC and successful treatment characterized by diffuse ADC values.

fused representation of MP-MRI data. A more intelligent approach to quantitatively fusing orthogonal (complimentary) channels of information, is to optimally weight the contributions of individual data streams for improved classification. Additionally, all of these quantitative data integration strategies involving MP-MRI have purely been focussed on pre-RT imaging alone. To the best of our knowledge, there does not exist any computerized detection methods in the context of MP-MRI that can quantify changes on pre-, post-RT for early determination of therapy effectiveness. A few major challenges associated with developing such an automated scheme for pre-, post-RT evaluation include, (a) developing elastic registration tools to deal with changes in shape and size of the prostate gland pre-, post-RT, (b) accurate alignment of various MP imaging protocols for computing voxel level absolute difference of the imaging markers (reflective of treatment changes), and (c) optimized weighted quantitative integration of imaging marker changes across MP-MRI.

In this paper we present a novel MP quantitative data integration scheme for evaluating pre-, post-RT related changes, that, (1) provides a common framework across pre-, post- patient studies via registration, segmentation and classification modules, to overcome the aforementioned challenges associated with pre-, post- data alignment, (2) accurately quantifies post-RT imaging marker changes ("hotspots") on a per-voxel level, on T2w MRI, MRS, and DWI, and (3) intelligently combines "changes in imaging markers" across individual MP-MRI modalities for accurately assessing pre-, post-RT changes ("hotspots"), identified as, (a) successful treatment (CaP on pre-RT, no CaP on post-RT), (b) new CaP foci (no CaP on pre-RT, CaP on post-RT) and (c) local recurrence (CaP on pre-RT, CaP on post-RT but in a different location relative to the site of treatment). These treatment changes are captured by differences in imaging markers across different imaging modalities (T2w, MRS, DWI), and are combined by optimally weighting contributions of each MP-MRI modality based on their ability to accurately capture post-RT changes.

The rest of the paper is organized as follows. In Section 2, a brief system overview and description of the datasets employed in this work is provided. In Section 3, we describe our registration and segmentation modules for pre-, post-RT data alignment. Detailed description on generating a weighted multi-parametric difference map is provided in Section 4. Results and discussion are presented in Section 5, followed by concluding remarks in Section 6.

2 System Overview and Data Description

2.1 System Overview

Figure 2 presents an overview of our scheme illustrating the registration, segmentation, quantification and integration modules. In Module 1, T2w MRI, MRS and DWI pre-, post-treatment are brought into alignment using a spatially constrained 3-D affine registration scheme [12], that accounts for changes in overall shape and size of the prostate pre-, and post-RT. Module 2 involves accurate delineation of the prostate region of interest (ROI) on pre-, post-RT using a robust statistical shape model [13] that is able to compensate for the loss of image resolution post-RT. In Module 3, a difference map is generated for each of the individual T2w MRI, MRS and DWI protocols by taking an absolute difference of the corresponding imaging markers pre-, post-RT MRI on a per-voxel basis. The difference maps thus obtained on each of these imaging markers are then intelligently weighted based on their respective ability in capturing treatment related changes to yield a weighted, combined MP-MRI imaging marker difference map (Module 4).

2.2 Notation

We denote a pre-treatment T2w prostate MRI scene as $\mathscr{C}_{t2}^{pre} = (C, f_{t2}^{pre})$, where $f_{t2}^{pre}(c)$ is the associated intensity at every voxel location c on a 3D grid C. MRS data corresponding to $\mathscr{C}_{t2}^{pre}$ is obtained at a much coarser resolution, such that multiple voxels are located within a single MRS voxel. To obtain a voxel based MRS representation,

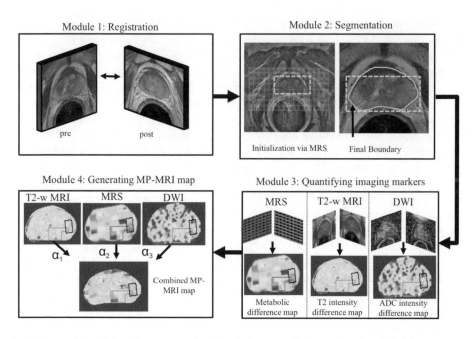

Fig. 2. Flowchart of the new strategy showing different modules, registration (Module 1), segmentation (Module 2), quantification of imaging markers (Module 3). The individual imaging marker difference maps are integrated via a weighted combination scheme to yield an integrated difference map, one that is more reflective of the disease specific changes, pre-, post, RT (Module 4).

we linearly interpolate acquired MRS information to a T2w MRI voxel resolution, thus yielding the corresponding spectral scene $\mathcal{C}_{mrs}^{pre} = (C, G^{pre})$, where $G^{pre}(c)$ is the associated MRS metabolic vector at every voxel $c \in C$ (representing the concentrations of different biochemicals, such as creatine, citrate, and choline). The DWI MRI scene is similarly defined as $\mathcal{C}_{adc}^{pre} = (C, f_{adc}^{pre})$, where $f_{adc}^{pre}(c)$ is the associated ADC intensity at every voxel location c on a 3D grid C (interpolated to a T2w MRI voxel resolution). Post-RT T2w MRI prostate image scene, $\widehat{\mathcal{C}}_{t2}^{post}$, is registered to $\mathcal{C}_{t2}^{pre}$ to yield the corresponding registered T2w MRI scene (post-RT) as $\mathcal{C}_{t2}^{post} = (C, f_{t2}^{post})$. MRS information (interpolated to T2w voxel resolution) is transformed to yield $\mathcal{C}_{mrs}^{post} = (C, G^{post})$. DWI image is similarly transformed to yield the corresponding registered DWI image as $\mathcal{C}_{adc}^{post} = (C, f_{adc}^{post})$.

2.3   Data Description

A total of 14 *in vivo* endorectal MP-MRI patient datasets were acquired at the University of California, San Francisco between 1998-2007. All patients underwent external beam radiotherapy after initial MRI (1.5 Tesla, GE Signa, endorectal coil), with supplementary, neo-adjuvant hormonal therapy. Post-RT, patients were reimaged via MRI (3 Tesla, GE Signa, endorectal coil). An expert spectroscopist labeled the spectral voxels as CaP and benign on the MRI/MRS pre- and post-RT studies, which was used as surrogate ground truth labels for CaP extent. Five out of the 14 studies included T2w, MRS, and ADC maps (from DWI), while the remaining 9 comprised MRS and T2w MRI alone. A total of 51 slices from the 14 patient studies (with T2w MRI and MRS information, acquired between 1998-2002) with CaP (pre-RT) constituted Dataset 1, and a total of 20 slices with CaP (pre-RT) from the 5 patients studies (with ADC, T2w and MRS information, acquired between 2002-2007) constituted Dataset 2. Based on the pre-, and post-RT CaP label information, regions of definite treatment change ("hotspots") were defined on each of the 51 images for Dataset 1, and 20 images for Dataset 2. These included regions of (1) successful treatment, (2) partially successful treatment, and (3) local recurrence (detailed in Table 1).

3 Registration and Segmentation of Multi-Parametric MR Imagery

3.1 Registration of Pre- and Post-treatment MR Imagery

Registration of $\mathscr{C}_{t2}^{pre}$ to $\widehat{\mathscr{C}}_{t2}^{post}$ is uniquely complicated by (1) changes in the overall shape and size of the prostate gland (which is known to shrink, post-RT [1]), (2) differing acquisition parameters, and (3) changes in imaging markers due to RT effects. We attempt to address these challenges by employing a mutual information (MI) based 3D registration scheme [12], comprising of following steps,

1. Post-RT MP-MRI data is first down-sampled to pre-RT image resolution. Bounding boxes containing the prostate on $\mathscr{C}_{t2}^{pre}$ and $\widehat{\mathscr{C}}_{t2}^{post}$ are then manually selected.
2. A spatially constrained MI similarity measure is used to drive the affine transformation of $\widehat{\mathscr{C}}_{t2}^{post}$ onto $\mathscr{C}_{t2}^{pre}$. Only those voxels of $\mathscr{C}_{t2}^{pre}$ and $\widehat{\mathscr{C}}_{t2}^{post}$ that fall within the bounding box (selected in Step 1) are considered in the calculation of MI (chosen for its robustness to non-linear intensity relationships [12]).
3. A 3D affine transformation with 12 degrees of freedom, encoding rotation, translation, shear, and scale, is implemented (as presented in [12]) to accurately align the prostate between $\mathscr{C}_{t2}^{pre}$ and $\widehat{\mathscr{C}}_{t2}^{post}$.

Alignment of T2w and ADC maps is done based on available voxel sizes and locations (automatically extracted from DICOM headers). In the case of post-RT ADC maps, the 3D transformation from Step 3 is applied to map all the data into the pre-treatment coordinate frame C (associated with $\mathscr{C}_{t2}^{pre}$). However, alignment of T2w MRI and MRS is done in 2D (since MRS, T2 are implicitly aligned pre-registration in 2D), by applying the transformation obtained in Step 3 along the X and Y-direction to obtain $\mathscr{C}_{mrs}^{post}$.

3.2 Automated Segmentation of Prostate Capsule on T2w MRI Data

This module utilizes a novel, fully automated Active Shape Model (ASM) scheme for delineation of the prostate capsule on *in vivo* T2w MR imagery [13]. This technique, developed by our group and presented in [13], leverages multi-protocol data as follows,

1. First, a texture-based support vector machine (SVM) classifier is constructed to be able to classify voxels within the prostate ROI.

2. A single midgland slice is selected from each test study. Corresponding MRS data is identified as either prostatic or extra-prostatic via a replicated k-means spectral clustering scheme [13]. This yields a bounding box of spectra from within the prostate.
3. The SVM classifier from Step 1 is used to identify prostatic voxels within the bounding box identified in Step 2, resulting in a boundary initialization.
4. The ASM transforms a known mean shape of the prostate (detailed in [13]) to the boundary initialization from Step 3, resulting in the gland capsule segmentation for this slice.
5. This segmentation is extended to the base and apex to yield a delineation of the prostate ROI (as described in [13]) on $\mathscr{C}_{t2}^{pre}$, $\mathscr{C}_{t2}^{post}$ as well as on the ADC map.

4   Weighted Combination of Imaging Marker Difference Maps for Identifying Treatment Related Changes Post-therapy

4.1   Feature Extraction for Individual T2, MRS and DWI Protocols

A difference map for each of the imaging markers, extracted from each of the individual MR protocols (T2, MRS, DWI) is computed for every scene $\mathscr{C}$, for every $c \in C$ as,

$$\Delta_i = |\mathscr{C}_i^{pre} - \mathscr{C}_i^{post}|, \tag{1}$$

where $i \in \{1, 2, ..., n\}$ is the imaging marker evaluated, $\mathscr{C}$ is the 3D image scene associated with each imaging marker i, and n is the total number of imaging markers.

A. Structural (T2w): All T2w MRI images, pre-, post- RT, were first corrected for bias-field and underwent intensity standardization [14]. A difference map (Δ_1) is then calculated by taking an absolute difference (L_1-norm) of T2w signal intensities across pre-, post- RT image scenes at every $c \in C$, using Equation 1.

B. Metabolic (MRS): Kurhanewicz et al [3] have suggested that ratios of area under the choline (A_{ch}), creatine (A_{cr}) and citrate peaks (A_{cit}) are highly indicative of the presence of CaP. However, only choline (A_{ch}) and creatine (A_{cr}) are considered post-RT, due to the known absence of citrate [5]. We calculated A_{ch} and A_{cr} using a composite trapezoidal rule within the pre-defined metabolic ranges on each spectrum, both pre-, and post-RT. A ratio of A_{ch}/A_{cr} was recorded and used to obtain a difference map (Δ_2) by taking a L_1 norm of A_{ch}/A_{cr} pre-, and post-RT as illustrated in Equation 1.

Table 1. Different RT outcomes with corresponding effects on CaP presence and extent

Treatment response	Residual CaP	New CaP occurrence	Number of studies
Successful treatment	N	N	5
Partially successful treatment	Y	N	3
Local recurrence	Y	Y	6
	N	Y	

C. Functional (ADC): DWI images were corrected for bias field and intensity standardized pre-, post-RT. Equation 1 is then employed to compute an ADC difference map (Δ_3) by taking an absolute difference of ADC signal intensities values across pre-, and registered post- RT on a per voxel basis.

4.2   Generating a Combined Multi-Parametric Weighted Map

Individual difference maps ($\Delta_1, \Delta_2, \Delta_3$) obtained from T2w, MRS and DWI, allow for quantification of the changes in imaging markers across each of the individual protocols. A MP-MRI weighted map can thus be obtained by leveraging each of the different marker difference maps as,

$$\mathscr{C}_{map} = \sum_{i=1}^{n} \alpha_i \times \Delta_i, \tag{2}$$

where $\alpha_i, i \in \{1,2,..,n\}$ reflects the contribution of each of the individual n imaging markers obtained via different MP-MRI protocols (T2w MRI, ADC, MRS) employed simultaneously to accurately quantify treatment-specific changes on MP-MRI.

Optimization of Weights. Weights are obtained via a rigorous optimization of imaging marker difference maps from a set of training images ($\tilde{D}$), and the learned weights are then assigned to the test image to obtain $\hat{D}$.

1. For each of the training images, $\tilde{D}_i$, a binary mask, $\tilde{D}_i^\theta$, is created by thresholding the intensity values between 0 and 1, such that $\tilde{D}_i^\theta = \tilde{D}_i \geq \theta$ for each $i, i \in \{1,...n\}$.
2. Sensitivity and specificity values at each threshold $\theta, \theta \in [0,1]$ are recorded and a receiver operating curve (ROC) is obtained for each $\tilde{D}_i$, for each $i, i \in \{1,...,n\}$. Binary map at the operating point of the ROC curve $\tilde{D}_i^\nu$ for each i is recorded, where ν is the operating point of the ROC curve.
3. $\tilde{D}_i^\nu$ is then used to create a MP-MRI map as, $\tilde{D}_{map} = \sum_{i=1}^{n} \alpha_i \times \tilde{D}_i^\nu$, where weights are such that $\sum_{i=1}^{n} \alpha_i = 1, \alpha_i \in [0,1]$.
4. Positive predictive value (Φ) is recorded for different values of α_i, $\alpha \in [0,1]$ based on the overlap of training MP-MRI image, $\tilde{D}_{map}$, with respect to expert delineated ground truth, D_{GT}. The values of α_i that maximize Φ in accurately identifying treatment changes are obtained as:

$$\{\tilde{\alpha}_1,...,\tilde{\alpha}_n\} = \arg\max_{\alpha_1,...,\alpha_n} (\Phi) \tag{3}$$

5. The maximum likelihood estimate (MLE) of $\tilde{\alpha}_i$ (mode of the distribution assuming each $\tilde{\alpha}_i$ is normally distributed) for each $i, i \in \{1,...,n\}$ across all training images, $\hat{\alpha}_i$, is then used to obtain the combined test image, $\hat{D} = \sum_{i=1}^{n} \hat{\alpha}_i \times \hat{D}_i$.

5   Results and Discussion

A leave-one-out cross validation strategy was used, where at each iteration, slices from a single patient study were held out from testing, while the remaining slices were used for training. The cross-validation process was repeated until all slices from all patient studies are evaluated. During each run of cross validation, test image, $\hat{D}$, is evaluated via ROC analysis for threshold $\theta, \theta \in [0, 1]$ based on overlap of thresholded binary image with respect to the expert delineated ground truth labels, D_{GT}, on a per-voxel basis.

5.1   Experiment 1: Quantifying Changes in Individual Imaging Markers Post-RT

Figure 3 shows scaled absolute difference images of T2w intensities (Figure 3(c), (i)), ADC values (Figure 3(d), (j)), ch/cr metabolites (Figure 3(e), (k)), and weighted MP-MRI maps (Figures 3(f), (l)) for single 2D slices from two different patient studies. The results were evaluated based on the overlap of ground truth labels ("hotspots") on a per-voxel basis. CaP on pre-RT is outlined in magenta, while the CaP on post-RT is outlined in black. Note that ADC (Figure 3(d), (j)) appears to identify more true positive regions (RT-changes) as compared to T2w MRI (Figure 3(c), (i)) and MRS (Figure 3(e), (k)). MRS (Figure 3(e), (k)) appears to pick fewer false positives associated with RT-related changes, as compared to ADC (Figure 3(d), (j)), and T2w MRI (Figure 3(c), (i)) across the two slices.

Table 3(a) shows the mean AUC and accuracy for Dataset 1 across 14 patient studies (with only T2w MRI and MRS data), while Table 3(b) shows the mean AUC and accuracy obtained for Dataset 2 (with DWI, T2w MRI and MRS) for 5 patient studies, obtained via a leave-one-out cross validation. It is worth noting that ADC difference maps outperformed T2w MRI and MRS difference maps, with an AUC of 70.2%, compared to 67.5% for MRS and 54.9% for T2w MRI, in accurately quantifying RT-related changes. The qualitative and quantitative results presented in this work corroborate with the findings in [6] which suggests that difference in ADC values might be an important imaging marker in evaluating pre-, post-RT changes.

Table 2. Summary of qualitative changes in MP-MR imaging parameters pre- and post-RT, and the corresponding quantitative features used in this work to characterize each of the marker differences for different protocols

	Pre-RT appearance	Post-RT appearance
T2w	low T2w signal intensity in peripheral zone	Hypo-intense regions, smooth texture No change in residual CaP regions
MRS	elevated levels of choline (A_{ch})/creatine (A_{cr}) reduced levels of citrate (A_{cit})	Nearly absent A_{cit}, polyamines in benign, CaP Residual CaP has elevated A_{ch}, A_{cr}
DWI	significantly low ADC compared to benign	Increased ADC compared to pre-RT Residual CaP lower ADC compared to benign areas

5.2   Experiment 2: Quantifying Changes via Weighted Combination of MP-MRI

The results presented in Figure 3 and Table 3 suggest that MP-MRI map outperformed each of the individual imaging marker differences $(\Delta_1, \Delta_2, \Delta_3)$ across both the datasets, in accurately quantifying treatment changes. The improved performance of combined

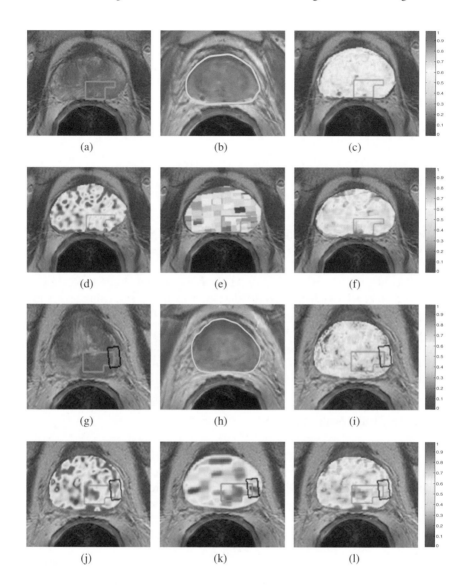

Fig. 3. (a), (g) show pre-RT T2w MRI image with the pre, post-RT CaP labels delineated in magenta (pre-RT CaP) and black (post-RT CaP) respectively. (b), (h) demonstrate the corresponding registered post-RT T2w MRI image with the segmented prostate region shown with the orange boundary. (c), (i) correspond to the scaled absolute T2w MRI image intensity difference heat maps. (d) and (j) show the corresponding difference heatmaps obtained by taking a difference of ADC values pre-, post- RT. Similarly, (e) and (k) show the heatmaps for metabolic marker A_{ch}/A_{cr}, and (f) and (l) show the corresponding weighted MP-MRI maps for two single slices from two different patient studies.

Table 3. Average AUC and accuracy obtained via leave-one-out cross validation for quantifying pre-, post-RT changes, obtained from T2w image intensity map, ch/cr map, ADC difference map and the weighted MP map for, (a) Dataset 1 (T2w MRI and MRS) over a total of 14 T2w MRI-MRS studies and, (b) Dataset 2 (T2w, MRS and DWI) over a total of 5 patient studies. Note that Dataset 2 which was acquired later compared to Dataset 1 used a more optimized set of MRI protocols, resulting in superior image quality.

Method	AUC	Accuracy
T2w intensity map	49.6 ± 9.0	51.7 ± 7.0
ch/cr map	55.9 ± 20.0	55.2 ± 11.3
MP-MRI map	**61.6 ± 7.5**	**63.0 ± 4.3**

(a)

Method	AUC	Accuracy
T2w intensity map	54.4 ± 8.3	54.9 ± 7.8
ch/cr map	68.6 ± 10.3	67.5 ± 9.0
ADC map	70.8 ± 7.0	70.2 ± 10.2
MP-MRI map	**73.2 ± 6.9**	**72.5 ± 8.0**

(b)

MP-MRI map clearly indicates the efficacy of optimal weighted combination of imaging markers in identifying treatment specific changes pre-, post RT. It is also interesting to note that a much higher AUC was obtained for Dataset 2 (AUC = 73.2%), as compared to Dataset 1 (AUC = 61.6%), when ADC was incorporated along with T2w MRI and MRS to create the weighted MP-MRI map. This is not surprising as a number of groups [2,4,15] have shown that that the inclusion of DWI in addition to the other MRI protocols, significantly improves CaP detection. Since Dataset 2 only comprised 5 patient studies, AUC values obtained via MP-MRI were not found to be statistically significantly different compared to AUC values obtained from DWI different maps using a paired student t-test.

6   Concluding Remarks

We presented a novel data integration strategy which optimally weights contributions from differences of individual imaging markers in accurately evaluating pre-, post-RT prostate cancer via MP-MRI. Different MRI protocols from pre- and post-RT MRI scans were first affinely registered, followed by automated segmentation of the prostate capsule using an active shape model. Functional, structural, and metabolic difference maps were then obtained individually using DWI, T2w, and MRS respectively, by taking a scaled absolute difference of the imaging markers pre-, post- RT. A combined weighted MP-MRI map is then created by leveraging differences across multiple imaging markers. Quantitative evaluation against expert delineated ground truth of treatment changes, yielded a high AUC and accuracy for the weighted MP-MRI map as compared to individual imaging markers. We believe that such an accurate per-voxel based quantitative evaluation of treatment changes pre-, post-RT will have a high clinical impact in monitoring treatment effectiveness, and could be used to modify treatment regimen early, in cases of studies with new foci or recurrence of CaP.

It is worth mentioning that differences in AUC across Dataset 1 and Dataset 2 were observed mainly because Dataset 2 was acquired later compared to Dataset 1, and used a more optimized set of MRI protocols, resulting in superior image quality. In future work, we intend to apply an elastic registration scheme to more accurately align pre-, post RT MP images and further extend this work for other treatment therapies such as proton-beam therapy and brachytheraphy. We also aim to incorporate additional MR protocols (such as dynamic contrast enhanced (DCE) MRI) to further improve efficacy of quantitative treatment evaluation using MP-MRI. The work presented here should set the stage for ultimately developing image based predictors for early treatment response and potentially long-term patient outcome. Additionally, the framework could be applied in the context of clinical trials for evaluating the comparative effectiveness of different prostate cancer treatment modalities.

References

1. Pucar, D., et al.: The role of imaging in the detection of prostate cancer local recurrence after radiation therapy and surgery. Curr. Opin. Urol. 18(1), 87–97 (2008)
2. Chen, M., et al.: Prostate cancer detection: Comparison of T2-w Imaging, DWI, proton MRSI, and the three techniques combined. Acta Radiologica 49(5), 602–610 (2008)
3. Kurhanewicz, J., et al.: Locally recurrent prostate cancer after EBRT: Diagnostic performance of 1.5T endorectal MRI and MRSI for detection. Radiology 256(2), 485–492 (2010)
4. Kim, C.K., et al.: Prediction of locally recurrent prostate cancer after radiation therapy: Incremental value of 3T diffusion-weighted MRI. JMRI 29(2), 391–397 (2009)
5. Coakley, F.V., et al.: Endorectal MRI and MRSI for locally recurrent prostate cancer after external beam radiation therapy: preliminary experience. Radiology 233(2), 441–448 (2004)
6. Song, I., et al.: Assessment of Response to Radiotherapy for Prostate Cancer: Value of Diffusion-Weighted MRI at 3T. Am. J. Roentgenol. 194(6), 477–482 (2010)
7. Westphalen, A., et al.: T2-Weighted endorectal MR imaging of prostate cancer after external beam radiation therapy. Int. Braz. J. Urol. 35(2), 171–180 (2009)
8. Zapotoczna, A., et al.: Current role and future perspectives of MRS in radiation oncology for prostate cancer. Neoplasia 9(6), 455–463 (2007)
9. Tiwari, P., et al.: Multimodal wavelet embedding representation for data combination: Integrating MRI and MRS for prostate cancer detection. NMR in Biomed (accepted 2011)
10. Langer, D., et al.: Prostate cancer detection with multi-parametric MRI: Logistic regression analysis of quantitative T2, DWI, and DCE MRI. JMRI 30(2), 327–334 (2009)
11. Ozer, S., et al.: Supervised and unsupervised methods for prostate cancer segmentation with multispectral mri. Med. Phy. 37, 1873–1883 (2010)
12. Chappelow, J., et al.: Elastic Registration of Multimodal Prostate MRI and Histology via Multi-Attribute Combined Mutual Information. Med. Phys. 38(4), 2005–2018 (2010)
13. Toth, R., et al.: A magnetic resonance spectroscopy driven initialization scheme for active shape model based prostate segmentation. Med. Img. Anal. 15, 214–225 (2010)
14. Madabhushi, A., Feldman, M., Metaxas, D., Tomaszewski, J., Chute, D.: Automated detection of prostatic adenocarcinoma from high resolution ex vivo mri. IEEE Transactions on Medical Imaging 24, 1611–1625 (2005)
15. Mazaheri, Y., et al.: Prostate cancer: Identification with combined diffusion-weighted MRI and 3d 1H MRSI correlation with pathologic findings. Radiology 246(2), 480–488 (2008)

Required Accuracy of MR-US Registration for Prostate Biopsies

Wendy J.M. van de Ven, Geert J.S. Litjens, Jelle O. Barentsz,
Thomas Hambrock, and Henkjan J. Huisman

Department of Radiology,
Radboud University Nijmegen Medical Centre,
Nijmegen, The Netherlands
W.vandeVen@rad.umcn.nl

Abstract. MR to TRUS guided biopsies can be a cost-effective solution for prostate biopsies. Prostate cancer can be detected on MRI and a biopsy can be directed towards a suspicious region. With the help of an accurate MR-US registration method the tumor can also be targeted under transrectal US guidance. For heterogeneous tumors, the needle should be guided towards the most aggressive part of the tumor. Not the tumor size, but the size of this smaller tumor hotspot determines the required accuracy of the registration. We investigate the percentage of tumors that are heterogeneous and the corresponding hotspot volume. Results show a hotspot in 63% of the tumors, with a median volume of 0.3 cm^3. By assuming a spherical shape, the required accuracy can be determined. For a 90% tumor hit-rate, the registration error should be less than 2.87 mm.

Keywords: MR-US registration, accuracy, hotspot, prostate biopsy.

1 Introduction

Prostate cancer is the second most common diagnosed malignancy in men in the western world, and one of the leading causes of death from cancer [7]. The current routine clinical standard method for making a definite diagnosis of prostate cancer is transrectal ultrasound (TRUS) guided biopsy. Prostate cancer is not visible on gray-scale ultrasound, thus TRUS is merely used to guide systematic biopsies. This systematic approach misses nearly a quarter of detectable cancers on the first biopsy [15]. Furthermore it underestimates the true Gleason score compared to radical prostatectomy specimens [12]. So the number of detected aggressive tumors is rather low with TRUS guided biopsy.

Magnetic resonance (MR) guided MR biopsy is a very promising technique for prostate biopsies. Firstly, multiparametric MR imaging (MRI) has proven to be an effective technique to detect prostate cancer. A combination of anatomical T2 weighted MRI, dynamic contrast enhanced MRI, and diffusion weighted MRI (DWI) improves the accuracy of prostate cancer localization over T2 weighted imaging alone [11,18]. Secondly, it has been shown that MR guided biopsy significantly increases the tumor detection rate as compared to TRUS systematic

A. Madabhushi et al. (Eds.): Prostate Cancer Imaging 2011, LNCS 6963, pp. 92–99, 2011.

biopsy [3]. Additionally, recent research has investigated the correlation between DWI and tumor aggressiveness. The apparent diffusion coefficient (ADC) determined at MRI has proven to be inversely correlated to the Gleason grade in peripheral zone prostate cancer [1,4,6]. It has moreover been shown that DWI guided biopsy determines Gleason grading in exact concordance with prostatectomy in 88% of the cases, which is substantially higher than TRUS systematic biopsy (55%) [2]. However, disadvantages of MR guided MR biopsy are that MRI is not widely available. It is also a relatively expensive method for taking prostate biopsies; the patient needs a detection MRI scan but then also a second MRI scan for guiding the biopsy.

An alternative is MR guided TRUS biopsy. MRI will still be used for the detection and localization of prostate cancer. These images can then enhance TRUS imaging and improve needle guidance, thereby taking advantages of both modalities. Accurate MR-TRUS registration is difficult and topic of current research. Recent works have investigated several MR to US registration methods, including rigid as well as nonrigid methods. Reported root mean square (RMS) target registration errors (TREs) lie within the range of $1.5 - 3.3$ mm [5,9,13,16]. However, these studies only look at the root mean square distance between TRUS-based and MRI-based segmentations of the prostate. Clinical studies using rigid fusion reported a significantly increased detection rate upon targeted prostate biopsy with MR-US fusion [8,14]. But there is to date no clinical study investigating the Gleason grading with MR guided TRUS biopsies. Accurate Gleason grading depends on accurate targeting of biopsies in the most aggressive tumor part.

In this paper, we investigate the required accuracy of the registration. To our knowledge, the current required accuracy is based on the widely used cutoff value of 0.5 cm^3 for clinically significant tumor volumes [5,9]. Some of the clinically significant tumors are heterogeneous, with only part of the volume containing highest Gleason grade tumor. For a correct grading, the biopsy needs to be targeted to the high-grade tumor volume part, thus requiring a higher registration accuracy. The required accuracy depends on the size of the most aggressive tumor part, the so-called tumor 'hotspot'. As aggressiveness showed an inverse relationship with ADC values, we define the darkest tumor region on the ADC map as tumor hotspot. We determine the hotspot sizes, as these are not yet known. We first investigate how many tumors are heterogeneous. Secondly, in case of a heterogeneous tumor, we determine the volume of the most aggressive part of the tumor. Using this hotspot volume, we estimate the required maximal registration error for taking a representative biopsy under MR to TRUS guidance.

2   Methods

2.1   Patient Data

For this study we used a dataset containing 51 consecutive patients with 62 different peripheral zone tumors, who where scheduled for radical prostatectomy between August 2006 and January 2009 [4]. Multiparametric MR imaging was performed at a 3.0-T MR system (Trio Tim; Siemens, Erlangen, Germany). Water diffusion was measured in three directions using b values of 0, 50, 500, and 800 s mm^{-2}. The ADC maps were automatically calculated by the imager software using all four b values.

After radical prostatectomy, prostate specimens were uniformly processed and entirely submitted for histologic investigation. Gleason grade and pathologic stage were determined for each individual tumor (see [4] for a summary of clinical characteristics). The entire tumor volume was outlined on each step-section. MR images were carefully aligned to these histopathologic step-sections. Regions of interest were then retrospectively annotated on the ADC map (Figs. 1a-e).

2.2   Automatic Hotspot Detection and Segmentation

The annotated ADC maps are used for an automatic detection of tumor hotspots. First, it is evaluated if the tumor is heterogeneous and thus contains a tumor hotspot. Second, the hotspot is automatically segmented and its volume can be determined.

The tumor hotspot is defined as the most aggressive part of the tumor, corresponding to the darkest region on the ADC map. We distinguished this region by an upper threshold of 1.07×10^{-3} mm^2 s^{-1}, which is based on Hambrock et al. [4]. This way, most of the high-grade tumors and half of the intermediate-grade tumors can be differentiated. To reduce image noise, a 3D Gaussian smoothing filter ($\sigma = 0.50$) is applied to the ADC map before analysis.

A tumor hotspot can be detected if the tumor contains a substantial amount of voxels both below and above the threshold of 1.07×10^{-3} mm^2 s^{-1}. We recorded a hotspot if its volume was between 5% and 95% of the total tumor volume. In this case the tumor is heterogeneous. Two types of homogeneous tumors can be distinguished: a tumor with almost all ADC values above the threshold (hotspot < 5%) and a tumor with most values below this threshold (hotspot > 95%).

When a hotspot is detected, a segmentation is needed before estimating its volume. The segmentation of the hotspot is done by means of a region growing, taking the minimum ADC value within the annotated region as seed point. In order to prevent leakage outside the tumor, the region growing is limited by the boundaries of the annotation (Fig. 1f).

2.3   Registration Accuracy

The required accuracy of MR-US registration methods depends on the smaller hotspot volume, not on the total tumor volume. Assuming that the tumor hotspot has a spherical shape, its volume can be used to determine its radius. Assuming negligible needle deflection, the tumor can be targeted when the TRE of the method is less than the radius.

By applying a procedure similar as described in Hu et al. [5], the clinical need for a TRE can be derived for a specified tumor hit-rate. Therefore, we furthermore assume that the targeting error is normally distributed and follows

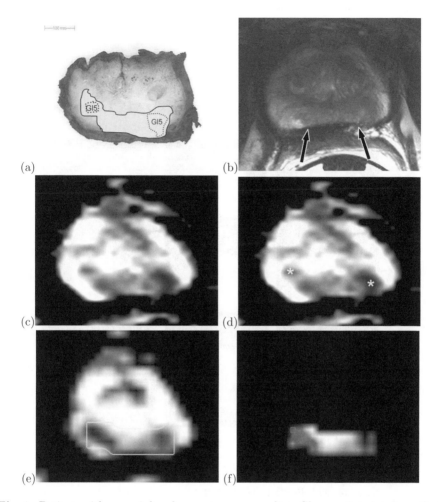

Fig. 1. Patient with a peripheral zone tumor revealing Gleason $3 + 4 + 5$ on final pathology. (a) Prostatectomy step-section with the tumor delineated in light blue. Regions with focal Gleason grade 5 on pathology are delineated with a dotted line. (b) Anatomical T2 weighted MR image. A large tumor region corresponding to the step-section is shown in the peripheral zone as indicated by the arrows. (c) On the ADC map, water restriction is clearly visible for the same lesion. (d) The Gleason 5 components are visible as dark regions (yellow asterisks). (e) Regions of interest annotated on the smoothed ADC map in correspondence with prostatectomy step-section (yellow delineation). (f) The segmentation of the hotspot finding based on ADC values (orange region). The red square indicates the seed point for the region growing.

a Maxwell-Boltzmann probability density function. The RMS TRE is then equal to $\sqrt{3}\sigma$. By determining the σ corresponding to the radius and the specified hit-rate, the threshold on the RMS TRE can be derived.

3   Results

Of the 62 peripheral zone tumors, 62.9% (39/62) were heterogeneous, 27.4% (17/62) had no hotspot at all, and 9.7% (6/62) were entirely dark on the ADC map. The numbers and volumes for each type are shown in Fig. 2. The heterogeneous tumors are somewhat larger than both homogeneous types, but not significantly different.

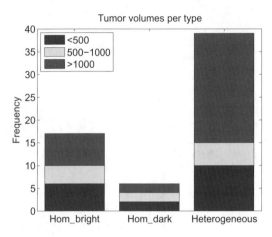

Fig. 2. Number of tumors for each type: homogeneous bright, homogeneous dark, and heterogeneous. Three volume ranges are indicated: $0 - 500$ mm^3, $500 - 1000$ mm^3, and > 1000 mm^3.

The heterogeneous tumors are important for determining the volume of the tumor hotspot. For these tumors, a boxplot for both the total tumor volume and the hotspot volume is shown in Fig. 3a. The distribution of the hotspot volumes is shown in a histogram in Fig. 3b. It can be seen that most of the hotspot volumes are below 500 mm^3, with a median of 297 mm^3.

For the estimation of the registration accuracy, we take the median tumor hotspot volume. The radius of a sphere with a volume of 297 mm^3 is 4.14 mm. For a tumor hit-rate of 90%, the threshold on the target registration error is 2.87 mm. Fig. 4a shows a graph of the TRE threshold as a function of the tumor hit-rate for the median hotspot volume. We also estimated the TRE threshold as a function of the hotspot volume for a fixed tumor hit-rate of 90% (Fig. 4b).

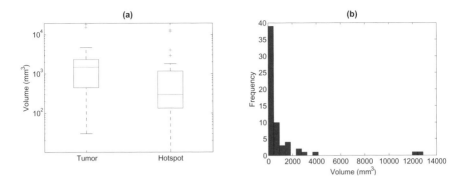

Fig. 3. (a) Boxplot showing the hotspot volumes in comparison with the total tumor volumes for heterogeneous tumors. (b) Distribution of the tumor hotspot volumes.

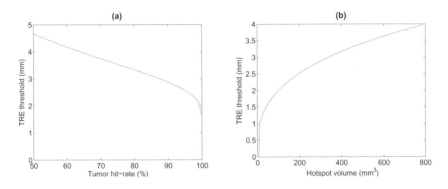

Fig. 4. (a) The TRE threshold as a function of the tumor hit-rate for the median tumor hotspot volume. (b) The TRE threshold as function of the hotspot volume for a 90% tumor hit-rate.

4   Discussion

We have shown that 62.9% of the peripheral zone tumors contain a hotspot. The median hotspot volume is 297 mm^3. To correctly assess the aggressiveness of the tumor, an accuracy of 2.87 mm is required (for the median volume and a 90% hit-rate).

However, there are some limitations to this study. First, the dataset is biased in that it only contains patients who are already scheduled for a prostatectomy. The tumors investigated are thus relatively large and aggressive. If data from a screening group would be taken, the mean tumor size will most likely decrease. The TRE threshold might then even be lower than 2.87 mm. Second, transition zone tumors were excluded. Transition zone tumors are known to have different ADC values than peripheral zone tumors [10,17]. Therefore, another threshold might be needed for the hotspot detection in this zone. Third, we took the median hotspot volume for estimating the required registration accuracy. By taking this value, we did not take into account the lower half of the tumor hotspots volumes. For smaller volumes, the TRE decreases as shown in Fig. 4b. So for increasing the hotspot detection rate for the smaller hotspots, the registration error should also be smaller. Furthermore, we only detected one hotspot per tumor. The example illustrated in Fig. 1 contains two hotspots of which only one was detected. This will increase the number of hotspots, but not the required accuracy.

Future work will focus on an accurate MR-US registration method (Toshiba Aplio XG ultrasound machine). The Gleason grading with MR guided TRUS biopsies and its correspondence with radical prostatectomy specimens can be investigated. It might also be interesting to explore the sizes of tumor hotspots on prostatectomy specimens and its correspondence with DWI.

References

1. de Souza, N.M., Riches, S.F., Vanas, N.J., Morgan, V.A., Ashley, S.A., Fisher, C., Payne, G.S., Parker, C.: Diffusion-weighted magnetic resonance imaging: a potential non-invasive marker of tumour aggressiveness in localized prostate cancer. Clin. Radiol. 63(7), 774–782 (2008)
2. Hambrock, H., Hoeks, C., Scheenen, T., Fütterer, J.J., Bouwense, S., van Oort, I., Schröder, F., Huisman, H.J., Barentsz, J.O.: Prospective assessment of prostate cancer aggressiveness using 3 Tesla diffusion weighted MR imaging guided biopsies versus a systematic 10-core transrectal ultrasound prostate biopsy cohort. Eur. Urol (submitted 2011)
3. Hambrock, T., Somford, D.M., Hoeks, C., Bouwense, S.A.W., Huisman, H., Yakar, D., van Oort, I.M., Witjes, J.A., Fütterer, J.J., Barentsz, J.O.: Magnetic resonance imaging guided prostate biopsy in men with repeat negative biopsies and increased prostate specific antigen. J. Urol. 183(2), 520–527 (2010)
4. Hambrock, T., Somford, D.M., Huisman, H.J., van Oort, I.M., Witjes, J.A., van de Kaa, C.A.H., Scheenen, T., Barentsz, J.O.: Relationship between apparent diffusion coefficients at 3.0-T MR imaging and Gleason grade in peripheral zone prostate cancer. Radiology 259(2), 453–461 (2011)
5. Hu, Y., Ahmed, H.U., Taylor, Z., Allen, C., Emberton, M., Hawkes, D., Barratt, D.: MR to ultrasound registration for image-guided prostate interventions. Med. Image Ana. (in Press 2011) (accepted Manuscript)
6. Itou, Y., Nakanishi, K., Narumi, Y., Nishizawa, Y., Tsukuma, H.: Clinical utility of apparent diffusion coefficient (ADC) values in patients with prostate cancer: can ADC values contribute to assess the aggressiveness of prostate cancer? J. Magn. Reson. Imaging 33(1), 167–172 (2011)
7. Jemal, A., Bray, F., Center, M.M., Ferlay, J., Ward, E., Forman, D.: Global cancer statistics. CA Cancer J. Clin. 61(2), 69–90 (2011)
8. Kadoury, S., Yan, P., Xu, S., Glossop, N., Choyke, P., Turkbey, B., Pinto, P., Wood, B.J., Kruecker, J.: Realtime TRUS/MRI fusion targeted-biopsy for prostate cancer: A clinical demonstration of increased positive biopsy rates. In: Madabhushi, A., Dowling, J., Yan, P., Fenster, A., Abolmaesumi, P., Hata, N. (eds.) MICCAI 2010. LNCS, vol. 6367, pp. 52–62. Springer, Heidelberg (2010)
9. Karnik, V.V., Fenster, A., Bax, J., Cool, D.W., Gardi, L., Gyacskov, I., Romagnoli, C., Ward, A.D.: Assessment of image registration accuracy in three-dimensional transrectal ultrasound guided prostate biopsy. Med. Phys. 37(2), 802–813 (2010)

10. Kim, J.H., Kim, J.K., Park, B.W., Kim, N., Cho, K.S.: Apparent diffusion coefficient: prostate cancer versus noncancerous tissue according to anatomical region. J. Magn. Reson. Imaging 28(5), 1173–1179 (2008)
11. Kitajima, K., Kaji, Y., Fukabori, Y.: Prostate cancer detection with 3 T MRI: comparison of diffusion-weighted imaging and dynamic contrast-enhanced MRI in combination with T2-weighted imaging. J. Magn. Reson. Imaging 31(3), 625–631 (2010)
12. Kvåle, R.: Concordance between Gleason scores of needle biopsies and radical prostatectomy specimens: a population-based study. BJU Int. 103(12), 1647–1654 (2009)
13. Martin, S., Baumann, M., Daanen, V., Troccaz, J.: MR prior based automatic segmentation of the prostate in TRUS images for MR/TRUS data fusion. In: Proceedings of the 2010 IEEE international conference on Biomedical imaging: From Nano to Macro, ISBI 2010, pp. 640–643. IEEE Press, Piscataway (2010)
14. Miyagawa, T., Ishikawa, S., Kimura, T., Suetomi, T., Tsutsumi, M., Irie, T., Kondoh, M., Mitake, T.: Real-time virtual sonography for navigation during targeted prostate biopsy using magnetic resonance imaging data. Int. J. Urol. 17(10), 855–860 (2010)
15. Roehl, K.A., Antenor, J.A.V., Catalona, W.J.: Serial biopsy results in prostate cancer screening study. J. Urol. 167(6), 2435–2439 (2002)
16. Singh, A.K., Kruecker, J., Xu, S., Glossop, N., Guion, P., Ullman, K., Choyke, P.L., Wood, B.J.: Initial clinical experience with real-time transrectal ultrasonography-magnetic resonance imaging fusion-guided prostate biopsy. BJU Int. 101(7), 841–845 (2008)
17. Tamada, T., Sone, T., Jo, Y., Toshimitsu, S., Yamashita, T., Yamamoto, A., Tanimoto, D., Ito, K.: Apparent diffusion coefficient values in peripheral and transition zones of the prostate: comparison between normal and malignant prostatic tissues and correlation with histologic grade. J. Magn. Reson. Imaging 28(3), 720–726 (2008)
18. Tanimoto, A., Nakashima, J., Kohno, H., Shinmoto, H., Kuribayashi, S.: Prostate cancer screening: the clinical value of diffusion-weighted imaging and dynamic MR imaging in combination with T2-weighted imaging. J. Magn. Reson. Imaging 25(1), 146–152 (2007)

A PET/CT Directed, 3D Ultrasound-Guided Biopsy System for Prostate Cancer

Baowei Fei [1,2,5,*], Viraj Master[3], Peter Nieh[3], Hamed Akbari[1], Xiaofeng Yang[1], Aaron Fenster[4], and David Schuster[1]

[1] Department of Radiology and Imaging Sciences
[2] Winship Cancer Institute
[3] Department of Urology, Emory University, Atlanta, GA 30329
[4] Imaging Research Laboratories, Robarts Research Institute, London, Ontario, Canada, N6A 5K8
[5] Department of Biomedical Engineering, Emory University and Georgia Institute of Technology, Atlanta, GA 30329
bfei@emory.edu

Abstract. Prostate cancer affects 1 in 6 men in the USA. Systematic transrectal ultrasound (TRUS)-guided biopsy is the standard method for a definitive diagnosis of prostate cancer. However, this *"blind"* biopsy approach can miss at least 20% of prostate cancers. In this study, we are developing a PET/CT directed, 3D ultrasound image-guided biopsy system for improved detection of prostate cancer. In order to plan biopsy in three dimensions, we developed an automatic segmentation method based wavelet transform for 3D TRUS images of the prostate. The segmentation was tested in five patients with a DICE overlap ratio of more than 91%. In order to incorporate PET/CT images into ultrasound-guided biopsy, we developed a nonrigid registration algorithm for TRUS and PET/CT images. The registration method has been tested in a prostate phantom with a target registration error (TRE) of less than 0.4 mm. The segmentation and registration methods are two key components of the multimodality molecular image-guided biopsy system.

Keywords: Molecular imaging, PET/CT, image segmentation, nonrigid image registration, wavelet transform, 3D ultrasound imaging, prostate cancer, image-guided biopsy.

1 Introduction

Systematic transrectal ultrasound (TRUS)-guided prostate biopsy is considered as the standard method for prostate cancer detection. The current biopsy technique has a significant sampling error and can miss at least 20% of cancers [1]. As a result, a patient may be informed of a negative biopsy result but may in fact be harboring an occult early-stage cancer. It is a difficult challenge for physicians to manage patients

---

* Corresponding author.

A. Madabhushi et al. (Eds.): Prostate Cancer Imaging 2011, LNCS 6963, pp. 100–108, 2011.

with false negative biopsies who, in fact, harbor curable prostate cancer as indicated by biochemical measurements such as rising prostate specific antigen (PSA), as well as patients diagnosed with early-stage disease.

Although ultrasound imaging is a preferred method for image-guided biopsy because it is performed in real time and because it is portable and cost effective, current ultrasound imaging technology has difficulty to differentiate carcinoma from benign prostate tissue. MR spectroscopic imaging (MRSI) is playing an increasing role in prostate cancer management [2-3]. Various PET imaging agents have been developed for prostate cancer detection and staging, these include ^{18}F-FDG [4], ^{11}C-choline [5], ^{18}F-fluorocholine [6], ^{11}C-acetate [7], ^{11}C-methionine [8], and other PET agents. ^{18}F-FDG is widely used in cancer applications. However, it has low sensitivity in the primary staging of prostate cancer and poor detection of abdominal-pelvic nodes because of excretion of tracers in the ureters, bladder, and bowel. PET imaging with new molecular imaging tracers such as FACBC has shown promising results for detecting and localizing prostate cancer in humans [9]. FACBC PET images show focal uptake at the tumor and thus could be ideal information to direct targeted biopsy. By combining PET/CT with 3D ultrasound images, multimodality image-guided targeted biopsy may be able to improve the detection of prostate cancer.

2   Multimodality Molecular Image-Guided Biopsy System

We focus on a PET/CT directed, 3D ultrasound-guided biopsy system (Fig. 1). The steps of targeted prostate biopsy are as follows. (1) Before undergoing prostate biopsy, the patient undergoes a PET/CT scan with FACBC as part of the examinations. The anatomic CT images will be combined with PET images for improved localization of the prostate and suspicious tumors. (2) During biopsy, 3D ultrasound images are acquired immediately before needle insertion. The 3D ultrasound images are registered with the PET/CT data for biopsy planning. Three-dimensional visualization tools guide the biopsy needle to a suspicious lesion. (3) At the end of each core biopsy, the needle tip position is recorded on the real-time ultrasound images. The location information of biopsy cores is saved and then restored in the re-biopsy procedure. This allows the physician to re-biopsy the same area for a follow-up examination. The location information of the biopsy cores can also be used to guide additional biopsy to different locations if the original biopsy was negative.

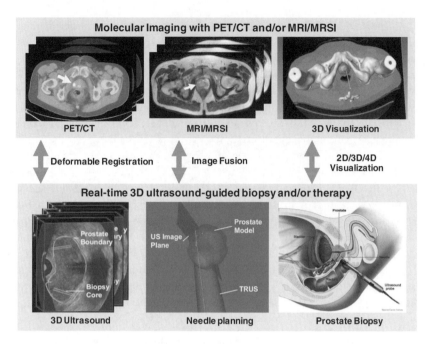

Fig. 1. Molecular image-directed, ultrasound-guided system for targeted biopsy. *Top:* The PET/CT and MRI/MRS were acquired from the same patient at our institution. PET/CT with FACBC shows a focal lesion within the prostate (white arrow). MR images also show the suspicious lesion in the gland. The 3D visualization of the pelvis and prostate can aid the insertion of the biopsy needle into a suspicious tumor target. *Bottom:* A mechanically assisted navigation device was developed to acquire 3D TRUS images from the patient. The prostate boundaries are segmented from each slice and are then used to generate a 3D model of the prostate. Real-time TRUS images are acquired and registered to the 3D model in order to guide the biopsy. To incorporate PET/CT into ultrasound-guided procedures, deformable registration, segmentation, fusion, and visualization are the key technologies.

3   Automatic Segmentation of 3D Prostate Ultrasound Images

Many methods for semi-automatic or automatic segmentation of the prostate in TRUS images have been proposed. Active shape models (ASM) was proposed to segment the prostate [10]. Knoll et al. proposed a deformable segmentation model that uses one-dimensional wavelet transform as a multi-scale contour parameterization tool to constrain the shape of the prostate model [11].

Our proposed method consists of the training and application stages. Two training TRUS images were used for wavelet features training and ten patients are used to make a predefined model. The prostate boundaries have been manually defined by specialists. A prostate shape model is created based on the allowable models of shape variations and its probability. This model is employed to modify the prostate boundaries. The prostate textures are locally captured by training the locally placed Wavelet-based support vector machines (W-SVMs). With integrating local texture features and geometrical data, W-SVMs can robustly differentiate the prostate tissue from the adjacent tissues. The trained W-SVMs are employed to tentatively label the respective voxels around the surface into prostate and non-prostate tissues based on their texture features from different Wavelet filters. Subsequently, after an affine transformation of the   shape model to the pre-defined prostate region that optimally matches with the texture features of the prostate boundary, the surface of the model is driven to the boundary between the tentatively labeled prostate and non-prostate tissues based on defined weighting functions and labeled voxels.

TRUS image textures can provide important features for accurately defining the prostate, especially for the regions where prostate boundaries are not clear. Biorthogonal wavelets 1.3, 1.5, and 4.4 are employed to extract the texture features of the prostate. Designing biorthogonal wavelets allows more degrees of freedom comparing to orthogonal wavelets. One additional degree of freedom is the possibility to construct symmetric wavelet functions. A number of W-SVMs on different regions of the surface model are placed and trained to adaptively label the tissue based on its texture and location. Each W-SVM is composed of 5 wavelet filter banks, voxel coordinates, and a Kernel Support Vector Machine (KSVM).

The wavelet filters are employed to extract texture features from TRUS images, and the KSVM is used to nonlinearly classify the Wavelet texture features for tissue differentiation. Each W-SVM corresponds to an individual sub-region in order to characterize and differentiate image textures locally and adaptively. All W-SVMs are trained to differentiate the texture features around its corresponding sub-regions in the training set. The trained W-SVMs are employed to tentatively label each voxel into prostate and non-prostate tissues in the application stage. To find more accurate segmentation, the set of W-SVMs is trained and applied in 3 planes (sagittal, coronal, transverse). Three sets of 2-D Wavelet filters were located at three orthogonal planes and were trained in each plane. Therefore, each voxel was tentatively labeled in three planes as prostate or non-prostate voxel. Fig. 2 shows the algorithm flowchart of the segmentation method.

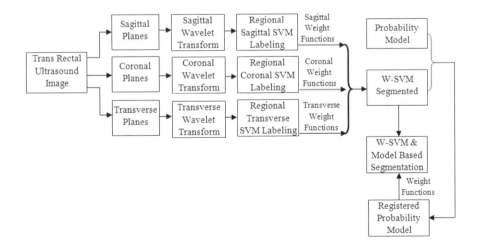

Fig. 2. The flowchart of the wavelet-based segmentation algorithm

A prostate probability model was used for modifying the segmentation. To build the prostate model, ten segmented prostates were registered using an affine transformation. Other registration methods can also be used to register the prostate of different patients [12-14]. In this study, we used the registration approach that is based on the principal axis transformation. This method was chosen because of its computational properties, speed and simplicity. The prostate volume was translated and rotated with respect to each other. The principal axis transformation is known from the classical theory of rigid bodies. A rigid body is uniquely located by knowledge of the position of its center of mass and its orientation (rotation) with respect to its center of mass. The center of mass, inertia matrix, and principal axes can be determined for any rigid body. For simple geometric shapes, the principal axes coincide with the axes of symmetry. In general, an orthogonal coordinate system is set up with their origin at the center of mass. When computed in the principal axis coordinate system, the inertia matrix is diagonal. The basic parameters that were used for registration of the prostate are the position of the center of mass and rotation of the prostate about the center of mass, and the lengths of the principle axes. These properties uniquely determine the location and geometry of the prostate in three-dimensional space. After overlaying these 10 registered volumes, a probability model was created for each voxel based on how many prostate models are labeled as a voxel of the prostate at that region.

4   Nonrigid Registration of TRUS and CT Images

Our non-rigid registration method includes three terms: (1) surface landmark matching, (2) internal landmark matching, (3) volume overlap matching. Let x_i^{CT} and y_j^{US} are surface landmarks of the prostate from the segmented CT and TRUS images, respectively, u_k^{CT} and v_l^{US} are internal landmarks e.g. urethra and calcification within the prostate on the CT and TRUS images, respectively. B_{CT} and B_{US} represent the bladder neck region on the CT and TRUS images, respectively.

Inspired by [16-18], we design an overall similarity function to integrate the similarities between same type of landmarks and add smoothness constraints on the estimated transformation between segmented CT and TRUS images. The transformation between CT and TRUS images are represented by a general function, which can be modeled by various function basis. In our study, we choose B-splines as the transformation basis. The similarity function is written as:

$$E(f) = \alpha E_{SS}(f\{x_i^{CT}, y_j^{US}\}) + \beta E_{IS}(f\{u_k^{CT}, v_l^{US}\}) + \gamma E_{VM}(f\{B_{CT}, B_{US}\}) + \lambda E_S(f)$$

Where

$$E_{SS}(f) = \sum_{i=1}^{I} \sum_{j=1}^{J} p_{ij} \left(\left\| y_j^{US} - f(x_i^{CT}) \right\|^2 \right) + \delta \sum_{i=1}^{I} \sum_{j=1}^{J} p_{ij} \log(p_{ij}) - \xi \sum_{i=1}^{I} \sum_{j=1}^{J} p_{ij}$$

$$E_{IS}(f) = \sum_{k=1}^{K} \sum_{l=1}^{L} q_{kl} \left\| v_l^{US} - f(u_k^{CT}) \right\|^2 + \tau \sum_{k=1}^{K} \sum_{l=1}^{L} q_{kl} \log(q_{kl}) - \eta \sum_{k=1}^{K} \sum_{l=1}^{L} q_{kl}$$

$$E_{VM}(f) = 1 - \frac{2*(f(B_{CT}) \cap B_{US})}{|f(B_{CT})| + |B_{US}|}$$

$$E_S(f) = \left\| \iiint_{(x,y,z) \in \Omega_M} \left(\frac{\partial^2 f}{\partial x^2} + \frac{\partial^2 f}{\partial y^2} + \frac{\partial^2 f}{\partial z^2} \right)^2 dxdydz \right\|^2$$

α, β, γ, and λ are the weights for each energy term. E_{SS} is the similarity for surface landmarks, and E_{IS} is the similarity for internal landmarks. E_{VM} is the energy term for the bladder-neck volume matching; and E_S is the smoothness constraint term. δ and τ are called the temperature parameter and its weighted term is an entropy term comes from the deterministic annealing technique [28]. ξ and η are the weight for the outlier rejection term. Matrixes p_{ij} and q_{kl} are the fuzzy correspondence matrixes [25]. f denotes the transformation between CT and TRUS images, which is B-spline transformation in our method.

The overall similarity function can be minimized by an alternating optimization algorithm that successively updates the correspondences matrixes p_{ij} and q_{kl}, and the transformation function f. First, with the fixed transformation f, the correspondence matrixes between landmarks are updated by minimizing $E(f)$. The updated correspondence matrixes are then treated as the temporary correspondences between landmarks. Second, with the fixed temporary correspondence matrixes p_{ij} and q_{kl}, the transformation function f is updated. The two steps are alternatively repeated until there are no updates of the correspondence matrixes.

5   Results

We developed a 3D ultrasound-guided biopsy system for the prostate. The system uses: (1) Passive mechanical components for guiding, tracking, and stabilizing the position of a commercially available, end-firing, transrectal ultrasound probe; (2) Software components for acquiring, storing, and reconstructing real- time, a series of 2D TRUS images into a 3D image; and (3) Software that displays a model of the 3D scene to guide a biopsy needle in three dimensions. The system allows real-time tracking and recording of the 3D position and orientation of the biopsy needle as a physician manipulates the ultrasound transducer.

The segmentation method was evaluated by five patient data sets of 3-D TRUS. Fig. 3 shows sample segmentation and its comparison with the corresponding gold standard. Quantitative performance assessment of the method was done by comparing the results with the corresponding gold standard data from manual segmentation. The Dice similarity and Sensitivity were used as performance assessment metrics in prostate classification algorithm. The numerical results of these evaluation criteria are shown in Table 1. The dice ratio is between 88.7%-95.0% among five prostate volumes. The mean and standard deviation of the dice function are 90.7% and 2.5%, respectively.

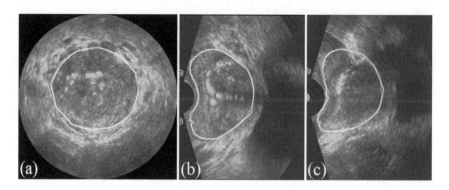

Fig. 3. 2-D segmentation results in different planes: red lines are the gold standard boundaries and green lines are the segmentation boundaries. (a) Coronal plane (b) Sagittal plane (c) Transverse plane.

Table 1. Quantitative evaluation results of the segmentation method

Patients	1	2	3	4	5	Mean	STD
DICE	90.2%	88.7%	88.9%	95.0%	90.8%	90.7%	2.5%
Sensitivity	91.2%	95.2%	82.3%	93.6%	91.1%	90.7%	4.9%

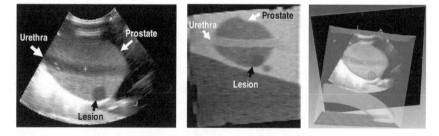

Fig. 4. An ultrasound image (*left*) is registered with an MR image (*middle*) of the same prostate phantom. The 3D visualization shows the relative location of the ultrasound plane within the 3D MR image (*right*) where green is the prostate and red is the lesion.

Fig. 4 shows the registration of ultrasound and MR images of a prostate phantom. The registration works well in the phantom experiment. We also evaluated the registration method using five sets of pre- and post-biopsy TRUS data of the same patients. The size of TRUS data is 244×244×175 voxels and the spatial resolution is 0.38×0.38×0.39 mm^3. We used pre-biopsy images as the reference images and registered the post-biopsy images of the same patient. For five sets of patient data, the target registration error (TRE) was 0.88 ± 0.16 mm and the maximum TRE is 1.08 ± 0.21 mm.

6   Discussion and Conclusion

We developed a PET/CT directed, 3D ultrasound-guided biopsy system for the prostate. In order to include other imaging modality such as PET/CT into 3D ultrasound-guided biopsy, we developed a 3D non-rigid registration method that combines point-based registration and volume overlap matching methods. The registration method was evaluated for TRUS and MR images. The registration method was also used to register 3D TRUS images acquired at different time points and thus can be used for potential use in TRUS-guided prostate re-biopsy. Our next step is to apply this registration method to CT and TRUS images and then incorporate PET/CT images into ultrasound image-guided targeted biopsy of the prostate in human patients.

In order to build a 3D model of the prostate, a set of Wavelet-based support vector machines and a shape model are developed and evaluated for automatic segmentation of the prostate TRUS images. Wavelet transform was employed for prostate texture extraction. A probability prostate model was incorporated into the approach to improve the robustness of the segmentation. With the model, even if the prostate has diverse appearance in different parts and weak boundary near bladder or rectum, the method is able to produce a relatively accurate segmentation in 3-D TRUS images.

Acknowledgement. This research is supported in part by NIH grant R01CA156775 (PI: Fei), Coulter Translational Research Grant (PI: Fei), Georgia Cancer Coalition Distinguished Clinicians and Scientists Award (PI: Fei), Emory Molecular and Translational Imaging Center (NIH P50CA128301), SPORE in Head and Neck Cancer (NIH P50CA128613), and Atlanta Clinical and Translational Science Institute (ACTSI) that is supported by the PHS Grant UL1 RR025008 from the Clinical and Translational Science Award program.

References

1. Roehl, K.A., Antenor, J.A., Catalona, W.J.: Serial biopsy results in prostate cancer screening study. J. Urol. 167(6), 2435–2439 (2002)
2. Jambor, I., Borra, R., Kemppainen, J., Lepomäki, V., Parkkola, R., Dean, K., Alanen, K., Arponen, E., Nurmi, M., Aronen, H.J., Minn, H.: Functional imaging of localized prostate cancer aggressiveness using 11C-acetate PET/CT and 1H-MR spectroscopy. J. Nucl. Med. 51(11), 1676–1683 (2010)
3. Carlani, M., Mancino, S., Bonanno, E., Finazzi Agrò, E., Simonetti, G.: Combined morphological, [1H]-MR spectroscopic and contrast-enhanced imaging of human prostate cancer with a 3-Tesla scanner: preliminary experience. Radiol Med. 113(5), 670–688 (2008)

4. Schöder, H., Herrmann, K., Gönen, M., Hricak, H., Eberhard, S., Scardino, P., Scher, H.I., Larson, S.M.: 2-[18F]fluoro-2-deoxyglucose positron emission tomography for the detection of disease in patients with prostate-specific antigen relapse after radical prostatectomy. Clin. Cancer Res. 11(13), 4761–4769 (2005)
5. Schilling, D., Schlemmer, H.P., Wagner, P.H., Böttcher, P., Merseburger, A.S., Aschoff, P., Bares, R., Pfannenberg, C., Ganswindt, U., Corvin, S., Stenzl, A.: Histological verification of 11C-choline-positron emission/computed tomography-positive lymph nodes in patients with biochemical failure after treatment for localized prostate cancer. BJU Int. 102(4), 446–451 (2008)
6. DeGrado, T.R., Coleman, R.E., Wang, S., Baldwin, S.W., Orr, M.D., Robertson, C.N., Polascik, T.J., Price, D.: Synthesis and evaluation of 18F-labeled choline as an oncologic tracer for positron emission tomography: initial findings in prostate cancer. Cancer Res. 61(1), 110–117 (2001)
7. Oyama, N., Akino, H., Kanamaru, H., Suzuki, Y., Muramoto, S., Yonekura, Y., Sadato, N., Yamamoto, K., Okada, K.: 11C-acetate PET imaging of prostate cancer. J. Nucl. Med. 43(2), 181–186 (2002)
8. Nuñez, R., Macapinlac, H.A., Yeung, H.W., Akhurst, T., Cai, S., Osman, I., Gonen, M., Riedel, E., Scher, H.I., Larson, S.: Combined 18F-FDG and 11C-methionine PET scans in patients with newly progressive metastatic prostate cancer. J. Nucl. Med. 43(1), 46–55 (2002)
9. Schuster, D.M., Votaw, J.R., Nieh, P.T., Yu, W., Nye, J.A., Master, V., Bowman, F.D., Issa, M.M., Goodman, M.: Initial experience with the radiotracer anti-1-amino-3-18F-fluorocyclobutane-1-carboxylic acid with PET/CT in prostate carcinoma. J. Nucl. Med. 48(1), 56–63 (2007)
10. Hodge, A.C., Fenster, A., Downey, D.B., Ladak, H.M.: Prostate boundary segmentation from ultrasound images using 2D active shape models: Optimisation and extension to 3D. Computer Methods and Programs in Biomedicine 84, 99–113 (2006)
11. Knoll, C., Alcaniz, M., Grau, V., Monserrat, C., Juan, M.C.: Outlining of the prostate using snakes with shape restrictions based on the wavelet transform. Pattern Recognit. 32, 1767–1781 (1999)
12. Fei, B., Duerk, J.L., Sodee, D.B., Wilson, D.L.: Semiautomatic nonrigid registration for the prostate and pelvic MR volumes. Academic Radiology 12, 815–824 (2005)
13. Fei, B., Lee, Z., Duerk, J.L., Lewin, J.S., Sodee, D.B., Wilson, D.L.: Registration and Fusion of SPECT, High Resolution MRI, and interventional MRI for Thermal Ablation of the Prostate Cancer. IEEE Transactions on Nuclear Science 51(1), 177–183 (2004)
14. Yang, X., Akbari, H., Halig, L., Fei, B.: 3D non-rigid registration using surface and local salient features for transrectal ultrasound image-guided prostate biopsy. In: Proc. SPIE 7964 (2011)
15. Alpert, N.M., Bradshaw, J.F., Kennedy, D., Correia, J.A.: The principal axes transformation a method for image registration. The Journal of Nuclear Medicine 31(10), 1717–1722 (1990)
16. Chui, H., Rangarajan, A.: A new point matching algorithm for non-rigid registration. Computer Vision and Image Understanding 89(2-3), 114–141 (2002)
17. Zhan, Y., Ou, Y., Feldman, M., Tomaszeweski, J., Davatzikos, C., Shen, D.: Registering histologic and MR images of prostate for image-based cancer detection. Acad. Radiol. 14, 1367–1381 (2007)
18. Yang, J., Blum, R.S., Williams, J.P., Sun, Y., Xu, C.: Non-rigid Image Registration Using Geometric Features and Local Salient Region Features. In: CVPR, pp. 1825–1832 (2006)

Improving Prostate Biopsy Protocol with a Computer Aided Detection Tool Based on Semi-supervised Learning

Francesca Galluzzo[2], Nicola Testoni[1], Luca De Marchi[1], Nicolò Speciale[1,2], and Guido Masetti[1,2]

[1] DEIS – Department of Electronics, Computer Sciences and Systems, Università di Bologna, v.le Risorgimento 2, I-40136 Bologna
[2] ARCES – Advanced Research Center on Electronic Systems, Università di Bologna, via Toffano 2, I-40125 Bologna
fgalluzzo@arces.unibo.it

Abstract. Prostate cancer is one of the most frequently diagnosed neoplasy and its presence can only be confirmed by biopsy. Due to the high number of false positives, Computer Aided Detection (CAD) systems can be used to reduce the number of cores requested for an accurate diagnosis. This work proposes a CAD procedure for cancer detection in Ultrasound images based on a learning scheme which exploits a novel semi-supervised learning (SSL) algorithm for reducing data collection effort and avoiding collected data wasting. The ground truth database comprises the RF-signals acquired during biopsies and the corresponding tissue samples histopathological outcome. A comparison to a state-of-art CAD scheme based on supervised learning demonstrates the effectiveness of the proposed SSL procedure at enhancing CAD performance. Experiments on ground truth images from biopsy findings show that the proposed CAD scheme is effective at improving the efficiency of the biopsy protocol.

Keywords: Computer Aided Detection (CAD), Tissue Characterization (TC), Semi-Supervised Learning (SSL), Prostate Cancer (PCa), Ultrasound Images.

1 Introduction

Prostate cancer (PCa) is a form of adenocarcinoma which affects the semen-secreting prostate gland cells. The current clinical procedure used to detect PCa is based on four diagnostic tools: Prostate Specific Antigen (PSA) evaluation, Prostate CAncer gene 3 (PCA3) test, Digital Rectal Examination (DRE), and Trans-Rectal Ultrasound (TRUS) image analysis. Results are combined in decision making for performing or repeating a prostate biopsy (PBx), as PBx is the only diagnostic tool able to confirm the presence of PCa. In fact, PCa patterns high variability limits TRUS diagnostic ability. As a consequence, PBx is not always lesion-directed but rather based on a systematic sampling of those areas where cancer incidence is higher. During PBx, up to 24 tissue samples or *cores*

A. Madabhushi et al. (Eds.): Prostate Cancer Imaging 2011, LNCS 6963, pp. 109–120, 2011.

are extracted [1][2]. A pathologist then checks for cancer cells. In this scenario, Computer Aided Detection (CAD) systems can be used to improve standard PBx protocol efficiency by providing physicians a second opinion.

The realization of an automatic CAD tool in ultrasound (US) imaging is hampered by the absence of an accurate mathematical model for the US signal traveling in prostate tissue which leads to the necessity of a large and consistent TRUS images database. Such a database, made up of the RF-signals acquired during biopsies along with the corresponding tissue histopathological outcomes, is available [3]. However, due to some ground truth uncertainty due to the unknown distribution of the pathology in each core, not all collected samples could be labeled *a priori* and employed to train the CAD system with standard Supervised Learning (SL) techniques [4]. Exploiting Semi-Supervised Learning (SSL) techniques [5] instead of the commonly used SL is an effective way to overcome these problems. In fact, being SSL methods capable to deal with unlabeled data, it is possible to train a CAD system using both labeled and unlabeled data. This reduces diagnosed samples collection effort and avoids collected data wasting.

This work presents a PCa CAD tool working on TRUS images based on a ground truth database detailed in Sec. 2, and a novel supervised/semi-supervised learning scheme. At its core there is the innovative SSL algorithm, SelfCo3Core, detailed in Sec. 3. The proposed tool is aimed at improving the current biopsy protocol by providing physicians a binary risk map highlighting suspect tissue areas, allowing them to perform a target-biopsy. In this way unnecessary samplings can be avoided without negative impinging on diagnosis accuracy.

A comparison between the proposed CAD and a state-of-art detection tool based on SL demonstrates the effectiveness of the SSL at enhancing CAD performance without requiring any additional labeled data and making use of the whole ground truth dataset. Experiments show that the proposed CAD is effective at improving the efficiency of the biopsy protocol by increasing the Positive Predicted Value (PPV) i.e. the probability of sampling a pathological core given a pathological patient. Both these evaluations are discussed in Sec. 4.

2   Signal Acquisition and Processing

2.1   System Overview

The proposed CAD tool combines information extracted from the RF echo signal and machine learning techniques to classify tissue, providing its characterization. The CAD processing flow consists of four main steps:

- Segmentation: RF signal is segmented into regular region of interest (ROI);
- Extraction: features highlighting data membership to a specific class are extracted from each ROI;
- Classification: selected ROI are classified as suspicious or not-suspicious basing on the extracted features;
- Rendering: classification result is rendered as a false color binary risk map overlapped to the original image.

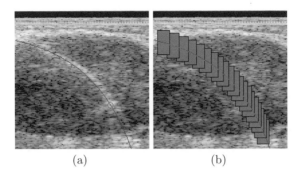

(a)   (b)

Fig. 1. Needle segmentation procedure: a) penetration track identification and b) automatically generated ROI

In this study two kinds of features were derived from the RF signal to characterize different tissue aspects. Shape and scale parameters of the Nakagami distributions estimated on the RF signal [6] give information about scatterer density, regularity and amplitude, whereas Unser Textural Features [7] represent the macroscopic appearance of scattering generated by tissue microstructure. To reduce the burden of feature's extraction while maintaining an high significance of the chosen features set, an hybrid feature selection algorithm was applied [8]. Classification is performed by means a non linear classifier based on the *kernel trick* principle [9] and selected by the SSL algorithm.

2.2   Ground Truth Database

The TRUS video-sequences database was collected in cooperation with the Department of Urology of S. Orsola Hospital in Bologna [3]. Up to now, it consists of 1323 video sequences belonging to 129 patient (79 healthy, 50 unhealthy).

To set up a consistent ground truth, biopsies were performed by the same operator and all acquisition parameters were kept fixed. Clinical parameters such age, PSA level, prostate volume and presence of focal lesion at TRUS were collected for each patient. During biopsy, the RF echo signal was recorded before, during and after each core extraction. Signal is acquired by a TECHNOS (Esaote s.p.a.) ultrasonographer equipped with a trans-rectal probe EC123 employed with US maximum frequency of 7.5MHz and combined with an hardware platform for US signal acquisition [10]. The echo signal was directly accessed just after A/D conversion and recorded to disk. After histopathological examination, each core length, sample position, presence of neoplastic lesion, histological classification, and lesion relative volume and Gleason score were also collected.

Acquired data were then processed providing that pathological information is confined within the bioptic core. To reliably associate RF signal to histology, only the image portion corresponding to the needle was used, as shown in Fig. 1. Needle track is manually detected within the core extraction frame, exploiting

Table 1. Ground Truth Database

Code	Description	#Cores	#ROI	Labels
M	PCa Percentage≥ 70%	39	780	Malign
UM	PCa Percentage <70%	128	2560	Unlabeled
U	Precancerous Lesions	123	2460	Unlabeled
BB	Benign Prostate Tissue from Benign Glands	557	11140	Benign
BM	Benign Prostate Tissue from Malign Glands	234	4680	Benign
BB*	Other Tissue from Benign Glands	180	3600	Benign
BM*	Other Tissue from Malign Glands	62	1240	Benign
Tot	129 patient (79 healthy, 50 unhealthy)	1323	26460	

its high reflectivity and almost fixed location. Segmentation proceeds automatically on each of the three frames preceding needle insertion once the maximum penetration depth is identified. Each core is further divided into 20 ROI.

Table 1 shows the structure of the resulting database. A univocal code identifying the pathological status is attributed to each core after histopathological evaluation. ROI labeling reckon that tumor distribution within each core is unknown, therefore only ROI belonging to malign cores with pathology covering more than 70% of the sample were labeled as suspicious. ROI belonging to the remaining malign cores were considered unlabeled as they cannot be accurately labeled *a priori* due to PCa imprecise localization. Also cores diagnosed with precancerous lesions were considered unlabeled as they are clearly neither benign nor equal to PCa. Finally, all ROI belonging to benign cores were labeled as not suspicious. ROI, along with their labels, constitute the ground truth. As shown by numbers reported in Tab. 1, large part of the collected data would be wasted, unless a learning procedure able to deal with unlabeled data is chosen.

3   The Learning Procedure

The proposed learning procedure is designed to achieve good prediction performance by reducing ground truth data collection costs and avoiding collected data wasting. To achieve this, a mixed SL/SSL approach was chosen. The learning procedure core is SelfCo3Core, a novel SSL algorithm combining two popular SSL techniques: Self-Training and Co-Training [5]. According to Co-Training style, it uses more than one classifier, but it can also be assimilated to Self-Training as the same soft-labeled data are used to refine all involved classifiers.

Three different classifiers are trained separately on labeled data complete feature set. Previous studies reported that features of different nature hardly are linearly correlated and that a nonlinear classification model can be able to extract valuable information from a mixed feature set and to reach higher accuracy levels [15]. On the other hand, complex classifier models fail in preserving features physical significance and their true dependence from the pathology.

In our approach, non linear classification models were obtained using the *kernel trick* technique. We employed a Fisher Linear Discriminant combined with a quadratic data mapping (QFLD)[4] since this classifier does not require any kernel parameter tuning. Also, we choose a Support Vector Machine (SVM)[4] and a

Kernel Fisher Discriminant (KFD)[11], both based on Gaussian kernels, because they are widely used, general purpose methods, usually effective in classification tasks akin to the discussed one. Still, any other classification algorithm could be used, as SelfCo3Core is a wrapper method. Since diversity among classifiers is guaranteed by using different classification algorithms, co-training necessity of two different features sets, is avoided.

Following training, classifiers label unlabeled data. Unanimous agreement on labeling is required to add data, along their predicted labels (soft-labeled data), to the training set. Class balancing is also considered for training set updating to avoid biasing. Classifiers are then re-trained and procedure is repeated.

Performance can be further improved using tumor core volume as an information about a group of unlabeled data to strengthen the algorithm. By comparing classifiers predictions with histology, only data whose estimated core volume is in good agreement with the real one are used for training set enlargement.

Classifiers strong enough to give a good prediction, together with unanimous agreement on labeling, avoid the necessity of an explicit measurement of labeling confidence, which is a drawback of both Self-Training and Co-Training, as it usually depends on the selected classification approach and it is often time consuming. In fact, it could be reasonably assumed that, if classifiers are different enough, the probability of all of them to predict a wrong label for a given unlabeled data is lower than the one achievable with majority voting. Additionally, the comparison between tumor core volume estimation and its real value reduces the probability of ground truth uncertainty to negative imping on labeling accuracy. All these constraints, along with class balance preservation, concur to obtain a stronger classification model at each algorithm iteration.

3.1   SelfCo3Core

Let L and U_s be some labeled and unlabeled set respectively, each drawn independently from the same data set D: while L contains ROI from M and BB cores (see Tab. 1), U_s is made up of ROI from UM and U cores. Let L_v be a labeled validation set drawn from D in such a way that cores from a given patient will belong either to L or to L_v. Let U_{tot} be a data set made up of all available unlabeled ROI and the corresponding tumor core volume. Let C_1, C_2 and C_3 be three suitably selected classification models.

On these bases, the SelfCo3Core repeats a sequence of operations until U_s is empty or there are no data for which classifiers unanimously agree on labeling. At the start of each iteration C_1, C_2 and C_3 are trained on L, and are let label U_s: three predictions are obtained for each u_i belonging to U_s. All the three classifiers are also tested over L_v and Validation Error (VE) is computed for each of them. Finally, they are used to classify U_{tot} computing an estimated tumor volume for each core. Collected information are used as follows:

– The best classifier is chosen as the one corresponding to the minimum VE;
– Soft-labeled data are selected as a subset of U_s basing on classifiers unanimous agreement on the predicted labels;

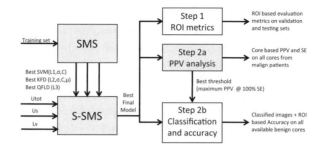

Fig. 2. Training and validation flows: training steps are represented by gray boxes while validations by white ones

- The selected subset is eventually shrunk according to tumor core volume estimation results: only data belonging to cores whose estimated core volume is within ±20% of the real one are considered;
- The selected subset is eventually shrunk according to class balancing;
- Selected soft-labeled data are added to L.

At the end of each iteration, classifiers are refined by the same copy of the soft-labeled data. At the end of all iterations, the so enlarged training set and the best classifier are returned as components of the final classification model.

Our learning procedure extends SelfCo3Core reckoning that classifier parameters can be conveniently tuned according to practical environment and that the initial labeled training set can be different for each classifier. If accurate parameters tuning and training set selection are performed, SelfCo3Core initial classifiers will be stronger and SSL performance will increase. As a consequence, we divided the learning procedure in two parts as shown in Fig. 2: a Supervised Model Selection (SMS) concerning the selection of the best model for each classifier kind involved into SSL, and a Semi-Supervised Model Selection (S-SMS) which uses SelfCo3Core to select the best final classification model.

3.2   Supervised Model Selection

SMS consists in the choice of the best training set for each involved classifier, the variance σ of the Gaussian kernel for both SVM and KFD, the best regularization constant C for SVM and for the 1D-SVM used for the KFD bias selection, and the best regularization constant μ for KFD. This selection is performed by means cross-validation: for several values of σ, C, and μ, a number of tests over different, randomly selected, training and validation sets are performed. Sizes of thees sets differs for each classifier as they are chosen according to the number of features and model parameter following [12]. The resulting ROI-based VE, Sensitivity (SE), Specificity (SP), Accuracy (ACC), and PPV averaged over different tests are analyzed for each model in order to select the best parameters and training sets as those corresponding to minimum mean VE. The choice of VE as

ROI-based criterion is arbitrary. The output of SMS is constituted by the training set $[X_{trn}, Y_{trn}]$ and the required parameters for each classifier.

3.3   Semi-supervised Model Selection

During S-SMS, the classification models chosen during SMS are employed into a SSL procedure based on SelfCo3Core, slightly modified to be combined with the previously described step. By using different training sets, selected by SMS, SSL starts with the best models according to SL. The labeled set for SelfCo3Core is therefore replaced by three sets L_1, L_2, L_3. Then, for a fixed number of times, unlabeled ROI are mixed and a portion of them is used as the unlabeled data set for SelfCo3core. Being SSL procedure performance dependent on both the number of ROI and their cores membership, this operation is repeated for different label rates, i.e. the number of labeled data w.r.t. the total amount of training data. SelfCo3Core is applied $N_{tests} \times N_p$ times, where N_{tests} is the number of different unlabeled data mix and N_p is the number of label rates considered. At the end, the $N_{tests} \times N_p$ values of the previously mentioned ROI-based performance statistics computed over L_v are used to select the best classification model, made up by an algorithm whose parameters where chosen during SMS, and a new, enlarged, training set. The model is chosen by a two step selection procedure: first a model for each label rate is selected, then a specific label rate is fixed. Both these steps are based on VE minimization.

4   Experimental Results

To evaluate the proposed CAD tool performance, two steps were taken as shown in Fig. 2. The first assesses learning efficiency by comparing the obtained classification models in terms of classification error over specific validation and testing sets. The second verifies the effectiveness of the whole detection tool in a clinical environment through the comparison to standard PBx protocol.

4.1   Step 1

To evaluate CAD performance, a comparison to a state-of-art classification system we previously developed [8] was performed. The reference system is a supervised trained non linear classifier combining feature extraction based on Generalized Discriminant Analysis (GDA)[13] with Gaussian kernel and a linear FLD[4]. For fair comparison SMS was extended to train also this classifier.

The dataset for this study is made up of 292 cores from the collected database. It contains ROI from BB cores (162 cores, 3240 ROI), ROI from M cores (23 cores, 460 ROI), and ROI from U and UM cores (107 cores, 2140 ROI). The total amount of labeled data was divided into three parts: a training set (512 ROI) and a validation set (124 ROI) used respectively into the SMS and S-SMS, and a testing set (280 ROI) used to evaluate the generalization ability of the obtained classification models. Class balancing was preserved within all these sets.

Table 2. Classification Errors of Compared Algorithms and Relative Improvments

Label Rate	GDA+FLD	SL	SSL	SSL vs SL	SSL vs GDA	Class. Alg.
15%	.328	.328	.320	2.38%	2.38%	KFD
20%	.328	.320	.312	2.44%	4.76%	SVM
24%	.328	.336	.320	4.65%	2.38%	QFLD
29%	.328	.328	.305	7.14%	7.14%	KFD
38%	.328	.320	.281	12.2%	14.3%	SVM
53%	**.328**	**.320**	**.258**	**19.5%**	**21.4%**	**SVM**
73%	.328	.320	.297	7.31%	9.52%	SVM
91%	.328	.320	.312	2.44%	4.76%	SVM

During SMS, 200 random data set of labeled ROI are generated and split into training and validation set. A Cross Validation (CV) over 30 values of σ equally distributed between 0.1 and 6, 3 values of C $(10, 100, 1000)$, and 2 values of μ $(10^{-3}, 10^{-4})$ was performed on each. Then, during S-SMS, SSL is performed for 10 different original unlabeled set and 8 different label rates ranging from 15% to 91%. Label rates were obtained by keeping different amount of unlabeled data while maintaining a fixed amount of labeled data. The validation set used to select the final model is the same used within SelfCo3Core internal runs.

Table 2 reports the outcomes of these selection steps. VE of the GDA+FLD classifier, of the final model generated by SelfCo3Core, and of its supervised trained counterpart are shown for each label rate as well as their relative improvements. Values obtained for the label rate selected by the S-SMS have been boldfaced. The final column reports the classification algorithm chosen by S-SMS. Results show that the final model generated by SSL outperforms its SL counterpart, confirming that SelfCo3Core is effective at enhancing learning performance w.r.t. a standard SL algorithm. This is highly pleasing as improvements are due only to the introduction of unlabeled ROI, unusable without a SSL approach. SelfCo3Core is hence effective at providing a performance enhancement without requiring any additional labeled data. The final model generated by SSL outperforms GDA+FLD too, confirming its efficacy for the target application: an improvement in excess of 20% is obtained at the selected label rate of 53%.

To evaluate obtained classification models in terms of generalization ability, their performance over a completely unknown test set were evaluated in terms of classification error. On this testing set the classification error of GDA+FLD is equal to 43.2%, while the ones of the final model generated by the SSL procedure and its supervised-trained counterpart are respectively equal to 40.0%, and 39.2%. The final model generated by our learning procedure outperforms both its supervised trained counterpart and the state-of-art classification model also operating on an unknown testing set, showing relative improvements respectively equal to 2% and 9.25%. It can thus be stated that SSL is also effective at enhancing prediction performance maintaining a good generalization ability.

4.2 Step 2

The standard PBx protocol efficiency can be conveniently expressed in terms of PPV. Known the gland to be pathological, PPV represents the probability of

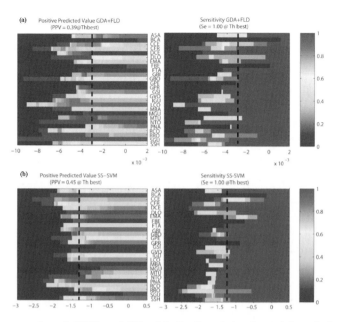

Fig. 3. The core based PPV and SE of both the state-of-art (a) and the proposed detection tool (b) for a selection of patients from the training dataset

a single core to be PCa positive according to the detection tool. This figure is low due to the high number of false positives, i.e. cores which were not useful for confirming the presence of PCa. To improve it, reducing the number of cores while maintaining the same detection rate over patients is mandatory.

To verify the effectiveness of the proposed method at achieving this goal, a so called *PPV Analysis* is performed: the classification model generated by the procedure described in Step 1 is tested over a set of 26 malign patients (247 cores) to evaluate PPV improvement w.r.t. randomized biopsy cores. This analysis can also be considered a further learning step, as CV is performed on classification model threshold to select the one maximizing the median PPV over the whole dataset under a 100% median sensitivity constraint over patients. CV is performed by varying the threshold value between the minimum and the maximum of the discriminant function: this allows to choose between models spanning from 100% ROI-based SP to 100% ROI-based SE. For each threshold value, the classification model is applied to the 247 cores and some core-based statistics are computed for each patients. A core is considered unhealthy if at least one of its ROI is classified as malign. The final threshold value is selected as the ones providing the largest median PPV over all pathological patients constrained to SE maximization. The proposed method was compared to the state of art CAD tool in order to evaluate the performance improvement.

Fig. 3 depicts the core based PPV and SE for two different classification models: GDA+FLD trained by using only SMS on Fig. 3a and SVM trained with the complete SMS/S-SMS learning procedure on Fig. 3b. Each horizontal bar represents a patient from the database, identified by a three letter code: the color in each bar indicates how the respective statistic changes as a function of the threshold over the given patient. The vertical dashed line is the best threshold Th_{best} selected by the system to discriminate between suspicious or not-suspicious ROI. At Th_{best} semi-supervised trained SVM (SS-SVM) provides a median PPV of 45%, while supervised trained GDA+FLD scores 39%, both with a median SE of 100%. As a comparison, on the same dataset, the standard PBx protocol features a PPV of 29%. The proposed method improves PPV of 55% without losing diagnostic power. Moreover, let p_0 be the standard PBx protocol PPV: the probability of correctly diagnosing PCa with N_0 cores is expressed by $[1 - (1 - p_0)N_0]$. Now, let $p_1 > p_0$ be the detection tool PPV: the number of cores can be reduced according to $N_1 = N_0[\log(1 - p_0)/\log(1 - p_1)]$. Our detection tool allows to reduce the number of cores from 12 to 6.

Using this threshold selection, the CAD tool is tuned for reducing false positives by avoiding false negatives. To confirm this statement, both the classification systems were tested on all available benign cores (260 cores), and ROI-based accuracy was measured for the same threshold value considered in the PPV analysis. At Th_{best}, GDA+FLD shows an accuracy of 91.3%, while SS-SVM resulted into 94.4%, in accord with theory.

A further step toward the verification of the effectiveness of the proposed detection tool as for PBx guide was taken by letting the CAD classify a video sequence of images and comparing classification results to the ground truth. The same evaluation was carried out on the reference tool: results were compared to assess performance enhancement. Examples of classified images and their corresponding B-mode with superimposed needle trace are shown for an unhealthy patient (Fig. 4a and 4b) and for an healthy one (Fig. 4c and 4d). The frames corresponding to PBx sampling (top) and the previous one with the overlapped binary risk map (bottom) elaborated by the reference CAD are shown on the left side; results of the proposed tool are on the right side. Patient were diagnosed as healty or unhealty as a result of histological analysis.

For the unhealthy patient, the considered tissue sample histology indicates a tumor volume equal to 90%, while tumor volume estimated considering the image portion marked by the CAD is equal to 70% for the new detection tool and to 84% for the state of art ones. For the healthy patient, the state of art classification system assigned to a benign core a tumor volume equal to 35%, while the proposed classification system does not highlight any presence of PCa in the tissue sample. Hence an unnecessary bioptic sampling would have been avoided for the healthy patient, while the presence of PCa would have been correctly diagnosed for the unhealthy one with an acceptable accuracy. These results confirm the effectiveness of the proposed classification framework at enhancing performance of both the state-of-art PBx protocol and CAD.

To be used for biopsy guide, the CAD tool must be able to preserve the real-time nature of the echographic examination. Exploiting the application intrinsic parallelism, both features extraction and classification steps can be implemented making full use of CUDA parallel processing capabilities [14]. That being so,

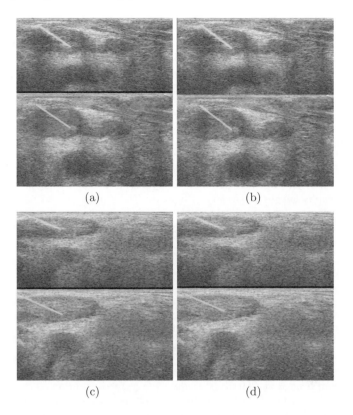

(a)   (b)

(c)   (d)

Fig. 4. Example of ground truth and classified images for both the state-of-art (left) and the proposed CAD tool (right): a-b) unhealthy patient, c-d) healthy patient

considering a 2792×250 image segmented into 10×100 pixels ROI, our detection tool is capable of delivering a frame rate as high as 30 fps, confirming its effectiveness for PBx guidance.

5   Conclusion

In this work a computer aided detection tool for prostate cancer detection in TRUS images was proposed. It is based on a TRUS video-sequences database realized in cooperation with physicians and a mixed supervised/semi-supervised learning procedure. The database was realized ensuring the exact correspondence between the RF-signal and the tissue sampled by biopsy in order to guarantee ground truth reliability. The core of the learning procedure is SelfCo3Core, a SSL algorithm which combines Self-Training and Co-Training and makes use of unanimous labeling agreement, class balancing, and tumor core volume knowledge to improve prediction performance. A comparison with a state-of-art detection tool based on SL demonstrate the effectiveness of SSL at enhancing prediction performance with an improvement on classification error greater than 20% on a validation set and equal to 9.25% on an unknown testing set. The proposed CAD is able to improve the PPV of the standard double sextant biopsy protocol of 55%. Consequently, the number of biopsy cores could be reduced from 12 to 6 without losing diagnostic power. Exploiting parallel computing the CAD is able to deliver a frame rate of 30 fps which confirms its effectiveness as real time biopsy guide.

References

1. De La Rosette, J., Giensen, R., Huynen, A., Aornink, R., Van Iersel, M.P., Debruyne, F., Wijkstra, H.: Automated Analysis and interpretation of transrectal ultrasonography images in patients with prostatitis. Europ. Urol. 27(1), 47–53 (1995)
2. Raja, J., Ramachandran, N., Munneke, G., Patel, U.: Current status of transrectal ultrasound-guided prostate biopsy in the diagnosis of prostate cancer. Clin. Rad. 61, 142–153 (2006)
3. Testoni, N., Speciale, N., Bertaccini, A., Marchiori, D., Fiorentino, M., Manferrari, M., Schiavina, R., Cividini, R., Galluzzo, F., Maggio, S., Biagi, E., Masotti, L., Masetti, G., Martorana, G.: A retrospective study to reduce prostate biopsy cores by a real time interactive tool. Arch. Ita. Urol. Androl. 82(4), 238–241 (2010), ISSN: 1124-356217
4. Theodoridis, S., Koutroumbas, K.: Pattern Recognition, 4th edn. Academic Press, London (2009), ISBN: 978-1-59749-272-0
5. Zhu, X., Goldberg, A.B.: Introduction to Semi-Supervised Learning. Synthesis Lectures on Artificial Intelligence and Machine Learning. Morgan & Claypool Publishers, San Francisco (2009)
6. Shankar, P.: A general statistical model for ultrasonic backscattering from tissues. IEEE Trans. Ultrason. Ferroelectr. Freq. Control 47(3), 727–736 (2000)
7. Unser, M.: Sum and difference Histograms for texture classification. IEEE Trans. Patt. Rec. Mach. Intell. 8, 118–125 (1986)
8. Maggio, S., Palladini, A., De Marchi, L., Alessandrini, M., Speciale, N., Masetti, G.: Predictive Deconvolution and hybrid Feature selection for computer aided detection of Prostate Cancer. IEEE Trans. Med. Imag. 29(2), 445–464 (2010)
9. Aizerman, M., Braverman, E., Rozonoer, L.: Theoretical foundations of the potential function method in pattern recognition learning. Automat. Rem. Contr. 25, 821–837 (1964)
10. Scabia, M., Biagi, E., Masotti, L.: Hardware and Software Platform for real-time processing and visualizationof echographic radiofrequency signals. IEEE Trans. Ultrason. Ferroelectr. Freq. Control 49(10), 1444–1452 (2002)
11. Mika, S., Ratsch, G., Weston, J., Scholkopf, B., Mullers, K.R.: Fisher discriminant analysis with kernels. In: Proc. of the 1999 Neural Net. Sig. Proc. (1999)
12. Guyon, I.: A scaling law for the validation-set training-set size ratio. AT&T Bell Laboratories, Berkeley (1997)
13. Baudat, G., Anouar, F.: Generalized discriminant analysis using a kernel approach. Neural Comput. 12, 2385–2404 (2000)
14. NVIDIA CUDA Compute Unified Device Architecture Programming Guide, NVIDIA Corporation (2007)
15. Moradi, M., Mousavi, P., Abolmaesumi, P.: Computer-aided diagnosis of prostate cancer with emphasis on ultrasound-based approaches: a review. Ultrasound in Medicine and Biology 33(7), 1010–1028 (2007)

Fusion of MRI to 3D TRUS for Mechanically-Assisted Targeted Prostate Biopsy: System Design and Initial Clinical Experience

Derek W. Cool[1,2,*], Jeff Bax[1], Cesare Romagnoli[2], Aaron D. Ward[3],
Lori Gardi[1], Vaishali Karnik[1], Jonathan Izawa[4],
Joseph Chin[4], and Aaron Fenster[1,2]

[1] Imaging Laboratories, Robarts Research Institute
[2] Department of Medical Imaging
[3] Lawson Health Research Institute
[4] Department of Surgery, Division of Urology
University of Western Ontario, London, ON, Canada

Abstract. This paper presents a mechanically-assisted 3D transrectal ultrasound (TRUS) biopsy system with MRI–3D TRUS fusion. The 3D TRUS system employs a 4 degree-of-freedom linkage for real-time TRUS probe tracking. MRI–TRUS fusion is achieved using a surface-based non-linear registration incorporating thin-plate splines to provide real-time overlays of suspicious MRI lesions on 3D TRUS for intrabiopsy targeted needle guidance. Clinical use of the system is demonstrated on a prospective cohort study of 25 patients with clinical findings concerning for prostate adenocarcinoma (PCa). The MRI–3D TRUS registration accuracy is quantified and compared with alternative algorithms for optimal performance. Results of the clinical study demonstrated a significantly higher rate of positive biopsy cores and a higher Gleason score cancer grading for targeted biopsies using the MRI–3D TRUS fusion as compared to the standard 12-core sextant biopsy distribution. Lesion targeted biopsy cores that were positive for PCa contained a significantly higher percentage of tumor within each biopsy sample compared to the sextant cores and in some patients resulted in identifying higher risk disease.

Keywords: Prostate, Biopsy, 3D TRUS, MRI, Registration.

1   Introduction

Prostate adenocarcinoma (PCa) is the most common non-cutaneous malignancy in American men with over 200,000 new cases diagnosed each year [1]. Screening tests such as the digital rectal examination (DRE) and the prostate specific antigen (PSA) blood test are sensitive for PCa; however, a definitive diagnosis

* This work has been supported by the Canadian Institute for Health Research (CIHR), Ontario Institute for Cancer Research (OICR), Prostate Cancer Research Foundation of Canada (PCRFC).

A. Madabhushi et al. (Eds.): Prostate Cancer Imaging 2011, LNCS 6963, pp. 121–133, 2011.

requires histopathological confirmation from a biopsy sample. Biopsies are currently performed clinically using 2D transrectal ultrasound (TRUS) for needle guidance. Unfortunately, ultrasound lacks the sensitivity to adequately visualize early-stage PCa. As a result, biopsies are placed systematically in a 6- to 12-core sextant distribution [9] within the prostate rather than targeted toward suspicious lesions. The false-negative rates for systematic sextant biopsies range up to 30% [19], which requires many to undergo multiple biopsy procedures before cancer is detected.

Contrary to TRUS, magnetic resonance imaging (MRI) has demonstrated a high sensitivity for detection of early stage PCa [23]. Substantial research has focused on the development of technologies to perform prostate biopsies within the bore of an MRI [11,15,5,2]. These systems exploit the increased visibility of PCa on MRI for targeting the biopsy needle toward suspicious lesions; however, the high costs of using MRI for needle interventions is prohibitive for most centers. Lattouf et al. investigated the use of 2D TRUS to indirectly target biopsy needles toward regions of the prostate containing suspicious lesions on MRI [17]. Unfortunately, results of their study showed no significant improvement over the standard sextant procedure. The restriction of TRUS to 2D spatial information and the lack of MRI–TRUS registration were suggested as potential causes for poorer than expected MRI-directed prostate biopsy clinical results [17].

Multiple 3D TRUS systems have been developed and investigated to improve the spatial information and to allow for the registration with MRI [8,4,22,18,3,21]. A hand-held 3D TRUS using a magnetic tracker to monitor 2D TRUS probe movement was developed by the research group from the national institute of health (NIH) and was used in MRI-3D TRUS biopsy patient study [22,12]. The MRI-3D TRUS biopsy study was performed under general anesthesia and involved 101 patients with either abnormal findings on MRI or a prior known history of PCa. Results demonstrated that targeted biopsies had higher positive biopsy core rates compared to sextant distribution biopsies for needles targeted toward highly suspicious lesions on MRI [12].

We previously developed a mechanically-assisted 3D TRUS system [4] that is capable of 3D prostate TRUS volume acquisitions in < 10 s and provides real-time 3D needle guidance and biopsy core 3D spatial recording. We have enhanced the 3D prostate biopsy system to allow for intra-biopsy fusion of pre-biopsy MRI for targeted biopsy of suspicious prostate lesions using 3D TRUS needle guidance. This article reports the initial clinical results of a prospective MRI-3D TRUS fusion biopsy study on a cohort of 25 patients biopsied without general anesthesia or conscious sedation. The complete 3D system is described, including biopsy workflow, intra- and inter-modality registration algorithms, and enhancements to the mechanical design not previously published. Finally, the accuracy of MRI–TRUS linear and nonlinear registrations are compared.

2   Biopsy System Design

2.1   Mechanical 3D TRUS System Design

The design and forward kinematics of our mechanical tracking system was described previously[4] and is summarized here with the system enhancements. The mechanical linkage consists of a passive 4 degree-of-freedom (DOF) tracking device, adaptable cradle and hydraulic support (Fig. 1). The adaptable cradle design fits most standard end-fire 2D TRUS probes. The tracking arms and transducer cradle are secured by the hydraulic support mechanism, which stabilizes the 4 DOF tracker linkage throughout the biopsy procedure. A mechanical spring-loaded counterbalancing system was developed since [4] to provide pose stabilization of the 4 DOF tracker linkage (Fig. 1). The counterbalancing system maintains the orientation of the TRUS probe and attached biopsy gun without manual support from the physician.

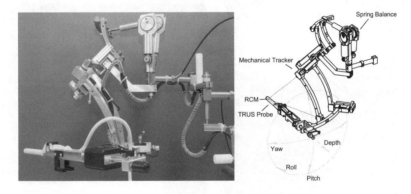

Fig. 1. A photograph (left) and a schematic diagram (right) of the 3D TRUS mechanical system are displayed. The spring balance mechanism, mechanical tracker linkage and RCM are identified on the on the schematic diagram.

   The tracking device is a spherical linkage assembly where the axis of each pinned connection converges to a common point to produce a remote center of motion (RCM). Two additional linkage arms were added to our previous design [4] (for a new total of 4) to allow for remote stabilization via the spring counterbalance system (Fig. 1). The mechanical linkages of the tracking device constrain the TRUS probe to two degrees of rotation (pitch and yaw) about the RCM to which the probe tip is aligned. The RCM is intended to minimize prostate motion during scanning and manipulation of the probe while allowing needle guidance to all prostate tissue. The probe is connected to the linkage by a sleeve, allowing the TRUS probe to freely pivot and slide about its long axis. The additional two DOF provided by the sleeve allows for probe insertion and longitudinal 180° probe rotation to generate a 3D volume (Fig. 2). 3D TRUS image generation requires a total of 8-10 seconds for acquisition and reconstruction.

The forward kinematics of the tracker linkage are defined in a spherical coordinate system:

$$\hat{\mathbf{r}} = \begin{bmatrix} x \\ y \\ z \end{bmatrix} = \begin{bmatrix} \cos\theta\sin\phi \\ \sin\theta\sin\phi \\ \cos\phi \end{bmatrix}, \tag{1}$$

where $\hat{\mathbf{r}}$ is the vector that defines the 3D orientation of the TRUS probe centered at the RCM. The angles, ϕ and θ represent the angles that TRUS probe makes with the z-axis and within the x-y plane, respectively. The orientation of the TRUS probe is calculated based on the rotational information of two encoders mounted at the pivots in the spherical linkage. Two additional encoders mounted onto the wrist joint (at the insertion of the cradle) measure the angle and insertion depth of the TRUS probe. The equations of motion for the tracker linkages are unchanged from [4], despite the addition of two linkage arms.

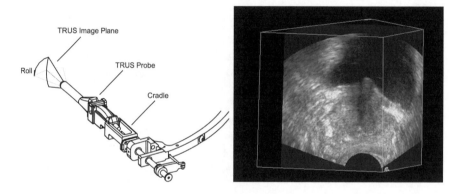

Fig. 2. Illustration of 3D TRUS image acquisition through rotation along the long axis of the TRUS probe (left). An example of a 3D TRUS prostate image volume from a biopsy patient (right).

2.2 MRI–TRUS Biopsy Workflow

MRI–3D TRUS prostate biopsy involves the fusion of a pre-biopsy MRI and identified lesions with intrabiopsy TRUS to provide targeted biopsy needle guidance. MRI/TRUS fusion is achieved through a chain of transformations from MRI to real-time TRUS, allowing for TRUS biopsy needle guidance toward suspicious lesions on MRI. The transformation pipeline is the following:

$$T_{US \to MRI} = T_{Pre-3DUS \to MRI} \cdot T_{3DUS \to 3DUS} \cdot T_{US \to 3DUS}, \tag{2}$$

where $T_{3DUS \to MRI}$ and $T_{3DUS \to 3DUS}$ represent the transformations from MRI to pre-biopsy 3D TRUS and pre-biopsy 3D TRUS to intrabiopsy 3D TRUS, respectively. $T_{US \to 3DUS}$ is the real-time TRUS probe position and orientation based on the mechanical tracking system (Sect. 2.1), which should be inherently coregistered with the intrabiopsy 3D TRUS volume assuming there is no prostate motion or deformation.

A pre-biopsy MRI is acquired for patients with abnormal PSA or DRE findings and any suspicious prostate lesions are identified and demarcated. MRI–TRUS registration, $T_{3DUS \to MRI}$, is performed in advance of the biopsy procedure using a pre-biopsy 3D TRUS image that is acquired on the same day as MRI scanning (Sect. 2.3). Pre-procedure TRUS imaging permits adequate time to ensure proper multimodal alignment without prolonging the patient's biopsy procedure or level of discomfort. Adequate time is important for MRI–TRUS prostate registrations, which typically involve a surface- or model-based registration algorithm that is inherently sensitive to the accuracy of the gland segmentation.

For the biopsy procedure, the pre-biopsy 3D TRUS volume—and coregistered MRI information—is registered with an intrabiopsy 3D TRUS scan that is acquired following initial sonographic assessment and prior to biopsy sampling. The TRUS–TRUS registration algorithm, $T_{3DUS \to 3DUS}$, outlined in [13] and summarized in Section 2.4, is a fully automatic, image-based block-matching metric that executes within 60s.

Replacement of the pre-biopsy 3D TRUS acquisition with intrabiopsy MRI–TRUS registration is possible; however, this would limit the opportunity to confirm proper MRI–TRUS registration and may negatively impact tracking correspondence as the time required for MRI–TRUS registration increases. The automatic image-based TRUS–TRUS registration allows for the intrabiopsy 3D TRUS scan to occur following ultrasound survey and immediately prior to the delivery of the targeted biopsies, thereby minimizing the likelihood of patient motion breaking real-time 2D TRUS to 3D TRUS correspondence inherent in $T_{US \to 3DUS}$.

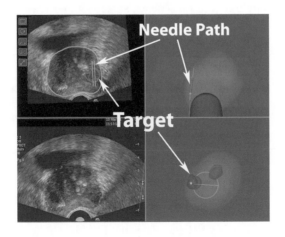

Fig. 3. The 3D TRUS User interface system

Following MRI–TRUS fusion, biopsy targeting is performed using the real-time needle guidance interface (Fig. 3). Surface models of the patient's prostate and tumor lesions identified on MRI are transformed from the pre-biopsy imaging and displayed in the intrabiopsy TRUS space (Fig. 3, right column windows). The real-time TRUS image is displayed adjacent to the intrabiopsy 3D TRUS image volume (Fig. 3, left column windows). The intrabiopsy 3D TRUS volume is dynamically sliced in real-time to match the mechanical tracked probe position, $T_{US \rightarrow 3DUS}$. Discordance between the real-time TRUS image and the dynamically sliced 3D TRUS plane indicates a spatial correspondence failure (typically due to patient or prostate motion). If severe, prostate motion correction can be completed by repeating 3D TRUS scan and repeating the automatic TRUS–TRUS registration to recalculate $T_{3DUS \rightarrow 3DUS}$.

Alignment of the expected path of the biopsy needle with the target lesion indicates the proper biopsy needle alignment. The biopsy needle is then delivered at the marked needle insertion depth and the location of each core is recorded for post-biopsy review and confirmation in 3D TRUS or MRI.

2.3   MRI-3D TRUS Registration

Successful targeting of suspicious MRI lesions under TRUS needle guidance requires accurate MRI–3D TRUS registration. Our proposed algorithm initializes with a landmark-based rigid registration followed by a surface-based thin-plate spline (TPS) non-linear deformation using respective prostate surface models.

Though more labor intensive, a landmark-based registration was selected over an iterative closest point (ICP) model-based approach, as qualitative assessment of initial ICP registrations lacked sufficient MRI–TRUS image correspondence. As part of our clinical study, a quantitative evaluation of landmark vs. ICP was performed (Sect. 2.5).

Following rigid alignment, a non-linear, surface-based registration using thin-plate splines (TPS) [6] is applied to compensate for prostate deformations caused by the MRI endorectal coil. Equal-angle radial segmentations of the prostate gland are performed for TRUS and MRI modalities. TRUS segmentation is performed using a semi-automatic algorithm developed previously [16]. The algorithm fits a 2D dynamic deformable contour (DDC) following a 4-point initialization on a single plane within the 3D TRUS volume. Radial propagation of the contour provides a contour initialize for each successive DDC through the 180° of prostate surface segmentation.

2.4   TRUS–TRUS Registration

TRUS–TRUS registration allows for alignment of intersession or intrasession 3D TRUS prostate volumes. Intersession registration maps the pre-biopsy 3D TRUS and the coregisterd MRI into the 3D TRUS volume acquired following initial sonographic assessment. Correction for intrasession prostate motion can also be achieved by applying the algorithm to subsequent 3D TRUS volumes acquired following loss of spatial correspondence.

We employ a block matching approach for image-based, TRUS–TRUS rigid registration, $T_{3DUS \to 3DUS}$ [7,20]. The registration algorithm is fully automatic without requiring user initialization. A mutual information image-based metric is used for the registration cost function. Our previous studies have demonstrated significantly lower TRE values for TRUS-TRUS registration with the image-based block matching algorithm compared to a surface-based approach [13,14]. The block-matching algorithm uses a coarse-to-fine, multiresolution hierarchal approach with a total registration time is approximately 60 s [13].

2.5 Patient Biopsy Study

Written informed consent was obtained from 25 patients (mean age: 58.0 ± 8.0 years) enrolled in an institutional review board (IRB) approved MRI-3D TRUS fusion prostate biopsy study. Study inclusion criteria included the following: 1) PSA > 4 ng/mL, 2) High clinical suspicion of PCa over prostatitis, 3) no prior diagnosis of PCa. The patient prostate volumes ranged from 15-132 cm^3 (mean: 50.4 ± 28.8 cm^3), with a mean PSA value of 8.3 ± 5.0 ng/mL. A cohort of 14 patients had one or more prior standard 2D TRUS biopsy procedures, while the remaining 11 patients had no prior prostate interventions. No patients had any prior MRI prostate imaging.

Multisequence prostate MRIs were collected on a 3T MRI (GE Healthcare, Waukesha, WA) using an endorectal coil. T2, diffusion weighted (DWI) and dynamic contrast enhanced (DCE) image sequences were analyzed by an expert radiologist and suspicious areas on the MRI were manually segmented. Patients were prospectively stratified into 1) high, 2) moderate, or 3) mild level of suspicion based on the MRI findings. Patients without any suspicious areas on MRI were classified as non-suspicious and excluded from calculation of positive biopsy core rates.

Prebiopsy and intrabiopsy 3D TRUS images were acquired using an end-fire, 9 MHz 2D TRUS probe (Philips, Bothell, WA) attached to the 3D mechanical tracking system described in Section 2.1. One to three targeted biopsy cores were taken from all suspicious lesions identified on MRI. All patients received a standard, random 12-core sextant biopsy as per the current clinical standard, in addition to any targeted biopsy cores. In patients with suspicious MRI lesions, the 12-core distribution cores served as an intrinsic control for statistical analysis of cancer detection. The 3D location of both targeted and sextant biopsy cores were recorded to allow for retrospective verification of needle placement and MRI correlation to histopathology Gleason prostate cancer grading [10].

As part of this study, 5 patients (20%) with prostatic micro-calcifications visible in both MRI and TRUS were identified for a retrospective, quantitative comparison of registration algorithms based on fiducial-target registration error (TRE).

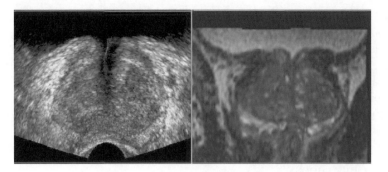

Fig. 4. Illustration of the 3D TRUS (left) and T2 MRI (right) coregistered using a landmark-based rigid followed by a TPS deformable registration (Sect. 2.3)

Table 1. Comparison of algorithm fiducial target registration error (TRE) for MRI-3D TRUS registration for a subset of 5 patients (Sect. 2.3)

		Mean TRE (mm)
Landmark-Based	Rigid	3.8 ± 0.8
	TPS	4.3 ± 1.2
Iterative Closest Point (ICP)	Rigid	5.1 ± 1.5
	TPS	5.2 ± 1.5

3   Results

Suspicious lesions were identified MRI in 76% (19/25) of patients enrolled in the MRI-3D TRUS fusion biopsy study. MRI-TRUS fusion was successfully performed on all 19 patients (Fig. 4); however, targeted biopsy was only performed on 18 of the 19 patients as TRUS-TRUS regsitration failed in one case and manual correction was not available at the time of the biopsy. Retrospective comparison of the MRI-TRUS registration on 5 patients showed a mean TRE = 4.3 ± 1.2 mm using TPS deformable registration following landmark-based initialization (Table 1). Landmark-based registration TRE was less than that of the ICP algorithm (5.2 ± 1.5 mm), although this result was not statistically significant. TRE values for landmark-based registration were non-significantly lower with rigid alignment alone compared to post-TPS deformation. Though not statistically significant, this finding could indicate a poor point correspondence between the two surfaces for TPS deformation leading to inaccurate gland distortion. It is also probable that the TPS surface-matching does not adequately model the deformation of the prostate internal architecture.

Prostate adenocarcinoma was identified in 42% (8/19) of all suspcious patients. Table 2 shows the PCa distribution based on level of suspicion. Cancer was not found on the standard 12-core sextant biopsy in any patients without suspicious lesions identified on MRI. Targeted biopsy cores were positive for PCa in 6 of the 8 patients found to be positive. Of the two patients not detected by targeted biopsy, one did not actually have any targeted biopsies performed, despite a moderately suspicious lesion, due to the registration failure described earlier. The other patient had PCa detected on sextant biopsy on the contralateral side, remote from the suspicious lesion. Retrospective analysis of the MRI did not reveal any imaging characteristics typical of malignancy.

Table 2. Breakdown of patient biopsy results based on the level of suspicion on MRI

	High Suspicion	Moderate Suspicion	Low Suspicion	No Suspicion
All Patient MRI Findings	7	7	5	6
Prostate Cancer Found	4	3	1	0
Targeted Biopsy Detection	4	2	0	0
Sextant Biopsy Detection	4	3	1	0
Prostate Cancer By Location				
Peripheral Zone	3	1	1	0
Transitional Zone	1	2	0	0

A total of 62 biopsy cores were targeted at 31 lesions with a 29.0% (18/62) rate of positive biopsy cores. Sextant distribution demonstrated to a total positive biopsy core rate of 9.6% (32/334) or 16.4% (31/189) when only biopsy cores within the prostate hemisphere of the suspicious lesion are considered. Figure 5 is a plot of positive rate of biopsy cores separated by MRI level of suspicion. Targeted biopsy cores had a higher rate of positive cores compared with the sextant distributed cores for both moderate (30.4% vs. 7.1%) and high (42.3% vs. 25.6%) suspicion lesions.

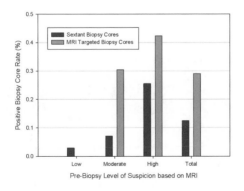

Fig. 5. Comparison of the biopsy core cancer rate for based on the level of suspicion as assessed on the MRI

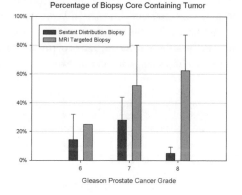

Percentage of Biopsy Core Containing Tumor

Gleason Prostate Cancer Grade

Fig. 6. Comparison of the biopsy core cancer rate for based on the level of suspicion as assessed on the MRI

For all patients, targeted biopsies demonstrated equal or higher Gleason score (GS) cancer grades compared to the sextant distribution biopsies. The mean GS score for positive biopsy cores was significantly higher ($p < 0.01$) for targeted biopsy cores (7.0 ± 0.5) compared to sextant cores (6.4 ± 0.7). Fifty percent or 3 of the 6 patients with cancer proven on targeted biopsy had upgraded or higher GS values when compared to the histopathology of the distributed biopsy cores. Two of these patients had clinically significant upgrading from low-risk (GS 6) to intermediate-risk (GS 7) disease based on the targeted biopsy cores.

PCa positive biopsy cores from targeted biopsies had significantly ($p < 0.001$) higher percentage of the core containing tumor compared to the sextant biopsies ($48 \pm 28\%$ and $16 \pm 17\%$, respectively). Statistical significance was also seen for moderate and high suspicion patients (Fig. 6). Figure 7 illustrates an example

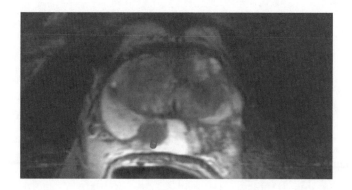

Fig. 7. Illustration of a targeted biopsy core (red) transformed back and recorded on the pre-biopsy T2 MRI, suggesting a successfully sampling of the suspicious hypointense lesion

case with a targeted biopsy core transformed back and displayed on the T2 MRI. For this patient the targeted biopsy core (red) successfully transected the hypointense lesion on MRI while the adjacent sextant core (not visualized) only sampled the edge of the lesion perimeter. The histopathology of targeted and sextant cores were GS 8, 45% tumor (high-risk disease) and GS 6, 5% tumor (low-risk disease), respectively.

4   Conclusion and Future Work

We have demonstrated the clinical application of a mechanically-assisted 3D TRUS biopsy system for successful targeting of suspicious lesions identified on MRI. Targeted biopsies produced significantly higher positive biopsy core rates, mean Gleason score cancer grades, and tumor volume sampled when compared to a standard 12-core sextant biopsy distribution. Landmark-based initialization with thin-plate spline deformable registration had a lower mean TRE for MRI-TRUS registration when compared to an ICP rigid initialization; however, both algorithms were greater than the 2.5 mm clinically driven target. Future work will focus on algorithm development to improve MRI-TRUS registration accuracy and minimize user interaction to make MRI-TRUS fusion biopsy more clinically practical.

References

1. American Cancer Society: Cancer facts and figures 2010. Tech. rep., American Cancer Society (2010)
2. Anastasiadis, A.G., Lichy, M.P., Nagele, U., Kuczyk, M.A., Merseburger, A.S., Hennenlotter, J., Corvin, S., Sievert, K.D., Claussen, C.D., Stenzl, A., Schlemmer, H.P.: Mri-guided biopsy of the prostate increases diagnostic performance in men with elevated or increasing psa levels after previous negative trus biopsies. Eur. Urol. 50(4), 738–748 (2006), discussion 748–9
3. Andriole, G.L., Bullock, T.L., Belani, J.S., Traxel, E., Yan, Y., Bostwick, D.G., Humphrey, P.A.: Is there a better way to biopsy the prostate? prospects for a novel transrectal systematic biopsy approach. Urology 70(suppl. 6), 22–26 (2007)
4. Bax, J., Cool, D., Gardi, L., Knight, K., Smith, D., Montreuil, J., Sherebrin, S., Romagnoli, C., Fenster, A.: Mechanically assisted 3d ultrasound guided prostate biopsy system. Med. Phys. 35(12), 5397–5410 (2008)
5. Beyersdorff, D., Winkel, A., Hamm, B., Lenk, S., Loening, S.A., Taupitz, M.: Mr imaging-guided prostate biopsy with a closed mr unit at 1.5 t: initial results. Radiology 234(2), 576–581 (2005)
6. Bookstein, F.: Principal warps: Thin-plate splines and the decomposition of deformations. IEEE Trans. Pattern Anal. Mach. Intell. 11(6), 567–585 (1989)
7. Chrisochoides, N., Fedorov, A., Kot, A., Archip, N., Black, P., Clatz, O., Golby, A., Kikinis, R., Warfield, S.K.: Toward real-time image guided neurosurgery using distributed and grid computing. In: ACM/IEEE Conference on Supercomputing (SC 2006), p. 37 (2006)

8. Cool, D., Sherebrin, S., Izawa, J., Chin, J., Fenster, A.: Design and evaluation of a 3d transrectal ultrasound prostate biopsy system. Med. Phys. 35(10), 4695–4707 (2008)
9. Eichler, K., Hempel, S., Wilby, J., Myers, L., Bachmann, L.M., Kleijnen, J.: Diagnostic value of systematic biopsy methods in the investigation of prostate cancer: a systematic review. J. Urol. 175(5), 1605–1612 (2006)
10. Gleason, D.: Histologic grading and clinical staging of prostatic carcinoma, pp. 171–198. Lea and Febiger, Philadelphia (1977)
11. Hata, N., Jinzaki, M., Kacher, D., Cormak, R., Gering, D., Nabavi, A., Silverman, S.G., D'Amico, A.V., Kikinis, R., Jolesz, F.A., Tempany, C.M.: Mr imaging-guided prostate biopsy with surgical navigation software: device validation and feasibility. Radiology 220(1), 263–268 (2001)
12. Kadoury, S., Yan, P., Xu, S., Glossop, N., Choyke, P., Turkbey, B., Pinto, P., Wood, B.J., Kruecker, J.: Realtime TRUS/MRI fusion targeted-biopsy for prostate cancer: A clinical demonstration of increased positive biopsy rates. In: Madabhushi, A., Dowling, J., Yan, P., Fenster, A., Abolmaesumi, P., Hata, N. (eds.) MICCAI 2010. LNCS, vol. 6367, pp. 52–62. Springer, Heidelberg (2010)
13. Karnik, V.V., Fenster, A., Bax, J., Cool, D.W., Gardi, L., Gyacskov, I., Romagnoli, C., Ward, A.D.: Assessment of image registration accuracy in three-dimensional transrectal ultrasound guided prostate biopsy. Med. Phys. 37(2), 802–813 (2010)
14. Karnik, V.V., Fenster, A., Bax, J., Romagnoli, C., Ward, A.D.: Evaluation of intersession 3d-trus to 3d-trus image registration for repeat prostate biopsies. Medical physics 38(4), 1832–1843 (2011)
15. Krieger, A., Susil, R.C., Menard, C., Coleman, J.A., Fichtinger, G., Atalar, E., Whitcomb, L.L.: Design of a novel mri compatible manipulator for image guided prostate interventions. IEEE Trans. Biomed. Eng. 52(2), 306–313 (2005)
16. Ladak, H.M., Mao, F., Wang, Y., Downey, D.B., Steinman, D.A., Fenster, A.: Prostate boundary segmentation from 2d ultrasound images. Med. Phys. 27(8), 1777–1788 (2000)
17. Lattouf, J.B., Grubb, R.L., Lee, S.J., Bjurlin, M.A., Albert, P., Singh, A.K., Ocak, I., Choyke, P., Coleman, J.A.: Magnetic resonance imaging-directed transrectal ultrasonography-guided biopsies in patients at risk of prostate cancer. BJU Int. 99(5), 1041–1046 (2007)
18. Long, J.A., Daanen, V., Moreau-Gaudry, A., Troccaz, J., Rambeaud, J.J., Descotes, J.L.: Prostate biopsies guided by three-dimensional real-time (4-d) transrectal ultrasonography on a phantom: comparative study versus two-dimensional transrectal ultrasound-guided biopsies. Eur. Urol. 52(4), 1097–1104 (2007)
19. Norberg, M., Egevad, L., Holmberg, L., Sparen, P., Norlen, B.J., Busch, C.: The sextant protocol for ultrasound-guided core biopsies of the prostate underestimates the presence of cancer. Urology 50(4), 562–566 (1997)
20. Ourselin, S., Roche, A., Prima, S., Ayache, N.: Block matching: A general framework to improve robustness of rigid registration of medical images. In: Delp, S.L., DiGoia, A.M., Jaramaz, B. (eds.) MICCAI 2000. LNCS, vol. 1935, pp. 557–566. Springer, Heidelberg (2000)

21. Shen, F., Shinohara, K., Kumar, D., Khemka, A., Simoneau, A.R., Werahera, P.N., Li, L., Guo, Y., Narayanan, R., Wei, L., Barqawi, A., Crawford, E.D., Davatzikos, C., Suri, J.S.: Three-dimensional sonography with needle tracking: role in diagnosis and treatment of prostate cancer. J. Ultrasound Med. 27(6), 895–905 (2008)
22. Singh, A.K., Kruecker, J., Xu, S., Glossop, N., Guion, P., Ullman, K., Choyke, P.L., Wood, B.J.: Initial clinical experience with real-time transrectal ultrasonography-magnetic resonance imaging fusion-guided prostate biopsy. BJU Int. 101(7), 841–845 (2008)
23. Zakian, K.L., Sircar, K., Hricak, H., Chen, H.N., Shukla-Dave, A., Eberhardt, S., Muruganandham, M., Ebora, L., Kattan, M.W., Reuter, V.E., Scardino, P.T., Koutcher, J.A.: Correlation of proton mr spectroscopic imaging with gleason score based on step-section pathologic analysis after radical prostatectomy. Radiology 234(3), 804–814 (2005)

Validation of Direct Registration of Whole-Mount Prostate Digital Histopathology to *ex vivo* MR Images

Eli Gibson[1], Cathie Crukley[1,2], José Gomez[3], Madeleine Moussa[3],
Joseph L. Chin[4], Glenn Bauman[2,5], Aaron Fenster[1,2,5,6], and Aaron D. Ward[2]

[1] Robarts Research Institute, London, Canada
[2] Lawson Health Research Institute, London, Canada
[3] Department of Pathology, The University of Western Ontario, London, Canada
[4] Department of Urology, The University of Western Ontario, London, Canada
[5] Department of Oncology, The University of Western Ontario, London, Canada
[6] Department of Medical Biophysics, The University of Western Ontario, London, Canada

Abstract. Accurate determination of cancer stage and grade from *in vivo* prostate imaging could improve biopsy guidance, therapy selection and, possibly, focal therapy guidance. Validating prostate cancer imaging ideally requires accurate 3D registration of *in vivo* imaging to histopathology, which is facilitated by intermediate histology-*ex vivo* imaging registration.

This work introduces and evaluates a direct registration with fiducial-based local refinement of digital prostate histopathology to *ex vivo* magnetic resonance (MR) images that obviates three elements typical of existing methods: (1) guidance of specimen slicing, (2) imaging/photography of sliced tissue blocks, and (3) registration guidance based on anatomical image features. The mean target registration error (TRE) of 98 intrinsic landmarks across 21 histology images was calculated for the proposed direct registration (0.7 mm) and compared to existing approaches: indirect using tissue block MR images (0.8 mm) and image-guided-slicing-based (1.0 mm). The local refinement was also shown to improve existing approaches to achieve a similar mean TRE (0.7 mm).

Keywords: prostate cancer, histology, registration, imaging.

1 Introduction

Prostate cancer is the most common non-cutaneous cancer in North American men. The current clinical standard for prostate cancer diagnosis is two-dimensional (2D) transrectal ultrasound (TRUS) guided biopsy, with a 29% rate of underestimation and 14% rate of overestimation of cancer grade [12]. The resulting over-diagnosis may lead to unnecessary treatments, which may have severe side effects, including incontinence and erectile dysfunction. Accurate localization (or detailed "mapping") of cancerous lesions on *in vivo* imaging

A. Madabhushi et al. (Eds.): Prostate Cancer Imaging 2011, LNCS 6963, pp. 134–145, 2011.
© Springer-Verlag Berlin Heidelberg 2011

could support improved biopsy guidance, therapy selection and, possibly, guidance of "focal therapy", whereby one would target only the lesion of interest and spare the rest of the prostate. Focal therapy of the prostate has the potential to treat early prostate cancer effectively without some of the life-altering complications associated with surgery and other forms of prostate therapy. Ideally, validation of imaging modalities for staging and grading of prostate cancer requires accurate 3D registration of imaging to histopathology, where correct assessments of stage and grade can be made.

Registration of histology to *in vivo* imaging is a multi-modality non-linear registration of 2D data that is sparse (in the through plane direction) to a dense 3D *in vivo* image. Construction of a 3D histology volume is practical when closely spaced parallel histology sections are taken [7,14]; however, data for registration-based validations of prostate imaging are typically taken from clinical specimens, where each histology section is sampled from a separate 3-5 mm thick tissue block [2], and the relative positions and orientations of the histology sections taken from within each tissue block are variable. Avoiding 2D to 3D registration via the accurate construction of a 3D histology volume is challenging because of this variability and sparseness [1]. The variability also introduces challenges to methods that guide the slicing of the tissue block to align with imaging [1,16], or orient imaging to align with tissue block slicing [6]. The differences in image content and scale and substantial deformations introduce challenges for direct 2D to 3D registration. Tissue deformation, due to resection, fixation and histoprocessing, is best modeled as non-linear [8], which allows out-of-plane deformation. At the same time, the lack of 3D context for the histology image makes the correct determination of out-of-plane correspondence challenging. This is exacerbated by the difference in image content, as histology image content derives from tissue affinity for chemical stains, information not represented in most 3D medical images. Due to these challenges in registering histology to *in vivo* images, many studies (e.g. [17,4]) resort instead to using a subjective visual correspondence of regions of interest visible in both images, with limitations of unknown accuracy and repeatability. These limitations limit the conclusions that can be drawn from these studies, especially where correspondence of small lesions is concerned.

The focus of this work is on an intermediate registration of histology images to images of *ex vivo* fixed specimens. Conducting this intermediate registration can leverage the reduced deformation, higher resolution imaging and non-anatomical fiducials to circumvent these challenges, and has been adopted as a common strategy in registration-based validations. Registration to *ex vivo* MR images using the same scanner, coils and pulse sequence as *in vivo* imaging addresses many of the challenges of a registration to *in vivo* imaging, reducing the problem to a tractable single-modality 3D *ex vivo-in vivo* registration. Additionally, preliminary validation of imaging modalities or image processing on *ex vivo* specimens [11] requires accurate 3D registration of *ex vivo* imaging to histopathology.

Many existing methods [2,18] address the registration of *ex vivo* imaging to histology by controlling the position and orientation of specimen slicing into tissue blocks, often using *image guidance* and specialized/custom slicing equipment. This can introduce operator variability and disrupts the standard clinical slicing procedure by constraining the position and orientation of slicing. *Indirect* methods use additional 2D [15,5] or 3D [3,19] imaging of sliced tissue blocks to retrospectively determine the locations from which histology sections were sampled, which can be costly and time-consuming, and can suffer from an accumulation of errors. Registrations using anatomic image features hold the potential for full automation in principle, but they depend on the presence of image features often disrupted by the inherent variability of prostate appearance and, as observed by Ou et al. [13], by the very cancer foci that these methods aim to register.

This work describes and evaluates a simplified approach, developed in our laboratory, to the registration of digital prostate histopathology to *ex vivo* magnetic resonance (MR) images based on extrinsic fiducials applied within and on the surface of the specimen. Our approach eliminates the need for three elements typical of existing methods: (1) guidance of specimen slicing, (2) imaging/photography of sliced specimen tissue blocks, and (3) dependence on the appearance of salient anatomical structures within the image to guide registration. Thus, the method is robust, is less time consuming, reduces the need for specialized equipment, and is more amenable to implementation in multi-centre studies. Furthermore, since this registration is driven entirely by extrinsic fiducials, the process is robust to disease-related appearance variability, which is critical for aligning cancerous regions. We calculated a sub-millimeter 3D target registration error (TRE) using intrinsic anatomical landmarks, showing that the method performs as well as or better than existing, more complex methods. We also demonstrated that the local optimization component of our method can be used to improve registrations generated from other methods and is robust to a variety of initializations.

2   Materials and Methods

2.1   Materials

Six radical prostatectomy specimens were collected as part of an ongoing study, yielding 21 whole-mount histological sections in total. Specimen MR images were acquired with the tissue immersed in Christo-Lube (Lubrication Technology, USA) to provide a black background and minimize boundary artefacts, on a 3T Discovery MR750 (GE Healthcare, Waukesha, WI, USA) using an endorectal receive coil and two MRI protocols: T1-weighted (3D SPGR, TR 6.5 ms, TE 2.5 ms, bandwidth ±31.25 kHz, 8 averages, FOV 14x14x6.2 cm, slice thickness 0.4 mm, 256x192 matrix, 312 slices, flip angle 15 degrees, 25 min) and T2-weighted (3D FSE, TR 2000 ms, TE 151.5 ms, bandwidth ±125 kHz, 3 averages, FOV 14x14x6.2 cm, slice thickness 0.4 mm, 320x192 matrix, 312 slices, 25 min). Histology slides were digitized on a ScanScope GL (Aperio Technologies, Vista, CA,

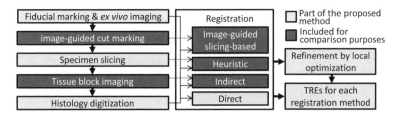

Fig. 1. Specimen processing. Light grey steps are required for the simplified registration process. Dark grey steps are only required for the comparison to existing methods and for intrinsic-fiducial-based validation. Note that the proposed direct method relies on the smallest number of inputs.

USA) bright field slide scanning system with a 0.5 μm resolution and downsampled to a 30 μm resolution.

2.2   Methods

Specimen Processing. The overall process for the simplified histology to *ex vivo* registration is shown in Figure 1 in light grey. Formalin-fixed prostate specimens were marked with fiducials, then imaged with MRI. After the removal of the prostatic apex from the inferior aspect of the gland, the midgland was transversely sliced into 4.4 mm thick tissue blocks. After whole-mount paraffin embedding, 4 μm-thick sections were cut from each block and stained with hematoxylin and eosin, and the resulting slides were digitized. Because of the constraints of the ongoing study from which specimens were drawn, the removal of the apex was performed using an image-guided slicing method [18]. This enabled a comparison to the image-guided slicing method. MR images of the 4.4 mm-thick tissue blocks were collected to enable a comparison to a method that uses tissue block imaging [3].

Fiducial Markers. Ten strand-shaped fiducials visible on both histology and T1-weighted MR images (details can be found in [18]) were added to each specimen: 7 surface-mounted fiducials (kidney tissue strands infused with gadolinium contrast) (h_{1-7} in Figure 2) and 3 internal fiducials (thread infused with blue tissue ink and gadolinium contrast) (h_{8-10} in Figure 2). The internal fiducials were introduced using a Quincke cannula (BD Medical Inc., USA), which cleanly separates tissue without any tissue removal, and are removed before slicing leaving only ink. Application of these fiducials took ~90 minutes per specimen. These fiducials have been used in 20 clinical prostatectomy specimens at our institution and have been found to be entirely non-disruptive to the pathologists' clinical assessments.

The two end points of each fiducial strand were placed near the apex and base, respectively. Neighbouring pairs of surface-mounted fiducials were placed at approximate 45° angles to each other, forming Z and arrowhead-configurations

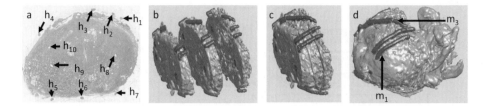

Fig. 2. Registration data stages: (a) histology (b) tissue block MR images (c) reassembled tissue blocks (d) whole specimen MR images. (b-d) Surface reconstructions with fiducial markers highlighted in red. *The registration introduced in this work aligns (a) to (d) directly, while the indirect registration [3] aligns (a) to (b) to (c) to (d).*

on the anterior and posterior side respectively, supporting the determination of the inferior-superior positions of cross-sectional surfaces passing through the fiducials.

The fiducial tracks were located on the whole-specimen and tissue block MR images at ~1 mm intervals centered along each fiducial track, and interpolated to ~0.2 mm intervals using cubic splines. Fiducials were localized in 3D Slicer (Surgical Planning Lab, Harvard Medical School, Boston, USA) on a 3-plane view for MR images and a 1-plane view for histology. While these localizations are readily automatable, manual localizations were used for this study, taking 30 minutes per specimen. On T1-weighted MR images, fiducials have strong signal due to gadolinium contrast. On histology, internal fiducials are marked by the distinctive hue of blue tissue ink, and surface-mounted fiducials can be identified by the characteristic texture of kidney tissue.

Registration. The presented registration of histology images to whole specimen *ex vivo* MR images consists of a search to identify an initial correspondence, followed by a local optimization. This optimization can be applied to not only the direct initialization presented in this work, but also to other initializations. The following sections describe initializations from (A) the direct registration introduced in this work, and three methods for purposes of comparison described below: (B) an existing indirect registration using tissue block MR images [3], (C) a heuristic registration based on procedural information, and (D) an existing registration based on image guidance of slicing [18]. The extrinsic-fiducial-based local optimization that can be applied to any of these initializations is then presented.

A) *Direct* Registration. To register histology images to whole-specimen MR images, we used a landmark-based approach. On the histology image, the cross-section of the i-th fiducial gives a 2D point $\boldsymbol{h}_i$ (Figure 2a), which corresponds to a 3D point $m_i(s_i \in [0,1])$ (Figure 2d) along the parametric curve defined by the corresponding fiducial in the MR image. For the 10 points in each histology image, this correspondence was encoded as a 10D vector $\boldsymbol{s} = [s_1, s_2, \cdots, s_{10}]$.

Each possible vector s determines a least-squares best-fit 2D-3D affine transformation A_s mapping fiducials on histology near to their corresponding points on whole-specimen MR images; one such correspondence vector,

$$\bar{s} = argmin_s \sum_{i=1}^{10} ||A_s h_i - m_i(s_i)||^2, \qquad (1)$$

yields the transformation $A_{\bar{s}}$ having the minimal residual error. Because an exhaustive search of this 10D space would be computationally prohibitive and a greedy minimization may find a local minimum, we instead selected a triplet of fiducials $[i_1, i_2, i_3]$ corresponding to three dimensions of s, defining a 3D correspondence vector $t = [s_{i_1}, s_{i_2}, s_{i_3}]$, and the unique 2D-3D affine transformation A_t that maps $[h_{i_1}, h_{i_2}, h_{i_3}]$ to $[m_{i_1}(s_{i_1}), m_{i_2}(s_{i_2}), m_{i_3}(s_{i_3})]$. An exhaustive search of this reduced space of 3D correspondence vectors,

$$\bar{t} = argmin_t \sum_{i=1}^{10} ||A_t h_i - C(A_t h_i, m_i))||^2, \qquad (2)$$

yields a transformation $A_{\bar{t}}$ with the minimal residual (computed from all ten fiducials, using closest point correspondence, where $C(p, m)$ is the closest point on parametric curve m to point p). The fiducial triplet was manually selected to exclude fiducials not present on histology and to include widely spaced fiducials and at least one diagonal fiducial. The closest point correspondence determines a least-squares best-fit affine transformation.

B) *Indirect* Registration using Tissue Block MR images. In this method [3], histology was registered to whole-specimen MR images in three steps, with MR images of the sliced tissue blocks as an intermediate registration target: (1) histology (Figure 2a) was registered to tissue block MR images (Figure 2b), using the registration algorithm described in the preceding paragraph, but with m_i denoting a segment of fiducial on a tissue block; (2) tissue block images were virtually reassembled automatically (Figure 2c) by aligning corresponding end points of each fiducial on either side of each tissue block cut using a least squares best-fit rigid transform, and (3) the assembly was registered to whole-specimen MR images (Figure 2d), using the registration algorithm described in the preceding paragraph, but using rigid transformations and with h_i as 3D fiducial points in the assembly. These transformations were composed into an affine transformation.

C) *Heuristic*-based Registration. In this approach, we used information about the specimen processing procedure to inform registration. This method is used to demonstrate that the local refinement described below is robust even to coarse initial registrations. Because the specimens were sliced using image-guided slicing [18] that constrains slicing to be aligned with an *in vivo* imaging plane, a heuristic was developed to identify this plane on the *ex vivo* image. First, clinical constraints on the slicing are imposed: the transverse apical cut must yield a prostatic apex at least 1 cm thick and must include the entire urethral opening. Second, the prostate is rotated approximately 20° by the endorectal coil during *in vivo* imaging, so the slicing (intended to lie in the axial imaging plane) will be rotated 70° clockwise from the posterior wall (as viewed from patient left). Third, all of the histology images are taken from the mid-gland and thus include the fiducial markers, so any fiducial visible on histology must pass through the first cut. Fourth, subsequent cuts are made parallel to the first cut at 4.4 mm intervals. Correspondences between fiducial cross-sections on histology h_i and the intersection of fiducials with a plane, determined using the above heuristics, on the *ex vivo* image determined a least-squares best-fit affine transformation.

D) *Image-guided* **Slicing-based Registration.** In image-guided specimen slicing [18], a specific oblique plane in each *ex vivo* image was targeted for the first cut (which removes the prostatic apex) based on a manual registration to *in vivo* imaging and clinical criteria. After identifying a desired cutting plane, landmarks (exit points of internal fiducials) were identified on the whole-specimen image, with corresponding landmarks localized on the physical prostate surface using a tracked stylus. Rigid registration of these landmarks identified the cutting plane on the specimen, which was marked for cutting. The cut was guided by a slotted forceps. By carefully controlling the first cut, with subsequent cutting at known intervals, the histology was localized in the *ex vivo* image. This image guidance method was adapted to yield a least-squares best-fit affine transform from a correspondence between fiducial cross-sections on histology h_i and intersections of the fiducials with the *intended* cutting plane on the *ex vivo* image.

Local Refinement. Each registration yielded a transformation A from histology to *ex vivo* imaging that, for a good registration, should yield a near-optimal 10D fiducial correspondence vector $[s_i|m_i(s_i) = C(Ah_i, m_i), i = 1..10]$. This vector was used to initialize a search for the optimal 10D correspondence vector $\bar{s}$. The search for the correspondence vector $\bar{s}$ comprises the minimization of the residual fiducial registration error used a greedy Nelder-Mead simplex-based minimization [10] in the 10D correspondence space (Equation 1). We used this minimization to refine initializations from each of the four registrations, and these refined transformations were also evaluated.

2.3   Validation

The TRE of each of the four registration methods, with and without local refinement, was calculated as the 3D post-registration misalignment of intrinsic landmarks identified on histology and on whole-specimen MR images. Because such landmarks are challenging to identify, tissue block MR was used to facilitate the process. Tissue block MR images have a higher density of salient features because the Christo-Lube fills internal ducts that are exposed by the slicing,

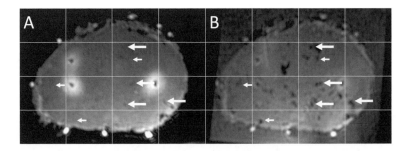

Fig. 3. Co-registered T1-weighted MR images of whole specimen (A) and tissue block (B). Barely visible (e.g. large arrows) or invisible (e.g. small arrows) ducts on the whole specimen image are visible on the tissue block image due to Christo-Lube contrast.

creating contrast, as shown in Figure 3. Correspondences of a few such salient features were used to approximately align the histology and whole-specimen MR images, facilitating the challenging further search for subtle, anatomically homologous landmark pairs in the histology and whole-specimen MR images. 98 corresponding intrinsic landmark pairs across 21 histology sections were thus identified. No information about intrinsic landmarks was available to any registration.

3 Results

Three histology images and the MR images co-registered using the method described in this paper are shown in Figure 4.

The mean and standard deviation of the TREs for the four registration methods with and without local refinement are shown in Table 1. Statistical analyses were performed in Prism 5.04 (Graphpad Software, Inc., San Diego, USA). To compare the mean TREs of the presented direct method with local refinement to existing methods, and to assess the improvement given by local refinement of existing methods, we used a repeated-measures ANOVA of TREs from the direct, indirect and image-guided slicing methods with and without local refinement, followed by post-hoc analysis with Bonferroni multiple comparison correction of particular comparisons of interest. The means of the 6 methods were unequal ($p < 0.0001$). Post hoc analysis showed that the direct method with local refinement had a lower mean TRE than the existing image-guided slicing (95% CI: 0.21 to 0.42 mm) and the existing indirect registration (95% CI: 0.02 to 0.23 mm). Post hoc analysis also showed that local refinement lowered the mean TRE of the image-guided method (95% CI: 0.22 to 0.43 mm) and the indirect registration (95% CI: 0.04 to 0.25 mm). To assess the difference in mean TRE of all the methods after local refinement, we used a repeated-measures ANOVA of the TREs. This test failed to show a statistically significant difference between the mean TREs with local refinement ($p = 0.38$, union of pairwise 95% CIs, -0.05 to 0.05 mm).

The direct registration required 3 hours per specimen including the application of fiducials, imaging of the intact specimen, localization of fiducials and computational registration of histology to whole specimen MR images. The indirect and image-guided slicing methods required 5 and 11 hours respectively for all processing steps.

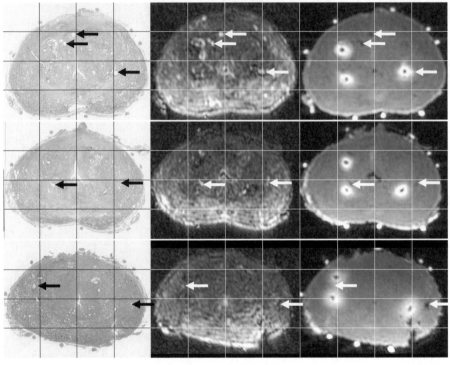

Histology   T2-weighted MR images   T1-weighted MR images

Fig. 4. Three histology images co-registered to MR images using the registration method described in this paper. Intrinsic landmarks are shown by arrows.

Table 1. Mean (std) TRE of four registration methods with and without local refinement (LR)

Registration	Heuristic	Indirect	Direct	Image-guided
Mean TRE (std) w/o LR (mm)	2.36 (1.74)	0.82 (0.43)	0.76 (0.41)	1.00 (0.58)
Mean TRE (std) w/ LR (mm)	0.68 (0.36)	0.67 (0.36)	0.69 (0.38)	0.68 (0.36)

4 Discussion and Conclusions

The direct registration presented in this work is less disruptive to the clinical workflow, requires 2 and 8 hours less to perform than the existing indirect and image-guided slicing methods, respectively, and is a promising replacement for current methods to register histology to *ex vivo* imaging. The shorter processing time would facilitate integration of the method into standard clinical workflows without delaying diagnosis.

Quantitative measurement of TRE in histology to imaging registrations is important in interpreting conclusions from registration-based validations. Unfortunately, the identification of homologous landmarks in histology and other imaging modalities is challenging, and often omitted in such studies. Our presented method for identifying such homologous landmarks using an initial alignment based on tissue block MR images enabled the localization of 98 landmarks to robustly quantify TRE. The 0.69 mm TRE of the presented method was shown to be lower than that of two existing methods computed on the same dataset, and compares favourably to the 0.82 mm [9], 0.82 mm [20] and 0.79 mm [13] TREs reported in the few existing studies of methods that have quantified the TRE.

The local refinement is a software-only improvement that can improve the accuracy of existing registrations. The similarity of TREs resulting from this refinement across the various initializations, including the heuristic with high initial error, suggests that the optimizer is robust to varying initializations, yielding mean TREs within 0.05 mm with 95% confidence. This permits the selection of the most appropriate registration for a given research question (e.g. a permitting a radiologist to sample histology from a specific imaging plane of diagnostic interest using image-guided slicing) while maintaining high registration accuracy.

The collection of further data to strengthen these preliminary conclusions is ongoing work in our laboratory, including processing additional specimens and assessing the fiducial localization variability. This data set of imaging and intrinsic fiducials, to be publicly released when complete, will provide a valuable benchmark for future validation of histology to prostate imaging registration.

These registrations assume a linear transformation is sufficient to account for histology to *ex vivo* deformation. With histology processes designed for whole mount processing, we have found that local deformations and significant tears can be avoided, even in our clinical pathology laboratory where specimens are processed by multiple technologists, most of whom are not specialized in whole-mount prostate histology. In the case of data where such deformations have not been eliminated, more flexible transformation classes could be considered.

Integrating this method into a pipeline to register histology to fused multi-modality *in vivo* images is part of ongoing research in our laboratory. In this context, the minimum acceptable TRE is based on the need to overlap cancer foci on histology with the anatomically homologous voxels on imaging. As the collected *in vivo* imaging resolutions range from 1-5 mm (e.g. T2W 3D FSE with 1.4 mm slice thickness and dynamic contrast enhanced perfusion CT with 5mm slice thickness used in an ongoing study at our institution), and the smallest clinically relevant tumours have radii of 3-5 mm, the TRE of 0.69 mm in the histology to *ex vivo* registration is small relative to the minimum acceptable error. Thus one may be confident imaging of the prostate and targeting small cancers for focal therapy based on the fused images can accurately access the lesion(s) without jeopardizing clinical outcome.

Acknowledgements. This work was supported by the National Sciences and Engineering Research Council, the Ontario Institute for Cancer Research and the Canadian Institutes of Health Research [funding reference number CTP 87515].

References

1. Chappelow, J., Bloch, B.N., Rofsky, N., Genega, E., Lenkinski, R., DeWolf, W., Madabhushi, A.: Elastic registration of multimodal prostate mri and histology via multiattribute combined mutual information. Medical Physics 38(4), 2005–2018 (2011)
2. Chen, L.H., Ho, H., Lazaro, R., Thng, C.H., Yuen, J., Ng, W.S., Cheng, C.: Optimum slicing of radical prostatectomy specimens for correlation between histopathology and medical images. Int J. Comput. Assist. Radiol. Surg. 5(5), 471–487 (2010)
3. Gibson, E., Crukley, C., Gómez-Lemus, J.A., Moussa, M., Bauman, G., Fenster, A., Ward, A.D.: Tissue block MRI for slice-orientation-independent registration of digital histology images to ex vivo MRI of the prostate. In: IEEE International Symposium on Biomedical Imaging, Chicago, USA (March 2011)
4. Itou, Y., Nakanishi, K., Narumi, Y., Nishizawa, Y., Tsukuma, H.: Clinical utility of apparent diffusion coefficient (adc) values in patients with prostate cancer: Can adc values contribute to assess the aggressiveness of prostate cancer? Journal of Magnetic Resonance Imaging 33(1), 167–172 (2011)
5. Jackson, A.S., Reinsberg, S.A., Sohaib, S.A., Charles-Edwards, E.M., Jhavar, S., Christmas, T.J., Thompson, A.C., Bailey, M.J., Corbishley, C.M., Fisher, C., Leach, M.O., Dearnaley, D.P.: Dynamic contrast-enhanced MRI for prostate cancer localization. Br. J. Radiol. 82(974), 148–156 (2009)
6. Jhavar, S.G., Fisher, C., Jackson, A., Reinsberg, S.A., Dennis, N., Falconer, A., Dearnaley, D., Edwards, S.E., Edwards, S.M., Leach, M.O., Cummings, C., Christmas, T., Thompson, A., Woodhouse, C., Sandhu, S., Cooper, C.S., Eeles, R.A.: Processing of radical prostatectomy specimens for correlation of data from histopathological, molecular biological, and radiological studies: a new whole organ technique. J. Clin. Pathol. 58(5), 504–508 (2005)
7. Kiessling, F., Le-Huu, M., Kunert, T., Thorn, M., Vosseler, S., Schmidt, K., Hoffend, J., Meinzer, H.-P., Fusenig, N.E., Semmler, W.: Improved correlation of histological data with dce mri parameter maps by 3d reconstruction, reslicing and parameterization of the histological images. European Radiology 15, 1079–1086 (2005)
8. Kim, B., Boes, J.L., Frey, K.A., Meyer, C.R.: Mutual information for automated unwarping of rat brain autoradiographs. NeuroImage 5(1), 31–40 (1997)
9. Kimm, S.Y., Tarin, T.V., Lee, J.H., Nishimura, D.G., Jensen, K.C., Hu, B.S., Lee, D.S., Brooks, J.D.: Correlation of histologic sections and magnetic resonance imaging in ex-vivo human prostate specimens. The Journal of Urology 181(suppl. 4), 783 (2009)

10. Lagarias, J.C., Reeds, J.A., Wright, M.H., Wright, P.E.: Convergence properties of the nelder–mead simplex method in low dimensions. SIAM Journal on Optimization 9(1), 112–147 (1998)
11. Madabhushi, A., Feldman, M.D., Metaxas, D.N., Tomaszeweski, J., Chute, D.: Automated detection of prostatic adenocarcinoma from high-resolution ex vivo MRI. IEEE Transactions on Medical Imaging 24(12), 1611–1625 (2005)
12. Moreira Leite, K.R., Camara-Lopes, L.H., Dall'Oglio, M.F., Cury, J., Antunes, A.A., Sanudo, A., Srougi, M.: Upgrading the Gleason score in extended prostate biopsy: implications for treatment choice. Int. J. Radiat. Oncol. Biol. Phys. 73(2), 353–356 (2009)
13. Ou, Y., Shen, D., Feldman, M., Tomaszewski, J., Davatzikos, C.: Non-rigid registration between histological and MR images of the prostate: A joint segmentation and registration framework. In: IEEE CVPR Workshops, pp. 125–132 (2009)
14. Ourselin, S., Roche, A., Subsol, G., Pennec, X., Ayache, N.: Reconstructing a 3d structure from serial histological sections. Image and Vision Computing 19(1-2), 25–31 (2001)
15. Park, H., Piert, M.R., Khan, A., Shah, R., Hussain, H., Siddiqui, J., Chenevert, T.L., Meyer, C.R.: Registration methodology for histological sections and in vivo imaging of human prostate. Acad. Radiol. 15(8), 1027–1039 (2008)
16. Shah, V., Pohida, T., Turkbey, B., Mani, H., Merino, M., Pinto, P.A., Choyke, P., Bernardo, M.: A method for correlating in vivo prostate magnetic resonance imaging and histopathology using individualized magnetic resonance -based molds. Rev. Sci. Instrum. 80(10), 104–301 (2009)
17. Vargas, H.A., Akin, O., Franiel, T., Mazaheri, Y., Zheng, J., Moskowitz, C., Udo, K., Eastham, J., Hricak, H.: Diffusion-weighted endorectal mr imaging at 3 t for prostate cancer: Tumor detection and assessment of aggressiveness. Radiology 259(3), 775–784 (2011)
18. Ward, A.D., Crukley, C., McKenzie, C., Montreuil, J., Gibson, E., Gomez, J.A., Moussa, M., Bauman, G., Fenster, A.: Registration of in vivo prostate magnetic resonance images to digital histopathology images. In: Madabhushi, A., Dowling, J., Yan, P., Fenster, A., Abolmaesumi, P., Hata, N. (eds.) MICCAI 2010. LNCS, vol. 6367, pp. 66–76. Springer, Heidelberg (2010)
19. Xu, J., Humphrey, P.A., Kibel, A.S., Snyder, A.Z., Narra, V.R., Ackerman, J.J., Song, S.K.: Magnetic resonance diffusion characteristics of histologically defined prostate cancer in humans. Magn. Reson. Med. 61(4), 842–850 (2009)
20. Zhan, Y., Ou, Y., Feldman, M., Tomaszewski, J., Davatzikos, C., Shen, D.: Registering histologic and MR images of prostate for image-based cancer detection. Academic Radiology 14(11), 1367–1381 (2007)

Variable Ranking with PCA: Finding Multiparametric MR Imaging Markers for Prostate Cancer Diagnosis and Grading

Shoshana Ginsburg[1], Pallavi Tiwari[1], John Kurhanewicz[2],
and Anant Madabhushi[1,*]

[1] Department of Biomedical Engineering, Rutgers University, USA
srosskam@eden.rutgers.edu, pallavit@eden.rutgers.edu,
anantm@rci.rutgers.edu
[2] Department of Radiology, University of California, San Francisco, USA

Abstract. Although multiparametric (MP) MRI (MP–MRI) is a valuable tool for prostate cancer (CaP) diagnosis, considerable challenges remain in the ability to quantitatively combine different MRI parameters to train integrated, fused meta–classifiers for *in vivo* disease detection and characterization. To deal with the large number of MRI parameters, dimensionality reduction schemes such as principal component analysis (PCA) are needed to embed the data into a reduced subspace to facilitate classifier building. However, while features in the embedding space do not provide physical interpretability, direct feature selection in the high–dimensional space is encumbered by the curse of dimensionality. The goal of this work is to identify the most discriminating MP–MRI features for CaP diagnosis and grading based on their contributions in the reduced embedding obtained by performing PCA on the full MP–MRI feature space. In this work we demonstrate that a scheme called variable importance projection (VIP) can be employed in conjunction with PCA to identify the most discriminatory attributes. We apply our new PCA–VIP scheme to discover MP–MRI markers for discrimination between (a) CaP and benign tissue using 12 studies comprised of T2–w, DWI, and DCE MRI protocols and (b) high and low grade CaP using 36 MRS studies. The PCA–VIP score identified ADC values obtained from Diffusion and Gabor gradient texture features extracted from T2–w MRI as being most significant for CaP diagnosis. Our method also identified 3 metabolites that play a role in CaP detection—polyamine, citrate, and choline—and 4 metabolites that differentially express in low and high grade CaP: citrate, choline, polyamine, and creatine. The PCA–VIP scheme offers an alternative to traditional feature selection schemes that are encumbered by the curse of dimensionality.

* Thanks to funding agencies: the Wallace H. Coulter Foundation, National Cancer Institute (R01CA136535-01, R01CA140772-01, R03CA143991-01), The Cancer Institute of New Jersey, The Society for Imaging Informatics in Medicine, the Department of Defense (W81XWH-09), and Rutgers University Presidential Fellowship.

A. Madabhushi et al. (Eds.): Prostate Cancer Imaging 2011, LNCS 6963, pp. 146–157, 2011.

1   Introduction

Prostate cancer (CaP), the second leading cause of cancer–related deaths among men [1], is typically diagnosed by a sextant trans–rectal ultrasound evaluation. Nevertheless, sensitivity of this diagnostic method is very poor due to the low resolution provided by ultrasound [2]. As a result, clinicians have explored employing T2–w MRI [3] and magnetic resonance spectroscopy (MRS) imaging [4] for CaP diagnosis and grading. While multiparametric (MP) MRI (MP–MRI) holds great promise for CaP diagnosis [4, 5, 6], there remains a need to identify the most discriminating imaging markers for identifying aggressive CaP *in vivo*, to assist clinicians in understanding the underlying disease processes and empower patients in deciding whether to pursue treatment or follow a watch–and–wait policy [7].

Furthermore, CaP diagnosis on MP–MRI is associated with high interobserver variability [8, 9]. For example, while metabolic concentrations of citrate, creatine, and choline present in MRS imaging have been shown to be linked to CaP presence and Gleason grade [4], the citrate and creatine peaks are often difficult to distinguish on MRS, resulting in inconsistent measurements by different observers [10]. In order to increase accuracy and reproducibility of CaP detection and grading on MP–MRI, researchers have turned to automated machine learning approaches to build integrated, fused classifiers that quantitatively combine multiple MRI parameters [11, 12, 13, 14, 15].

Nevertheless, building classifiers in high–dimensional spaces is encumbered by the curse of dimensionality [16]. Consequently, dimensionality reduction schemes such as principal component analysis (PCA) are needed to embed the data in a lower dimensional space where classification can be performed. While PCA–based classifiers provide substantial benefit for combining multiple MRI parameters to build integrated meta–classifiers [17], PCA does not allow for easy identification of the features in the original, high–dimensional space that are most relevant for classification [18]. At the same time, feature selection schemes that identify important features in the original space are often limited by dependencies and interactive effects among features [19]. Hence, there remains a need for methods to identify features that contribute most to PCA embeddings.

In this work we present an innovative scheme for computing a measure of variable importance in projections (VIP) that considers both the structure of the reduced dimensional PCA embedding and the class labels. Thus, the VIP method scores features based on the significance of their contributions in the PCA embedding where classifiers can be built. Whereas the concept of VIP exists for partial least squares [20], in this work we demonstrate that VIP can be extended in the context of PCA as well. Unlike other feature selection schemes, PCA–VIP is not encumbered by the curse of dimensionality because the most contributory features are identified in the reduced embedding space.

In this work we apply PCA–VIP to identify MP–MRI markers to distinguish between (a) benign tissue and CaP on 12 T2–w, DWI, and DCE MRI studies and (b) low and high grade CaP on 22 MRS studies. The former dataset has ground truth annotation of spatial extent of CaP *in vivo*, and the latter has ground truth annotation of both diagnosis and spatial extent of CaP *in vivo*. Our methodology comprises the following main steps. First PCA is applied to the MP–MRI features, which include spectral peaks on MRS and texture features on MRI, at the voxel level. PCA–VIP scores are assigned to the high–dimensional features, and the high–dimensional features with the highest PCA–VIP scores are identified. The PCA–VIP scheme is then evaluated via a classifier trained using the features with high PCA–VIP scores. The performance of this classifier is then compared against one that operates in the full high–dimensional space, the hypothesis being that the lack of statistically significant differences between the two classifiers will reflect that only the most class discriminatory attributes are being identified via PCA–VIP.

The remainder of this paper is organized as follows. In Section 2 we discuss PCA and how variable importance is determined by PCA–VIP. We apply our PCA–VIP methodology in Section 3 to identify MP–MR imaging markers for discrimination of (a) benign tissue and CaP and (b) high and low grade CaP on MP–MRI, and in Section 4 we provide some concluding remarks.

2   Variable Importance in Projection for PCA

2.1   Principal Component Analysis

PCA [21] attempts to find a linear transformation to maximize the variance in the data and applies this transformation to obtain the most uncorrelated features. The orthogonal eigenvectors of the data matrix $\mathbf{X}$ express the variance in the data, and the h eigenvectors that comprise most of the variance in the data are the principal components. Thus, PCA forms the following model:

$$\mathbf{X} = \mathbf{TP}^\mathsf{T}, \tag{1}$$

where $\mathbf{T}$ is made up of the h principal component vectors $\mathbf{t}_i$, $i \in \{1, ..., h\}$, as columns and $\mathbf{P}^\mathsf{T}$ is comprised of the h loading vectors $\mathbf{p}_i$ as rows.

2.2   Variable Importance in PCA Projections

The features that contribute most to the ith dimension of the PCA transformation can be identified as those with the largest weights in the ith loading vector; the fraction $\left(\frac{p_{ji}}{||\mathbf{p}_i||}\right)^2$ reveals how much the jth feature contributes to the ith principal component in the low–dimensional embedding. The overall importance of the jth feature to classification can be calculated by summing its contribution to each dimension of the PCA embedding and weighting these values by (a) the regression coefficients b_i, which relate the data back to the class labels, and (b) the transformed data $\mathbf{t}_i$. Thus, although PCA is itself an unsupervised method, the exploitation of class labels in computing the PCA–VIP leads to the identification of features that provide good class discrimination. The variable importance in projections (VIP) for PCA (PCA–VIP) is computed for each feature as follows:

$$\pi_j = \sqrt{m \frac{\sum_{i=1}^{h} b_i^2 \mathbf{t}_i^\mathsf{T} \mathbf{t}_i \left(\frac{p_{ji}}{||\mathbf{p}_i||} \right)^2}{\sum_{i=1}^{h} b_i^2 \mathbf{t}_i^\mathsf{T} \mathbf{t}_i}}, \qquad (2)$$

where m is the number of features in the original, high–dimensional feature space, and the b_i are the coefficients that solve the regression equation

$$\mathbf{y} = \mathbf{T}\mathbf{b}^\mathsf{T}, \qquad (3)$$

which correlates the principal components with the outcome vector $\mathbf{y}$. The degree to which a feature contributes to classification in the PCA transformed space is directly proportional to its associated PCA–VIP scores. Thus, features with PCA–VIP scores near 0 have little predictive power, and the features with the highest PCA–VIP scores contribute the most to class discrimination on the PCA embedding.

3 Experimental Results and Discussion

3.1 Identification of Imaging Markers for CaP Diagnosis

Data. A total of 12 pre–operative, endorectal *in vivo* 3 Tesla MR imaging studies including T2–w, DWI, and DCE MRI in men with organ confined prostate cancer were obtained prior to radical prostatectomy. Surgical specimens were then sectioned and examined by a trained pathologist to accurately delineate CaP presence and extent. Registration of multimodal imagery with histology was performed using Multiple–Attribute Combined Mutual Information (MACMI) [22], a non–rigid registration scheme that performs non–linear image warping at multiple image scales via a hierarchical B–spline mesh grid optimization scheme. 39 corresponding histological sections were brought into spatial alignment with corresponding T2–w, DWI, and DCE MRI slices to determine ground truth spatial extent of CaP on MRI.

Feature Extraction. A series of 18 voxel–wise image features, including six features from each of the T2–w, DWI, and DCE MRI protocols, were extracted from each of the 39 MP–MRI slices for discrimination between benign tissue and CaP. For each voxel on the T2–w and DCE MRI slices three co–occurrence features (contrast inverse moment, contrast average, and correlation), the magnitude gradient, and a Gabor feature combining all orientations of the Gabor filter via the l_∞ norm were extracted [14]. Additionally, the T2–w and ADC intensity values were taken as the sixth feature for each protocol. The six features extracted from DCE MRI were the post–contrast intensity values at each time point.

Table 1. Description of MP–MRI datasets used for CaP diagnosis and grading. Contributory features, as well as their associated PCA–VIP scores, are listed for each MRI protocol: T2–w, DWI, DCE, and MRS. Standard deviation of performance measures obtained by boot–strapping are shown in parentheses, and the feature from each MRI protocol with the highest PCA–VIP score is shown in bold.

MRI Protocol	Classes	Contributory Features	PCA–VIP
T2–w MRI	benign/CaP (12 studies)	**Gabor gradient**	1.63(0.002)
		Intensity value	.962(0.029)
DCE MRI	benign/CaP (12 studies)	**Time point 2**	1.56(0.002)
		Time point 6	.987(0.001)
ADC MRI	benign/CaP (12 studies)	**Intensity value**	2.27(0.002)
		Gabor gradient	1.82(0.019)
MRS	benign/CaP (22 studies)	**Polyamine**	2.92(0.137)
		Citrate	2.27(0.116)
		Choline	1.88(0.364)
		Creatine	1.04(0.216)
MRS	low/high grade (9 studies)	**Citrate**	2.18(0.107)
		Choline	2.14(0.113)
		Polyamine	2.13(0.130)
		Creatine	2.09(0.106)

MP–MR Imaging Marker Identification. CaP detection on MP–MRI was performed by representing each voxel within the prostate by the 18 extracted features and transforming this voxel–wise data using PCA. PCA–VIP scores were then calculated by boot–strapping for each of the 18 features. Randomized boot–strapping was performed by randomly selecting 8 of the 12 patient studies to obtain a PCA embedding and compute the PCA–VIP scores therewith. This randomized boot–strapping process was repeated 50 times, and the average values and standard deviatons of PCA–VIP scores were obtained from boot–strapping. Features associated with high PCA–VIP scores were identified as imaging markers for CaP diagnosis.

Evaluation. The probabilistic boosting tree (PBT) [25], which iteratively generates a decision tree structure of a predefined size and whose nodes combine classifier predictions from several weak classifiers, was employed to construct C^{all}, a classifier using all 18 features, and C^{VIP}, a classifier using the four features associated with the highest PCA–VIP scores. Since PBTs necessitate the use of atleast two features, this classifier could not be used to evaluate individual feature performance. Consequently, the naive Bayes classifier [26] was employed to construct classifiers $C^1, ..., C^4$ using each of the four features used in C^{VIP}.

Performance of each of C^1, C^2, C^3, C^4, C^{all}, and C^{VIP} was evaluated by accuracy and AUC estimates obtained via cross–validation, which was done by performing classification of each prostate voxel in the 12 studies. For each of the 12 studies, six classifiers—C^{all}, C^{VIP}, and C^k, $k \in \{1, ..., 4\}$—were trained on a random selection of 9 other studies, and each voxel in the prosate was classified as benign or CaP by each classifier. This process was repeated 50 times, and the average values and standard deviations of the performance measures over the 50 iterations were obtained for each of the six classifiers.

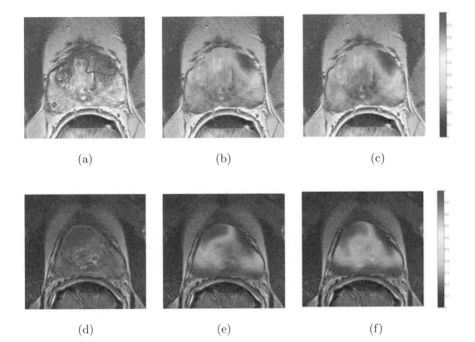

(a)   (b)   (c)

(d)   (e)   (f)

Fig. 1. Sample prostate T2–w MRI slices in (a) and (d) have CaP ground truth shown in red. Heat map representations of the probabilities that voxels within the prostate contain CaP are shown in (b) and (e) when C^{all} is used for classification and in (c) and (f) when C^{VIP} is used for classification. Red voxels denote high probability of CaP, while cool colors denote high probability that a voxel corresponds to benign tissue. The probability maps in (b) and (e) are similar to (c) and (f), respectively, demonstrating that eliminating features with low PCA–VIP scores does not significantly impact overall classifier performance.

Results and Discussion. PCA–VIP scores obtained for each of the 18 image features are shown in Table 1. The Gabor gradient features [23] extracted from both the T2–w MRI and ADC maps emerge as contributory to the PCA embedding for discriminating benign and CaP regions. The importance of Gabor wavelet features lies in their ability to quantify the visual appearance of CaP, typically documented by radiologists as a region of low signal intensity with incomplete stromal septations within its focus (on T2–w MRI). The Gabor operator attempts to match such localized frequency characteristics across multiple scales and orientations, allowing quantification of features that are used in visual processing [24]. Additional features whose importance is revealed by the PCA–VIP score are the ADC and the DCE intensity value at the second time point, which corresponds to peak enhancement (see Table 1). In fact, it is visually apparent on MRI that CaP voxels tend to have significantly lower ADC values and quicker contrast enhancement on DCE compared to benign voxels.

Table 2. Classification performance for C^{all}, C^{VIP}, C^1, C^2, C^3, and C^4 for CaP diagnosis on T2–w/DWI/DCE MRI. Standard deviation of performance measures from the 50 iterations are shown in parentheses.

	C^{all}	C^{VIP}	C^1	C^2	C^3	C^4
Accuracy	0.78(0.007)	0.78(0.006)	0.57(0.010)	0.47(0.007)	0.65(0.007)	0.49(0.013)
AUC	0.64(0.011)	0.64(0.011)	0.63(0.007)	0.53(0.009)	0.59(0.006)	0.55(0.014)

Qualitative results, displayed in Figure 1, illustrate that classification does not change significantly when features with low PCA–VIP scores are eliminated from the classification model. Quantitative results (see Table 2) confirm that classification accuracy and AUC are similar for C^{all} and C^{VIP}. The fact that classifier performance is not weakened significantly when C^{VIP} is used instead of C^{all} suggests that most of the relevant information captured by the 18 extracted features is contained within these four features. The results shown in Table 2 also indicate that combining the four features with high PCA–VIP scores provides for greater classification accuracy than using any of the features individually for classification.

3.2   Identifying Imaging Markers for CaP Grading

Data. A total of 22 pre–operative, endorectal *in vivo* 3 Tesla T2–w MRI, MRS studies were obtained. Upon radical prostatectomy, "ground truth" CaP extent and grade were manually delineated by an expert by visually registering corresponding histological and radiological sections. Class labels for the individual spectral voxels, assigned via a combination of manual registration of histology and MRI and subsequent expert inspection, were used as the surrogate ground truth for CaP detection and grading. The 22 studies comprised a total of 794 CaP and 1056 benign voxels, and 9 of these studies were found to contain 179 low grade CaP voxels and 231 high grade CaP voxels. Each voxel is associated with a 171–dimensional spectral vector, which encodes the metabolic concentrations of choline, polyamine, creatine, and citrate.

Feature Extraction. Three–dimensional MRS imaging data were processed and aligned with the corresponding T2–w imaging data. The raw spectral data was filtered with a 3 Hz Gaussian filter, Fourier transformed, baseline corrected, and phase and frequency aligned based upon the water peak using the methods in [27, 28]. Post baseline and frequency correction, choline, polyamine, creatine, and citrate peak areas were estimated using the composite trapezoidal rule [29].

MP–MR Imaging Marker Identification. Metabolic imaging markers that contribute to accurate diagnosis and Gleason grading of CaP spectra on MRS were identified by representing each voxel within the prostate by the 171 spectral features and transforming this voxel–wise data using PCA. PCA–VIP scores were then calculated by boot–strapping for each of the 171 spectral features. Randomized boot–strapping was performed by randomly selecting 16 of the 22 patient studies (or 6 of the 9 patient studies with Gleason grade information) to obtain a PCA embedding. This randomized boot–strapping process was repeated 50 times, and the average values and standard deviatons of PCA–VIP scores were obtained from boot–strapping. Dominant metabolites were found by aligning PCA–VIP score curves (see Figure 2(a)) with the spectral vectors and identifying spectral peaks with the highest PCA–VIP scores.

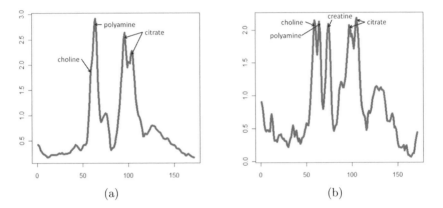

Fig. 2. PCA–VIP score curves for MRS spectra for discriminating between (a) benign tissue and CaP and (b) low and high grade CaP. Choline, polyamine, and citrate peaks emerge as contributory in classifying benign tissue and CaP, and choline, polyamine, creatine, and citrate differentially express in low and high grade CaP.

Evaluation. PBTs were employed to construct C^{all}, a classifier using all 171 spectral features, and C^{VIP}, a classifier using the peaks associated with the highest PCA–VIP scores. The naive Bayes classifier was employed to construct classifiers $C^1, ..., C^4$ using each of the peaks used in C^{VIP}. Classification performance was evaluated by accuracy and AUC estimates obtained via cross–validation. The average values and standard deviations of the performance measures over the 50 iterations are reported for C^{all}, C^{VIP}, C^1, C^2, C^3, and C^4.

Results and Discussion. PCA–VIP scores, shown in Figure 2, suggest that choline, polyamine, and citrate play a significant role in discrimination between CaP and benign tissue and that these three metabolities, as well as creatine, aid in differentiation of low and high grade CaP. Our results confirm the roles

Table 3. Classification performance for C^{all}, C^{VIP}, C^1, C^2, C^3, and C^4 for CaP diagnosis on MRS. Standard deviation of performance measures from the 50 iterations are shown in parentheses.

	C^{all}	C^{VIP}	C^1	C^2	C^3
Accuracy	0.78(0.001)	0.78(0.002)	0.69(0.002)	0.70(0.001)	0.70(0.002)
AUC	0.86(0.008)	0.74(0.008)	0.49(0.014)	0.56(0.014)	0.54(0.019)

of choline and citrate for CaP detection and grading of prostate, previously suggested in [4]. We find that although creatine is not a significant contributor to CaP detection, creatine appears to play an important role in differentiating between high and low grade CaP.

Table 4. Classification performance for C^{all}, C^{VIP}, C^1, C^2, C^3, and C^4 for CaP grading on MRS. Standard deviation of performance measures from the 50 iterations are shown in parentheses.

	C^{all}	C^{VIP}	C^1	C^2	C^3	C^4
Accuracy	0.72(0.043)	0.71(0.034)	0.58(0.062)	0.61(0.045)	0.56(0.069)	0.60(0.050)
AUC	0.76(0.061)	0.74(0.070)	0.54(0.107)	0.65(0.053)	0.60(0.090)	0.64(0.051)

Furthermore, PCA–VIP also reveals the importance of polyamine concentrations in distinguishing both CaP and benign tissue and low and high grade CaP. Low polyamine concentration was previously linked to CaP presence [4], and Swanson et. al. [30] suggested that cancer aggressiveness was associated with further reduction of polyamines. However, the number of cancerous samples in the Swanson study was small, so the findings could not be verified as being statistically significant. The results of this study strongly suggest that polyamine concentrations are differentially expressed in low and high grade CaP.

To quantitatively evaluate the discriminability of the metabolite features identified as important via PCA–VIP, PBT classifiers using only these metabolic concentrations were constructed to classify the individual spectra. Qualitative results, displayed in Figure 3 for discrimination between high and low grade spectra, illustrate higher sensitivity for C^{VIP} compared to C^{all}. Quantitative results (see Tables 3 and 4) confirm that both accuracy and AUC are similar for C^{VIP} and C^{all} for the CaP grading problem. For CaP diagnosis, C^{VIP} had a slightly lower AUC than C^{all}, suggesting that perhaps other, yet to be identified metabolites contribute to CaP–benign class separability. The results shown in Tables 3 and 4 also indicate that combining the peaks associated with high PCA–VIP scores provides for greater classification accuracy than using any of the metabolic peaks individually.

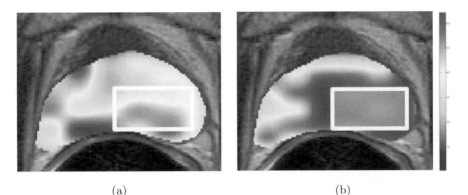

(a)   (b)

Fig. 3. Heat map representations of the probabilities that voxels within the prostate correspond to high grade CaP when (a) C^{all} and (b) C^{VIP} were used for classification. Ground truth presence of high grade CaP is shown within the white rectangles.

4   Concluding Remarks

We presented the PCA–VIP scheme, which facilitates interpretation of PCA models by quantifying the contributions of individual features on PCA embeddings. We demonstrated how PCA–VIP enables identification of imaging markers for CaP detection and grading on MP–MRI. The ability of PCA–VIP to correctly identify features that contribute to class discrimination was corroborated by the fact that classifier performance was largely unaffected by the elimination of features with low PCA–VIP scores. The work presented here could potentially be used for modulating the time and complexity of the prostate imaging exam by limiting the imaging acquisition to only those parameters found to be relevant.

Whereas traditional feature selection algorithms operate in the high dimensional feature space and are therefore encumbered by the curse of dimensionality, the PCA–VIP provides a means for feature selection, ranking, and weighting in the PCA embedding space. In future work we intend to explore the application of this scheme to other problem domains.

References

[1]   Jemal, A., et al.: Cancer Statistics. CA Cancer Journal for Clinicians 60(5), 277–300 (2010)
[2]   Borboroglu, P.G., et al.: Extensive repeat transrectal ultrasound guided prostate biopsy in patients with previous benign sextant biopsies. The Journal of Urology 163(1), 158–162 (2000)
[3]   Schiebler, M.L., et al.: Current role of MR imaging in the staging of adenocarcinoma of the prostate. Radiology 189(2), 339–352 (1993)
[4]   Kurhanewicz, J., et al.: Combined magnetic resonance imaging and spectroscopic imaging appraoch to molecular imaging of prostate cancer. Journal of Magnetic Resonance Imaging 16, 451–463 (2002)

[5]   Shukla–Dave, A., et al.: The utility of magnetic resonance imaging and spectroscopy for predicting insignificant prostate cancer: An initial analysis. BJU International 99, 786–793 (2007)

[6]   Langer, D.L., et al.: Prostate tissue composition and MR measurements: Investigating the relationsips between ADC, T2, Ktrans, ve, and corresponding histological features. Radiology 255, 485–494 (2010)

[7]   Klotz, L.: Active surveillance for prostate cancer: For whom? Journal of Clinical Oncology 23(32), 8165–8169 (2005)

[8]   May, F., et al.: Limited value of endorectal magnetic resonance imaging and transrectal ultrasonography in the staging of clinically localized prostate cancer. BJU International 87(1), 66–69 (2001)

[9]   Bonilla, J., et al.: Intra– and interobserver variability of MRI prostate volume measurements. Prostate 31(2), 98–102 (1997)

[10] Wetter, A., et al.: Combined MRI and MR spectroscopy of the prostate before radical prostatectomy. American Journal of Roentgenology 187, 724–730 (2006)

[11] Liu, X., et al.: Prostate cancer segmentation with simultaneous estimation of Markov random field parameters and class. IEEE Transactions on Medical Imaging 28(6), 906–915 (2009)

[12] Tiwari, P., et al.: A hierarchical spectral clustering and nonlinear dimensionality reduction scheme for detection of prostate cancer from magnetic resonance spectroscopy (MRS). Medical Physics 36(9), 3927–3939 (2009)

[13] Vos, P.C., et al.: Computer–assisted analysis of peripheral zone prostate lesions using T2–weighted and dynamic contrast enhanced T1–weighted MRI. Physics in Medicine and Biology 55(6), 1719 (2010)

[14] Viswanath, S., et al.: Enhanced multi–protocol analysis via intelligent supervised embedding (EMPrAvISE): Detecting prostate cancer on multi–parametric MRI. In: SPIE Medical Imaging, vol. 7963, pp.79630U

[15] Tiwari, P., et al.: Multimodal wavelet embedding representation for data combination (MaWERiC): Integrating magnetic resonance imaging and spectroscopy for prostate cancer detection. Accepted to: NMR in Medicine

[16] Duda, R., et al.: Pattern Classification, 2nd edn. Wiley-Interscience, Chichester (2000)

[17] Kelm, B.M., et al.: Automated estimation of tumor probability in prostate magnetic resonance spectroscopic imaging: Pattern recognition vs quantification. Magnetic Resonance in Medicine 57, 150–159 (2007)

[18] Craig, A., et al.: Scaling and normalization effects in NMR spectroscopic metabonomic data sets. Analytical Chemistry 78, 2262–2267 (2006)

[19] Yan, H., et al.: Correntropy based feature selection using binary projection. Pattern Recognition 44(12), 2834–2843 (2011)

[20] Chong, I.G., Jun, C.H.: Performance of some variable selection methods when multicollinearity is present. Chemometrics and Intelligent Laboratory Systems 78, 103–112 (2005)

[21] Esbensen, K.: Multivariate data analysis—in practice: An introduction to multivariate data analysis and experimental design. CAMO, Norway (2004)

[22] Chappelow, J., et al.: Elastic registration of multimodal prostate MRI and histology via multiattribute combined mutual information. Medical Physics 38, 2005–2018 (2011)

[23] Madabhushi, A., et al.: Automated detection of prostatic adenocarcinoma from high resolution ex vivo MRI. IEEE Transactions on Medical Imaging 24(12), 1611–1625 (2005)

[24] Bovik, A.C., et al.: Multichannel texture analysis using localized spatial filters. IEEE Transactions on Pattern Analysis and Machine Intelligence 12(1), 55–73 (1990)

[25] Quinlan, J.R.: C4.5: Programs for Machine Learning. Morgan Kaufmann, San Francisco (1993)

[26] Witten, I.H., Frank, E.: Data Mining: Practical Machine Learning Tools and Techniques. Elsevier, Amsterdam (2005)

[27] Nelson, S.J., Brown, T.: A new method for automatic quantification of 1-D spectra with low signal to noise ratio. Journal of Magnetic Resonance Imaging 84, 95–109 (1987)

[28] Nelson, S.J.: Analysis of volume MRI and MR spectroscopic imaging data for the evaluation of patients with brain tumors. Magnetic Resonance in Medicine 46, 228–239 (2001)

[29] Devos, A., et al.: Classification of brain tumours using short echo time 1H MR spectra. Journal of Magnetic Resonance 170(1), 164–175 (2004)

[30] Swanson, M.G., et al.: 1H HR–MAS investigation of four potential markers for prostate cancer. Proc. Intl. Soc. Mag. Reson. Med. 9 (2001)

Author Index